The Most Infamous Terrorist Groups in the World:
The History and Legacy of al-Qaeda, the Islamic State, the Nusra Front, and Boko Haram
By Charles River Editors

Al-Qaeda leader Ayman al-Zawahiri

D1726022

About Charles River Editors

Charles River Editors provides superior editing and original writing services across the digital publishing industry, with the expertise to create digital content for publishers across a vast range of subject matter. In addition to providing original digital content for third party publishers, we also republish civilization's greatest literary works, bringing them to new generations of readers via ebooks.

Sign up here to receive updates about free books as we publish them, and visit Our Kindle Author Page to browse today's free promotions and our most recently published Kindle titles.

Introduction
Al-Qaeda

A photo of Osama Bin Laden taken during an interview with Pakistani journalist Hamid Mir

"The correlation between the words and deeds of bin Laden, his lieutenants, and their allies was close to perfect—if they said they were going to do something, they were much more than likely to try to do it." – Michael Scheuer, CIA Station Chief

"[T]he ruling to kill the Americans and their allies—civilians and military—is an individual duty for every Muslim who can do it in any country in which it is possible to do it, in order to liberate the al-Aqsa Mosque and the holy mosque [in Mecca] from their grip, and in order for their armies to move out of all the lands of Islam, defeated and unable to threaten any Muslim. This is in accordance with the words of Almighty Allah, 'and fight the pagans all together as they fight you all together,' and 'fight them until there is no more tumult or oppression, and there prevail justice and faith in Allah.'" – A 1998 fatwa signed by Bin Laden and Ayman al-Zawahiri

Since the attacks on September 11, 2001, the world has struggled to define al-Qaeda, an amorphous, growing, and seemingly inexhaustible organization. Once a relatively organized group based in one country with a defined hierarchy and clear leadership, al-Qaeda has transformed into a transnational phenomenon over the last few decades, with branches and affiliates operating in dozens of countries across the world. Many call al-Qaeda an enemy, while some define it as an ideology, and others analyze it as a network. Of course, a small minority takes it up as their cause and an extension of their religion.

To that end, what is perhaps most clear about al-Qaeda is that there is no single definition that can comprehensively and precisely identify just what it is. Who can be described as an al-Qaeda terrorist? What is the exact makeup of al-Qaeda? These are all questions that are fairly straightforward and seem like they should be simple to answer – as they are with most other terrorist organizations – but in the case of al-Qaeda, there is no commonly accepted understanding. Bruce Hoffman, former director of RAND and a specialist in terrorism and counterterrorism affairs, wrote in 2003, "It is remarkable that more than a decade after its founding…al-Qaeda remains such a poorly understood phenomenon." He further noted, "Is [al-Qaeda] a monolithic, international terrorist organization with an identifiable command and control apparatus or is it a broader, more amorphous movement tenuously held together by a loosely networked transnational constituency?...Is al-Qaeda a concept or a virus? An army or an ideology? A populist transnational movement or a vast international criminal enterprise? All of the above? None of the above? Or, some of the above?"

The difficulty of defining al-Qaeda is reflected by the various ways the Arabic word qaeda can be translated. The most common translation is "base" or "foundation," but the word can also be used more ambiguously to mean "method," "principle," or "formula." Some maintain that the early founders of al-Qaeda were envisioning the name in the latter sense, while others believe that the name was applied to the group by outside powers. Osama bin Laden, the founder of al-Qaeda, stated in a February 2002 interview that the name al-Qaeda was "established a long time ago by mere chance," and that the group's training camp was called al-Qaeda ("the base"), a name that came to represent his entire organization.

Even greater frustration arises when attempting to physically identify what group or groups constitute al-Qaeda. Are all groups that pledge allegiance to al-Qaeda considered part of the franchise? Is there a difference between the "al-Qaeda core" based in Pakistan and the various affiliates and associates scattered across the world. If so, what is the relationship between them? While both groups have sworn allegiance to al-Qaeda's core leadership, is al-Qaida in the Arabian Peninsula in Yemen fighting for the same cause as al-Shabaab in Somalia or ISIS in Iraq and Syria?

Such questions may be difficult if not impossible to

answer with certainty, but the very fact that al-Qaeda eludes hard definitions indicate that it is more than a terrorist organization and more than a physical, identifiable entity. Al-Qaeda has and still continues to challenge people's abilities to analyze international politics and assess global security.

This book chronicles the birth and growth of al-Qaeda, including the key figures and events that impacted its formation, as well as the ideology of al-Qaeda and the historical context and environment that strengthened it. This book also looks at the various tactics and strategies al-Qaeda has employed to achieve its goals and further its ideology, especially its notorious terrorist attacks across the globe, and the various branches that have grown out of the core, including al-Qaeda in Iraq (AQI), al-Qaida in the Arabian Peninsula (AQAP), al-Qaeda in the Islamic Maghreb (AQIM), al-Shabaab in Somalia, and most recently, al-Nusrah Front in Syria. Along with pictures of important people, places, and events, you will learn about al-Qaeda like never before, in no time at all.

The Islamic State of Iraq and Syria

The emblem seal used by ISIS

Also known as ISIS, Da'esh, al-Qaeda in Iraq (AQI), and a host of other names, the Islamic State in Iraq and the Levant (ISIL) has increasingly gained attention over the years for its brutal tactics and seemingly blatant disregard for human rights, but it has recently dominated the global media spotlight and made headlines when it attacked and seized control of Mosul, the second largest city in Iraq, and drove out an Iraqi army force that was more than five times its size in June 2014. It has since laid claim to various territories throughout Iraq and the Levant, and it has established operational control and maintained administrative structures on both sides of the Iraqi-Syrian border. Most recently, it declared the restoration of a caliphate and renamed itself the Islamic State.

The ever-deteriorating crises in Iraq and Syria have continued to highlight the prolific activities of ISIS, but as a unified organization, ISIS is believed to consist of only a few thousand militants led by a shadowy and secretive leader named Abu Bakr al-Baghdadi. Nonetheless, despite its relatively small size, the group has taken on and at times successfully battled U.S. and Coalition forces, the Iraqi army, and other rival Iraqi and Syrian militant groups. The ferocity and fanaticism with which it fights, and the absolute commitment it has to the jihad in Iraq and the Levant, continue to set ISIS apart from other known terrorist organizations in the region.

One of the reasons ISIS has gone by so many different names is because it has rebranded itself numerous times in the past. After starting as an al-Qaeda-inspired Sunni Islamist brigade that emerged from the ashes of the jihadist struggle against foreign forces in Iraq, the group grew into a full-fledged al-Qaeda branch, then evolved into a religiously motivated army, then finally separated from al-Qaeda to become the organization it is today. The frequent name changes are hardly cosmetic; they represent the multiple transformations the group has undergone and symbolize its flexibility and adaptability, which is also how the ISIL has not only survived for over a decade but even flourished as one of the most influential groups in the region. Today, the group attracts fighters who wish to join its ranks not just from across Iraq and the region but from all over the world.

The group has also experienced many periods of withdrawal and reemergence, further confounding the true nature and structure of the organization, which has been littered with in-fighting, rivalries, and leadership shuffles. But the group's terrorism and violent capabilities have been made quite clear in the Syrian civil war, the fighting in Iraq, and even attacks into other countries within the region. Operatives have claimed bombings and attacks in Lebanon and Jordan, and there are known recruiting cells in places as far away as Egypt, Morocco, and the U.K.

The funding that the group continues to receive is alarming as well, from private donations made by wealthy citizens and charities[1] in the Gulf to funds obtained through illicit activities such as extortion, kidnapping ransoms, involvement in underground trade of stolen antiquities, counterfeiting, and other criminal activities. In 2012, ISIS seized control of oil fields in Syria, and it is believed that the group is reaping profits by selling the oil at discounted prices to anyone willing to pay, including the very regime of Bashar Assad that the group is purporting to fight. In June 2014, when the group took over the city of Mosul, ISIS reportedly plundered a government vault at a Mosul bank and took millions of state money. Like any enterprise, its increasing notoriety and burgeoning reputation are bound to increase the donations from private donors who are interested in investing in what has become one of the most successful and well-known militant Islamist organizations in the world.

The Al-Nusra Front

---

[1] These charities are often front organizations that are established either by ISIL supporters or benefactors. In countries like Kuwait, Qatar, and Saudi Arabia, despite government crackdowns on terrorism financing, there is still a tacit understanding with the governments of these countries that allow organizations and private donors to send funds to Iraq and/or Syria, with the purpose of financing ISIL and similar radical groups. Analysts believe that ISIL continues to enjoy a steady stream of funds, arms, and supplies from politically motivated players operating from the safety of U.S.-allied countries like Saudi Arabia and Qatar.

A Voice of America picture of Al-Nusra Front supporters

Since the Arab Spring uprising of 2011, reports of terrorist attacks around the world have flooded international media. Syria, a country about one and half times the size of Texas, has become the central battleground for many terrorist groups; those the world often focuses on and has heard much of--such as the Islamic State of Iraq and the Levant (also known as ISIS and Da'ash, but from here on referred to as ISIL)--and those the world rarely hears about and is unable to make distinctions between others--such as Jabhat Al-Nusra. Despite the lack of focused attention on its activities, Jabhat Al-Nusra (or, the Nusra Front as it is sometimes referred to) has built quite a reputation in Syria and the greater Middle East for its seemingly endless supply of weapons, ability to ally with strategic partners, and its peculiar mix of international, albeit notorious, supporters inside the country.

Jabhat Al-Nusra's formal name is, "Jabhat Al-Nusra li-Ahl al-Sham," or, the "Victorious Support Front for the People of Sham (or, Syria)" and the group first emerged on the international scene in early 2012 as a localized Syrian affiliate of Al-Qaeda in Iraq. The group has carried out numerous terrorist attacks and kidnappings, and has been involved in a variety of battles against Bashar Assad's Syrian government forces as well as against other anti-government factions such as ISIL. The complexity of the Syrian Civil War is most definitely reflected in the complexity of the groups fighting for power within and around its borders; Jabhat Al-Nusra is no exception. The group's relationship with ISIL, Al-Qaeda, and the other militant factions within Syria is complicated and appears often conflictual: as of the time of this writing, Jabhat Al-Nusra had announced its split from Al-Qaeda in Iraq (AQI) but analysts believe this is nothing more than a re-branding technique to attract all fighting elements in Syria to be under its own umbrella of control.

Abu Muhammad Al-Julani (real name, Ahmad Hussein Al-Shar'a) is currently the top leader of Jabhat Al-Nusra and one of its founding members. Al-Julani boasts a long career with jihadist groups in the region and his ties to Al-Qaeda are particularly strong which has served Al-Nusra very well over the last few years, especially when it comes to drawing upon resources and increasing recruitment for the cause. Al-Julani and Jabhat Al-Nusra aim to continue to increase recruitment and integrate all Syrian revolutionary factions into one larger group, thereby beginning the establishment of their own version of an Islamic caliphate in Syria. While their idea to build a caliphate in Syria is certainly not unique, their approach to this effort has most recently centered on finding consensus among warring factions to maximize efforts against Bashar Assad's regime forces as well as experimenting with efforts of control in occupied cities around Syria.

The international community's response to the Syria Civil War has been quite disorganized. The United States was quick to support the protester movements across the region during the Arab Spring which put Syrian President Bashar Assad on high alert. As the war commenced inside Syria, Russia was quick to rush to Assad's defense and aid both inside the country and to the international community more generally. This situation pitted the U.S. and Russia against each other once again which left the Syrian people in between. Jabhat Al-Nusra took this as an opportunity to fill in the gap where the world's superpowers failed them. Not only is Al-Nusra attempting to gain legitimacy within the country, they want to show the world they are the only force fighting for the Sunnis of Syria. From the summer of 2014 to 2016, the U.S.-led coalition has focused much of its effort on destroying the brutal ISIL whose territory encompasses parts of both Iraq and Syria. Al-Nusra has capitalized on ISIL's time in the spotlight and carved its own niche among Syrians, developing relationships and carrying out small scale battles against the Assad regime and rival rebel militant groups around the country. This has been particularly attractive to countries like Turkey and Qatar, whose feel their own position in the region may shift depending on the outcome of the war and the United States' changing relationship with Iran. Al-Nusra certainly appears more appealing than ISIL. In late July 2016, Al-Nusra evolved once more by changing its name to Jabhat Fatah Al-Sham and officially cutting ties with Al-Qaeda. According to analysts, this move is just another step in a long-term effort for Al-Nusra to make itself seem different than the other groups it competes with in the region and to shake loose Al-Qaeda's baggage.

This book explores the development of a highly specialized terrorist group, one that adapts quickly to situations on the ground as the conflict progresses and learns from other groups mistakes. Al-Nusra is relatively agile and seemingly less vicious than ISIL, which is why it both attracts and repels the international community. Examining Al-Nusra's bridging of online and offline battlefields and its internal structure allows readers to understand how this group developed so rapidly in the war. Understanding how Syrian civilians live under Al-Nusra controls allows readers to understand the similarities and differences with ISIL, whose caliphate it is often compared to. These various components paint the picture of "Al-Nusra the terrorist group, but also one of the group as "Al-Nusra the Syrian defender."

Boko Haram

A picture of Abubakar Shekau, the leader of Boko Haram, in late 2014

"Boko Haram are better armed and are better motivated than our own troops. Given the present state of affairs, it is absolutely impossible for us to defeat Boko Haram." - Kashim Shettima, governor of Borno

On the morning of April 15, 2004, the world woke up to the extraordinary news of the kidnap in a little known hamlet of Nigeria of some 276, primarily Christian schoolgirls, by the radical militant Nigerian insurgent group Boko Haram. Almost overnight, the group, which had resided somewhat on the fringes of global consciousness up until that point, found itself at the forefront as international public outrage, culminating in a social media campaign headed by First Lady Michelle Obama, demanded the immediate return of the kidnapped girls.

Those demands, while laudable, simply served to project a hitherto local and regional jihadist movement, operating in the gray hinterland of the African Sahel region, into an organization with an international profile and a place in the pantheon of globally recognized terror organizations. If anything, the headlines have probably imbued Boko Haram with more punch than it can practically wield, for in reality the organization, at least for the time being, it remains less a jihadist movement that a localized terror insurgency with very locally defined objectives. If Boko Haram does indeed nurture international ambitions, which increasingly it appears to, then these perhaps are a fringe expression of a movement that appears in on the whole, again at least for the time being, to be too haphazard, and chaotic in its administration and leadership to really find a home amongst the larger and better known international organizations.

The Most Infamous Terrorist Groups in the World: The History and Legacy of al-Qaeda, the Islamic State, the Nusra Front, and Boko Haram

Al-Qaeda
The Origins and Emergence of Al-Qaeda

"[T]his matter isn't about any specific person and...is not about the al-Qa`idah Organization. We are the children of an Islamic Nation, with Prophet Muhammad as its leader, our Lord is one...and all the true believers are brothers. So the situation isn't like the West portrays it, that there is an 'organization' with a specific name (such as 'al-Qa`idah') and so on. That particular name is very old. It was born without any intention from us. Brother Abu Ubaida...created a military base to train the young men to fight against the vicious, arrogant, brutal, terrorizing Soviet empire... So this place was called 'The Base', as in a training base, so this name grew and became. We aren't separated from this nation. We are the children of a nation, and we are an inseparable part of it, and from those public...which spread from the far east, from the Philippines, to Indonesia, to Malaysia, to India, to Pakistan, reaching Mauritania...and so we discuss the conscience of this nation." – Osama bin Laden, 2001

The origins of al-Qaeda can be traced to the 1980s, when the world was in the midst of the Cold War, and specifically to the battlefronts of Afghanistan. The Soviet War in Afghanistan (1979-1989) was a key element in the eventual collapse of the Soviet Union, and it was also significant in the formation of al-Qaeda because it fomented the influx of non-Afghan Muslim fighters into the country, leading to the proliferation of religiously motivated militancy and one of the most prominent cases of the foreign fighter phenomenon. As the conflict intensified, thousands of young Muslims from around the world flocked to Afghanistan to fight as *mujahideen* in what was being called a *jihad*, or holy war, against the invasion by a non-Muslim superpower.

Osama bin Laden was one of these *mujahideen*. Born in Saudi Arabia in 1957 to an affluent family of Yemeni origin, the man most commonly known as the primary founder and leader of al-Qaeda was the son of a successful billionaire construction magnate with close ties to the Saudi royal family. Raised as a Wahhabi Muslim[2] by his strict and pious father, young Osama bin Laden lived a privileged life, studying at an elite school and eventually entering King Abdulaziz University in Jeddah to study economics. In university, bin Laden began studying religion even more fervently, and he frequently met with members of the Saudi chapter of the Muslim Brotherhood.[3] In time, he became an advent adherent of the Palestinian theologian Abdallah Azzam, who was a strong proponent of *jihad* as a means to rid Muslim land of foreign invaders, and under the mentorship of Azzam and other influential Islamist ideologues, bin Laden increasingly took up militant Islamist views.

---

[2] Wahhabism, commonly characterized as a Salafist and ultraconservative branch of Islam, is the dominant faith in Saudi Arabia. It is an austere form of Islam that is centered on strict and literal interpretation of the Qur'an.

[3] Lawrence Wright, *The Looming Tower: Al-Qaeda and the Road to 9/11* (New York: Random House, 2006), 78.

Azzam

Shortly after the start of the Soviet invasion of Afghanistan in December 1979, bin Laden made the decision to travel to Afghanistan to join Azzam there, and he eventually established himself as a financier and recruiter for the *mujahideen* in Afghanistan. He worked very closely with Azzam, who issued a *fatwa* (religious decree) that called upon Muslims all over the world to join the Afghan jihad, and together, the two of them established Maktab al-Khidamat (MAK), or the Services Bureau, in Peshawar. What started as a loosely organized network of fighters quickly turned into a structured vehicle to raise funds and channel foreign fighters into the war. Though the MAK played a minimal role in the war itself, some cite the MAK as the predecessor to al-Qaeda, and there's no question that the networks it created and the trained fighters it produced were instrumental in the formation of al-Qaeda.

After several years of supporting the Afghan *jihad*, and as the war in Afghanistan was coming to a close, bin Laden began to extend his ambitions beyond Afghanistan to a more global stage. He no longer saw Afghanistan as the only land in need of Islamic liberation but the entire world as his battleground, and *jihad* as his war that had yet to be won. His mentor, Abdullah Azzam, agreed, writing in April 1988 that a "pioneering vanguard" needed to be formed that would pave the way for the ideal Islamic society. To both bin Laden and Azzam, Afghanistan was just the beginning: "We shall continue the jihad no matter how long the way, until the last breath and the last beat of the pulse—or until we see the Islamic state established."[4]

In August 1988, bin Laden and his associates met in Peshawar, Pakistan, to discuss the formation of a global organization from what they had already began building in Afghanistan, a recruiting, training, and financing structure for Islamic militants.[5] Though the men present at this meeting all had varied backgrounds, including different countries of origins, social status, and battle experience, they were all united by one common goal of reclaiming Muslim land and establishing an Islamic state. The men acknowledged the need for a united front that was bigger than the MAK, and that the next step must be taken. Thus, in a quiet suburb of Peshawar, at a secretive meeting of the most committed jihadists, al-Qaeda was formed.

Abdullah Azzam wanted this new organization to act as

---

[4] Wright, *The Looming Tower,* 130.
[5] Peter L. Bergen, *The Osama Bin Laden I Know* (New York: Free Press, 2006), 80-81.

a global force of Muslim fighters that could intervene in any conflict or country where Muslims were perceived to be threatened. He was focused on a more traditional interpretation of *jihad*, the reclamation of once Muslim lands in places like Palestine and Andalus[6]. But bin Laden, on the other hand, took up a more radical interpretation and sought the violent overthrow of Muslim rulers he deemed as apostates and infidels. Bin Laden's experience as a recruiter, logistical coordinator, and financier for the Afghan and Arab resistance in Afghanistan did not just give him confidence, credibility, and expertise but also made him believe that Muslims could take effective military action inspired by select Islamic principles. He desired to crush the apostate regime of Egypt, where the country's leaders had established ties with Israel and Western powers, and he also wanted to destroy the blasphemy that was Israel's existence in the Middle East. He wished to topple presidents, kings, and entire states, and with the victory in Afghanistan, he believed that this was now possible.

As such, the birth of al-Qaeda produced what would be an irreparable rift between bin Laden and his mentor, but this divergence didn't end up mattering much because Azzam was assassinated by unknown assailants in November 1989, only about a year after the founding of al-Qaeda. [7] With Azzam gone, Osama bin Laden assumed full control of his nascent but steadily growing

---

[6] Andalus (also known as Islamic Iberia) was a medieval Islamic (Moorish) state that was formed in present-day southern Spain and Portugal, as well as parts of southern France. Andalus was eventually conquered by the Christian kingdoms in the north. However, Islamic culture is still evident in southern Spain, particularly in Cordoba, which was the capital of Andalus.

[7] Bergen, *The Osama Bin Laden I Know*, 74.

organization.

In addition to bin Laden and Azzam, several other notable figures played a role in the formation and growth of al-Qaeda, the most prominent being Dr. Ayman al-Zawahiri. Ayman al-Zawahiri was born on June 19, 1951 and raised in Cairo, Egypt, where he grew up in turbulent times. The Arab world was still reeling from the creation of the state of Israel, and throughout his early years, al-Zawahiri felt anger when Egypt suffered an embarrassing defeat in the 1967 Six Day War against Israel. He was also excited when the Islamist movement of the Muslim Brotherhood was gaining momentum.

Al-Zawahiri was known to be a man with a pensive and quiet demeanor, and pious to a degree that made even his family uncomfortable. Perhaps as an early indication of his future militancy, al-Zawahiri started an underground cell devoted to overthrowing the Egyptian government at the young age of fifteen.[8] This cell eventually grew to become the Egyptian al-Jihad, which later merged with al-Qaeda.

A physician by education and training, al-Zawahiri traveled to Peshawar, Pakistan in 1981 to work in a Red Crescent hospital treating wounded refugees. While in Pakistan, he had several opportunities to make furtive trips across the border into Afghanistan, and it was there that he witnessed with his own eyes the valor, courage, and dedication of the fighters who called themselves *mujahideen.* Al-Zawahiri eventually returned to Cairo "full of stories about the 'miracles' that were taking place in the *jihad* against the Soviets."[9]

---

[8] Wright, *The Looming Tower,* 37.

In 1981, al-Zawahiri was one of hundreds who were detained following the assassination of Egyptian President Anwar Sadat by an al-Jihad cell (though purportedly without al-Zawahiri's knowledge). For years, al-Zawahiri was kept in detainment, and some have said that the severe torture he endured in the dark prisons of Cairo was what eventually led the quiet, polite, well-educated doctor down the vengeful path of *jihad*. Upon his release, al-Zawahiri traveled to Saudi Arabia, and it is there that sources say he first met Osama bin Laden.[10] In 1986, he traveled to Peshawar and began working at a hospital there. Bin Laden frequently visited him, and two grew close; al-Zawahiri shared his dream of the toppling of the political order and establishment of an Islamic state in Egypt, and in turn, he listened to bin Laden's own goals.

When bin Laden left for Sudan, he and al-Zawahiri and bin Laden went their separate ways, and Egyptian al-Jihad under al-Zawahiri's leadership repeatedly experienced failed attacks and foiled assassination plots against Egyptian government officials. Though al-Jihad's November 1995 bombing of the Egyptian Embassy in Islamabad was a success, bin Laden severely disapproved of it because the bombing triggered an immense round-up of suspected militants in Pakistan, which was the best route into Afghanistan. With declining support and depleting funds, Ayman al-Zawahiri formally decided to merge what was left of his al-Jihad with al-Qaeda in 1998.

Al-Zawahiri gained significant experience and loyalty during his years at bin Laden's side. Often described as

[9] Ibid., 45.
[10] Ibid., 61.

bin Laden's "top lieutenant" and identified by some as the "real brains" of the organization, al-Zawahiri now leads today's al-Qaeda following the death of Osama bin Laden in 2011.[11] David Wright wrote about the relationship between Osama bin Laden and Ayman al-Zawahiri as such: "Each man filled a need in the other. Zawahiri wanted money and contacts, which bin Laden had in abundance. Bin Laden, an idealist given to causes, sought direction; Zawahiri, a seasoned propagandist, supplied it. They were not friends but allies. Each believed he could use the other, and each was pulled in a direction he never intended to go. The Egyptian had little interest in Afghanistan except as a staging area for the revolution in his own country. He planned to use the Afghan jihad as an opportunity to rebuild his shattered organization. In bin Laden, he found a wealthy, charismatic, and pliable sponsor. The young Saudi was a devout Salafist but not much of a political thinker. Until he met Zawahiri, he had never voiced opposition to his own government or other repressive Arab regimes. His main interest was in expelling the infidel invader from a Muslim land, but he also nursed an ill-formed longing to punish America and the West for what he believed were crimes against Islam. The dynamic of the two men's relationship made Zawahiri and bin Laden into people they would never have been individually; moreover, the organization they would create, al-Qaeda, would be a vector of these two forces, one Egyptian and one Saudi."[12]

---

[11] Scott Baldauf, "The 'Cave Man' and Al Qaeda," *The Christian Science Monitor,* October 31, 2001, http://www.csmonitor.com/2001/1031/p6s1-wosc.html.

[12] Wright, *The Looming Tower,* 127.

Furthermore, al-Zawahiri was essential in the formation of the al-Qaeda concept of global *jihad* in the organization's early years. Since al-Zawahiri was so narrowly focused on *jihad* in Egypt and bin Laden so broadly caught up in *jihad* anywhere there were infidel invaders on Muslim land, each man was forced to compromise in order to accommodate the goals of the other. Bin Laden was kept from professing aims that were too ambiguous and unrealistic, whereas al-Zawahiri was encouraged to expand his focus outside Egypt and look at the entire world as potential areas of operations. As a result of the cooperation between the two men, al-Qaeda's path of global *jihad* was set.

Much has been written about the true nature of foreign (and especially American) involvement in the funding, training, and arming of the *mujahideen* in Afghanistan, and how this eventually contributed to the formation of al-Qaeda. Theories revolving around covert CIA operations exist, but these theories still have no supporting evidence. What is definitively known is that the U.S. government viewed the Afghan *mujahideen* as a potent force in the fight against the Soviets, and accordingly, the U.S. funneled substantial amounts of funds, weapons, and arms to militant groups in Afghanistan. Though the U.S. has revealed that it covertly supported Afghan *mujahideen* factions (estimates indicate an amount of approximately $3 billion from 1981-1991), it has categorically denied directly financing any non-Afghan volunteers, including Osama bin Laden's group.[13]

---

[13] U.S. Library of Congress, Congressional Research Service, *Al Qaeda: Profile and Threat Assessment,* by Kenneth Katzman, CRS Report RL33038 (Washington, DC: Office of Congressional Information

Despite official denials, many articles and reports have been written about secret CIA operations in Afghanistan. For example, Ahmed Rashid wrote in his piece on the Taliban: "With the active encouragement of the CIA and Pakistan's ISI [Inter-Service Intelligence], who wanted to turn the Afghan Jihad into a global war waged by all Muslim states against the Soviet Union, some 35,000 Muslim radicals from 40 Islamic countries joined Afghanistan's fight between 1982 and 1992. Tens of thousands more came to study in Pakistani madrasahs. Eventually, more than 100,000 foreign Muslim radicals were directly influenced by the Afghan jihad."[14] Whether U.S. funding or support contributed in any way to the founding of al-Qaeda, and how much it impacted the growth of the organization if there was any, cannot be determined. Speculations about CIA complicity abound, but to date, there is no concrete evidence pointing to U.S. involvement in the physical establishment of bin Laden's al-Qaeda, whether financially, operationally, or logistically. In fact, Ayman al-Zawahiri, the former leader of the Egyptian Islamic Jihad, lieutenant of bin Laden, and current leader of al-Qaeda, clearly stated in his autobiography, *Knights under the Prophet's Banner*, "The truth that everyone should learn is that the United States did not give one penny in aid to the mujahideen. Is it possible that Osama bin Laden who, in his lectures in the year 1987, called for the boycott of U.S. goods as a form of support for the Intifada in Palestine, is a U.S. agent in

---

and Publishing, August 17, 2005).

[14] Ahmed Rashid, "The Taliban: Exporting Extremism," *Foreign Affairs,* November-December 1999, http://www.foreignaffairs.com/articles/55600/ahmed-rashid/the-taliban-exporting-extremism.

Afghanistan?"[15]

Saudi Arabia is also often accused of having a role in the formation of al-Qaeda. Abu Musab al-Suri, a long-time Syrian associate of bin Laden, wrote in his book *The International Islamic Resistance Call*, that "the truth is that Saudi intelligence agencies did have involvement with bin Laden, and elements of their apparatus did send assistance from Saudi Arabia," while denying any links between bin Laden and the CIA.

However, neither al-Suri nor al-Zawahiri's statements can be taken at face value, because both individuals had significant reason to hide any ties between al-Qaeda and the CIA. Furthermore, al-Qaeda's goal of defeating apostate powers like America and Saudi Arabia has been and still is one of the key rallying points of the group.

In sum, the formation of al-Qaeda was impacted by many factors, including the foreign fighter phenomenon in Afghanistan, charismatic leadership, and a committed membership. The very fact that countries like the U.S. completely overlooked these Arab *mujahideen* factions in Afghanistan and deemed them as allies also meant that bin Laden was relatively free to act with impunity and without scrutiny in forming and building his organization, at least during this initial phase. As a result, what began as a small group of less than two dozen fighters began to snowball into a larger organization that would eventually top most countries' lists of the most dangerous terrorist organization, but even still, plenty of things about the origins of al-Qaeda remain murky. As journalist Adam Curtis pointed out, "The reality was that bin Laden and

---

[15] Bergen, *The Osama Bin Laden I Know*, 61.

Ayman al-Zawahiri had become the focus of a loose association of disillusioned Islamist militants who were attracted by the new strategy. But there was no organization. These were militants who mostly planned their own operations and looked to bin Laden for funding and assistance. He was not their commander. There is also no evidence that bin Laden used the term 'al-Qaeda' to refer to the name of a group until after September 11 attacks, when he realized that this was the term the Americans had given it."

The Ideology of Al-Qaeda

"Islam is different from any other religion; it's a way of life. We were trying to understand what Islam has to say about how we eat, who we marry, how we talk. We read Sayyid Qutb. He was the one who most affected our generation." - Mohammed Jamal Khalifa, a college friend of bin Laden's

"While the leadership's own theological platform is essentially Salafi, the organization's umbrella is sufficiently wide to encompass various schools of thought and political leanings. Al-Qaeda counts among its members and supporters people associated with Wahhabism, Shafi'ism, Malikism, and Hanafism. There are even some whose beliefs and practices are directly at odds with Salafism, such as Yunis Khalis, one of the leaders of the Afghan mujahedin. He is a mystic who visits tombs of saints and seeks their blessings—practices inimical to bin Laden's Wahhabi-Salafi school of thought. The only exception to this pan-Islamic policy is Shi'ism. Al-Qaeda seems implacably opposed to it, as it holds Shi'ism to be heresy. In Iraq it has openly declared war on the Badr Brigades, who have fully cooperated with the US, and now considers even Shi'i civilians to be legitimate targets for acts of violence." – Abdel Bari Atwan

As a movement advocating the return of Muslims to the fundamental tenets of Islam, Islamic fundamentalism emerged in the 1920s, but it was only in the late 1970s to 1980s that the movement began to gain significant political traction in the Middle East. Starting from this period, fundamentalism swept across the region to fill the ideological void felt by many Muslims, thereby providing what was largely deemed as a much needed blueprint for the role of Islam, of Muslims, and of the Middle East in the future of the world.

Several factors can be attributed to why Islamic fundamentalism blossomed in this era, but there were three key events that decidedly contributed to this phenomenon, and ultimately to the emergence of such radical ideologies like that of al-Qaeda. These events were the 1973 oil boom and the rise of Saudi Arabia, the Iranian Revolution of 1979, and the Soviet War in Afghanistan from 1979-1989. In a period that featured an increasing realization that the secular state had failed and Muslims were in a state of civilizational and political crisis and decline, these three events created a region-wide social and political environment in which Muslims brought to light new fundamentalist ideological interpretations of their religion, their countries, their politics, and their existence.

In October 1973, the Organization of the Petroleum Exporting Countries (OPEC), a Saudi-led economic cartel formed by oil-producing countries, initiated an oil embargo against the U.S. and other countries in protest of Western support of Israel against Arab nations in the Yom Kippur War of 1973. The embargo and the subsequent quadrupling of oil prices had devastating effects on U.S. and world economies, while also exposing the sheer severity of Western dependency on oil. As a result, the oil-rich monarchies, particularly Saudi Arabia, gained much notoriety and prestige among Arabs. People in the region could look to conservative Saudi Arabia – for decades branded as "American-made" and historically shunned to the fringes of Middle Eastern politics that was, at this time, overflowing with Nasserites and Arab socialism – suddenly bringing major countries to bend to its will. King Faysal was touted as the victorious hero, and Saudi Arabia the epitome of oil wealth and power, an Arab nation that stood apart from the rest not only in terms of unprecedented political sway but also in economic power. Whereas affluence and nobility were associated with Westernized suits and uncovered heads a decade ago, the rise of Saudi Arabia made devotion to Islamic practices a mark of prestige.

Meanwhile, oil money flooded into Saudi Arabia and was subsequently used to finance a campaign for its own Saudi brand of Islam: Wahhabism, the same branch of Islam Osama bin Laden practiced. The Saudis extended a sympathetic hand to fundamentalists, who inherently shared Wahhabism's anti-secular, puritanical streak, and from the 1970s onward, Saudi Arabia began to fund the activities and proliferation of Islamic educational institutions called *madrasas*, bankrolling its Wahhabism across the region and giving it basis in these religious schools. Saudi Arabia invested not so much in roads or bridges but more in the building of mosques and other Islamic causes, and the Saudis' mass distribution of radical Islamic texts across the region fell into the hands of many, particularly the youth. These efforts transformed the region into one rife with religious conservatism, which further made it more receptive to fundamentalism.

The explosive growth of Saudi-funded *madrasas* continued and became increasingly important during the Soviet occupation of Afghanistan, as extremist *madrasas* emerged in the Pakistan-Afghanistan region that focused more on *jihad* against the infidels than on Islamic scholarship. Saudi oil wealth was therefore used to give birth to a certain regional milieu, and equally important, it provided an institutional base that allowed for and encouraged fundamentalist interpretations of Islam.

The second key event was the 1979 Iranian Revolution, which led to the toppling of the Western backed Pahlavi dynasty in Iran and its replacement with a purely Islamic republic under Ayatollah Khomeini. The revolution was an event that enhanced Islamic fundamentalism as a viable alternative ideology for opposition against and overthrow of long-established secular regime, and its success in Iran confirmed the failure of the secular state model and proved the power of Islam. Fundamentalists could now point to Iran as proof that Islam could overthrow an entire system that was backed by the West, achieving what all other ideologies like Marxism and Leninism failed miserably to do. Iran thus became the concrete example of progress and independence as achieved through Islam, and from Lebanon to Palestine, Senegal to Malaysia, and even in Muslim communities in Europe, there was an identifiable surge in Islamist enthusiasm. Even Osama bin Laden was heavily inspired by this revolution, despite the fact that it was a Shi'a victory; there is evidence that bin Laden was so impressed with Shi'a radicalism and the Iranian Revolution that he gladly received assistance from Iranian backed militant groups like Hezbollah despite being a Sunni fundamentalist.[16]

[16] *The 9/11 Commission Report: Final Report of the National Commission on Terrorist Attacks Upon the United States*, official government edition (Washington, DC: U.S. Government Printing Office, 2004), 240.

Ayatollah Khomeini

In general, people do not personally and privately adopt a certain ideology or belief system simply and solely because an authority, or the state, or certain scriptures tell them to; they do so because it offers an efficient solution and a realistic chance of success. Islamic fundamentalism at its core is about the creation of an Islamic state, and before Iran's revolution, this seemed a desperately intangible figment of imagination. The emergence of the Islamic state of Iran served as the much-needed success story, bringing the fundamentalist argument out of the realm of theories. The fact that the revolution was led by an exiled cleric was further proof that Islam can overcome seemingly impossible odds and bring about regime change, making the concept of the Islamic state actually viable in the minds of many. This realization and resurgence of a new kind of optimism resonated throughout the region.

The Soviet War in Afghanistan was the third significant event that precipitated the resurgence of political Islam and Islamic fundamentalism. The Afghan *jihad* and the subsequent Soviet withdrawal showed that Islam was capable of defeating a superpower, and it was the watershed event that took Islamic fundamentalism to an even higher level. Its impact went beyond the realm of Sunnis versus Shiites, or Iran versus Saudi Arabia, because the Afghan *jihad* transformed into an Islamic *jihad*, a holy war won by all Muslims of the world.

The significance of this event lay in the fact that Muslims came to Afghanistan to fight from all over the world and then returned to their respective home countries all across the world. Legions of young men traveled to Afghanistan, received military training, fought side-by-side, and eventually returned home, but their minds remained in Afghanistan. Throughout the 1980s, these young guerillas gathered, exchanged ideas, and created a community in which the Afghan war became a universal Islamic *jihad* that was neither particular to Afghanistan nor to any other single Muslim country, as it pertained to any and all Muslims as one united struggle. Once the notion of the Afghan war as an Islamic *jihad* spread, more and more Islamists travelled to Afghanistan, including Osama bin Laden, Abdullah Azzam, and the early founders of al-Qaeda.

While all of these events served as influences and provided the context and backdrop for al-Qaeda's worldview, al-Qaeda members subscribed to a particularly radical and political form of Islam. Such movements hold certain common beliefs, the most important of them being the idea that Islam is the comprehensive and exclusive solution for all political, economic, diplomatic, and social problems of the world. Islam is therefore interpreted as a political ideology rather than as a purely theological construct; it is taken outside of the religious realm it has historically occupied and into the secular domain of politics.

Following the Islamic fundamentalist trend, al-Qaeda's ideology was based on several key perceptions its founders had of the world. First, it was believed that Muslims across the world were under attack by corrupt and infidel powers and were being oppressed in Afghanistan, Iraq, Israel, the Palestinian territories, and

Egypt. As with other Islamic fundamentalist movements, al-Qaeda's ideology was based on the view that the Islamic civilization was steadily in decline, and this was the fault of non-Islamic powers like the West and Israel, as well as heretical Arab regimes that cooperated with the infidel countries. Second, whether they realized it or not, the founders of al-Qaeda based their grievances not on religion but on politics. Though the woes that they raised were dressed in religious and theocratic terms, the basic grievances were inherently based on politics, such as the lack of an Islamic political power, alleged exploitation of Muslim regimes by Western superpowers, and oppression of Arabs by apostate monarchs.

This is an important distinction to make, because al-Qaeda used and still continues to use religious text to legitimize its violent pursuit of political goals.[17] An apt example of this is how al-Qaeda uses the term *jihad* to legitimize and in many ways decriminalize its use of violence. In al-Qaeda's view, *jihad* is defined purely as a "war" that is obligatory for all Muslims to undertake against any enemies of Islam, particularly non-Muslims, polytheists, and those who support them. However, in the Qur'anic sense, and according to most Islamic scholars, *jihad* simply means a "struggle" or "striving", such as struggling against one's inner evil and striving for goodness and excellence. Thus, the acutely violent nature associated with it is a misuse of the term. It is true that the Qur'an is full of references to *jihad,* and some lines order believers to "slay the idolaters wherever you find them"

---

[17] Note that as this is the very definition of terrorism: the use of violence or the threat of violence for the achievement of political goals.

and to "fight those who do not believe in God...until they pay the tax in acknowledgement of superiority and they are in a state of subjection."[18] However, Islamic scholars explain these lines by putting them into context and assert that these injunctions apply only when Muslims are invaded or persecuted, or when Islam itself is threatened, as the Qur'an also commands Muslims to "fight in the way of God against those who fight against you, and be not aggressive; surely God loves not aggression."[19] Over time, *jihad* has been used so frequently as an interchangeable term for "war" – not just by al-Qaeda but also by many other militant Islamist groups – that the term has mutated to become the legitimizing religious basis for waging violence.

Another example is al-Qaeda's use of the word *takfir*, which is a term used to describe the practice of excommunication of *kafirs*, or non-believers. In the traditional sense, *takfir* was employed only in rare circumstances when one Muslim accused another of abandoning his or her religious duties, thereby branding the accused as an apostate. In orthodox Islamic law, this is considered to be an extremely serious matter, so *takfir* requires stringent evidence and ample justifications for such accusations. However, al-Qaeda views this differently and has regularly used the term in an attempt to discredit other Muslims who oppose them, or to legitimize attacking and even killing fellow Muslims. This is despite the fact that the Qur'an explicitly states that Muslims must not kill except as punishment for murder.

---

[18] Wright, *The Looming Tower,* 108.
[19] Ibid., 108.

Moreover, according to the Qur'an, he who murders one innocent is judged "as if he had murdered all of mankind," and the killing of fellow Muslims is an even more punishable act. The Qur'an then concludes that those who do engage in the killing of Muslims will find that their "repayment is Hell, remaining in it timelessly, forever."[20] But even with such explicit condemnation of murder, al-Qaeda has successfully twisted and altered the term to its advantage.

In these ways, al-Qaeda has consistently misrepresented and politicized traditional religious tenets of Islam, using them to justify its ideology and its violent ways. Al-Qaeda's immediate goal is the overthrow of what it sees as heretical governments of Muslim states and replacing them with an Islamic state based on *sharia* law, and the only way to do this is through *jihad*. Al-Qaeda also claims that the current poverty and depravity of the Muslim world is to be blamed on the alliance between Zionists and Crusaders, their terms for Israel and the West. Any Muslim governments that have good relations with Israel and the West and do not adhere to al-Qaeda's politicized definition of Islam are deemed as apostates, and *takfir* must be declared against them.

Lawrence Wright in *The Looming Tower,* one of the most seminal books on al-Qaeda, shed light onto some of the training materials of al-Qaeda recruits in the 1990s. In recovered "class" notes, trainees listed the goals of the organization:

1. Establishing the rule of God on Earth.
2. Attaining martyrdom in the cause of God.

---

[20] Ibid., 124.

3.   Purification of the ranks of Islam from the elements of depravity.[21]

Additionally, the "enemies of Islam" were identified as:

1.   Heretics (the Mubaraks of the world)
2.   Shiites
3.   America
4.   Israel [22]

Though the above is from training notes taken by al-Qaeda recruits more than two decades ago, the content still resonates with al-Qaeda's ideology today. Islam, *sharia*, and the establishment of an Islamic state based on *sharia* law have been central to the al-Qaeda ideology, just as they were central to many of the Islamic fundamentalist and radical Islamist movements of the era. Thus, the basic foundations of al-Qaeda ideology were nothing new, as they were largely based on the tenets of other Islamic fundamentalist movements, such as the one instigated by Islamic theorist Sayyid Qutb, who in the 1950s and 1960s was one of the greatest proponents of strict compliance to *sharia* law and obedience to the principles of pure Islam.

---

[21] Ibid., 302.
[22] Ibid., 303.

Qutb

Many scholars have argued that the writings of Sayyid Qutb, often regarded as the father of modern Islamic fundamentalism, were essential in the formation of the al-Qaeda ideology. Qutb's goal of a world based on *sharia,* his rage against the secular government of Egypt, and his militant interpretation of *jihad* would later inspire the founding members of al-Qaeda, including Osama bin Laden and Abdullah Azzam. In what many call his most important work, *Milestones,* Qutb wrote that God had created Islam for the following purpose: "[Ignorant people] want Islam to become a mere collection of abstractions and theories, the subject of whose application is non-existent conditions. But the course prescribed by God for this religion is the same as it was earlier. First, belief ought to be imprinted on hearts and rule over consciences – that belief which demands that people should not bow before anyone except God or derive laws from any other source. Then, when such a group of people is ready and also against practical control of society, various laws will be legislated according to the practical needs of that society."[23] Qutb further went on to write that "[*sharia*] is not limited only to legal matters, as some people assign this narrow meaning to the *Sharia*. The fact is that attitudes, the way of living, the values, criteria, habits and traditions, are all legislated and affect people."[24] As such, al-Qaeda defines this unhindered and complete subjugation to God in all areas of life as the highest form of freedom for all.

Though there emerged many Islamist movements inspired by the work of Sayyid Qutb, al-Qaeda differed in that it was fully convinced that the creation of such an Islamic utopia could not happen peacefully. In a statement issued by al-Qaeda, bin Laden's foremost associate in Iraq, Abu Mus'ab al-Zarqawi, was quoted as saying, "There is no doubt that the Imamate [universal authority in all religious and secular affairs] is established by means of fealty from the proponents of valor—in other words, force."[25] Such a reorganization of the world would require

---

[23] Sayyid Qutb, "Milestones," in *Political Dissent: A Global Reader: Modern Sources*, ed. Derek Malone-France (Plymouth: Lexington Books, 2012), 229.

[24] James S. Robbins, "Al-Qaeda Versus Democracy," *The Journal of International Security Affairs* 9 (2005): 53-59.

[25] Ibid.

coercion and violence, not just against non-Muslims but even against Muslims if necessary. As noted before, it is significant that al-Qaeda sanctifies the killing of Muslims – an act strictly prohibited by the Qur'an – and legitimizes it as part of the collateral damage in the war for Islam.

It must be noted that these views held by al-Qaeda are decidedly unpopular among most of the Muslim population of the world, but it has historically not mattered all that much to al-Qaeda whether its beliefs have popular ground among the mainstream population or not. By and large, al-Qaeda has had little interest in gaining social support, nor does it feel the need to convince the large majority of the Muslim population that does not adhere to its beliefs. It simply believes that the world must be forcibly changed for the good of all Muslims, and that al-Qaeda is the vanguard of this change.

In sum, though al-Qaeda's ideology has taken inspiration from the Islamic fundamentalism movement of the 1900s, and particularly from the works of radical thinkers like Sayyid Qutb, the group took things one step further by building a perverse and distorted interpretation of the Qur'an and using this to justify its acts of killing and violence. And even more dangerous is that this corrupt interpretation of Islam has gained resonance and following in a very small but still formidable minority of Muslims. The al-Qaeda ideology has been key in the group's successful recruitment of hundreds of young extremist fighters from all over the world.

Al-Qaeda's Most Notorious Attacks of the 1990s

"America is a great power possessed of tremendous

military might and a wide-ranging economy, but all this is built on an unstable foundation which can be targeted, with special attention to its obvious weak spots. If America is hit in one hundredth of these weak spots, God willing, it will stumble, wither away and relinquish world leadership." – Osama bin Laden

"Any country that steps into the same trench as the Jews has only itself to blame." – Osama bin Laden

Ultimately, what has distinguished al-Qaeda from similar like-minded groups is that it has been responsible for some of the deadliest and most high-profile terrorist attacks in history, and to accomplish them, al-Qaeda has employed a number of tactics, most notably suicide bombings, car bombings, and hijackings. Most of its large-scale operations were extremely well planned, often over several months or even years, and the target has consistently been the United States.

Given that al-Qaeda's professed goals include toppling Arab regimes deemed apostates by bin Laden, or retribution against Israel, why was the U.S. the primary focus of all of al-Qaeda's attacks? In 1991, in response to the Iraqi invasion of Kuwait, the U.S. stationed troops in Saudi Arabia with the blessing of the Saudi king. Bin Laden was livid, not just because foreign boots were stampeding on what is popularly considered the holiest land in Islam but also because he had wanted to help defend the Saudi kingdom with his own group. By lashing out, bin Laden was caught up in the Saudi government's crackdown on dissidents and was ultimately forced into exile. Bin Laden took refuge in Sudan in 1992 and later in Afghanistan in 1996.

On December 29, 1992, two bombs detonated in Aden, Yemen. One exploded in the Movenpick Hotel, and another went off in the parking lot of the nearby Goldmohur Hotel. The bombers had targeted American troops who were on their way to Somalia to participate in a relief operation, but in actuality, the soldiers were not staying at either hotel. Widely cited as al-Qaeda's first bombing attacks, the double Aden bombings were also al-Qaeda's first operation that resulted in civilian deaths. An Australian tourist and a Yemeni hotel worker was killed, and several other Yemeni civilians were severely injured. Almost simultaneously, a group of al-Qaeda operatives were detained at the Aden airport as they prepared to launch rockets at U.S. military planes.[26]

Not only was al-Qaeda's first attack intended to target the U.S., it was also part of a larger plan centered on bin Laden's vision of a global *jihad*. At the time, the U.S. troops had been intervening in Somalia in response to the breaking out of a civil war that was destabilizing the country. Bin Laden, whose group had been training Somali militants to fight American forces, saw this intervention as yet another form of Western aggression and oppression. Most notably, the attack showed complete disregard for civilians, solidifying the al-Qaeda strategy of civilian casualties being acceptable in their war.

No Americans were killed, and the soldiers went on to Somalia, so the attack was barely noticed by U.S. security officials, but al-Qaeda rejoiced in the perceived success of

[26] Robert Windrem, "Al-Qaida Timeline: Plots and Attacks," *NBC News*, accessed June 12, 2014, http://www.nbcnews.com/id/4677978/ns/world_news-hunt_for_al_qaida/t/al-qaida-timeline-plots-attacks/#.U6I33fmSySp.

their operation, especially when the U.S. announced shortly after the December 29 bombings that it would no longer use Yemen as a base for soldiers deploying to Somalia. Thus, bin Laden claimed victory, and those recruits training with the still nascent al-Qaeda who had any doubts about the organization's prowess became further convinced that al-Qaeda was now the leading organization conducting *jihad* against the West. These attacks were a clear show of al-Qaeda's global goals.

Yemen also held special significance for bin Laden because Hadramawt (in eastern Yemen) was the birthplace of his father, and thus it was bin Laden's ancestral home. The supposed victory in Yemen thus held double the meaning for Osama bin Laden, and al-Qaeda's presence in Yemen and its neighboring countries would gradually strengthen over the decades, eventually leading to the formation of al-Qaeda in the Arabian Peninsula (AQAP).

On February 26, 1993, Ramzi Yousef parked a truck bomb below the North Tower of the World Trade Center in New York City, set the timing device on the bomb, and then swiftly departed. The subsequent detonation killed 6 people and caused plenty of damage, but Yousef had hoped to possibly knock both towers down and kill thousands.

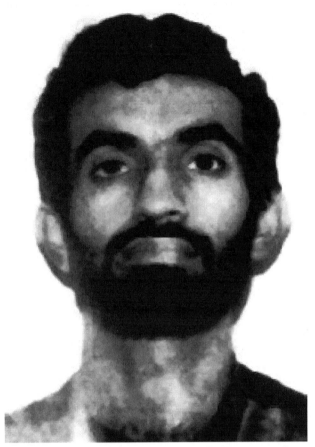

The FBI's photo of Yousef

Yousef became the first Islamist jihadist terrorist to successfully execute an attack on U.S. soil, but while this terrorist attack certainly got the country's attention, it is unclear how much involvement bin Laden or other senior leaders of al-Qaeda had in the planning and execution of this plot. Yousef was a product of an al-Qaeda camp in Afghanistan and had undergone explosives training there, but perhaps more notably, Yousef's uncle was Khalid Shaikh Mohammed [27], the alleged architect of the 9/11

---

[27] Khalid Sheikh Mohammad (often shortened to KSM) was detained in 2003 in Pakistan and currently in U.S. military custody at Guantanamo Bay prison. He was identified as the mastermind of the 9/11 attacks by the 9/11 Commission Report. It is alleged that he met up with his nephew Ramzi Yousef in the Philippines while Yousef was on the run, and together developed a hijacking plot called the "Bojinka" plot – the intended bombing of 12 U.S. commercial jets over the Pacific during a two-day span. For more details, see *The 9/11 Commission Report: Final Report of the National Commission on Terrorist Attacks Upon the United States*, official government edition. Washington, DC: U.S. Government Printing Office, 2004, 240.

attacks and a man who already had ties to Osama bin Laden.

Khalid Shaikh Mohammed

At the time of the 1993 attack, Khalid Shaikh Mohammed was mostly operating in Southeast Asia independently of al-Qaeda, and since the World Trade Center bombing's link to al-Qaeda remained unclear, few people stopped to reexamine, reassess, and realize the character and extent of the new threat facing the U.S. and the larger world. The subsequent trials of those involved in this 1993 plot did not bring al-Qaeda's network or Osama bin Laden to the attention of policymakers or the public.

Regardless of al-Qaeda's degree of involvement in the planning and execution of this attack, the fact that the attack was conducted on U.S. soil by foreigners who had easily slipped into American territory was astonishing. The FBI chased after the culprits ferociously, and the legal system prosecuted them so harshly and successfully that no one stopped to think about the bigger picture of how Ramzi Yousef and his accomplices had conducted such a sophisticated operation.

The attacks on 9/11 would make al-Qaeda a household name across the world, but the plot itself did not originate with bin Laden or his group. In the early '90s, before he joined al-Qaeda, Khalid Sheikh Mohammed was in the Philippines devising plots that focused on bombing international airliners. Working with his nephew, Ramzi Yousef, who had successfully fled the United States after bombing the World Trade Center in 1993, Khalid Sheikh Mohammed came up with a plot known as Operation Bojinka, which would have simultaneously detonated bombs on a dozen airliners over the Pacific Ocean while they were on their way to the United States.

Operation Bojinka was well on its way to being attempted when a chemical fire started in Yousef's apartment, forcing him to flee and leave the bomb making materials in the complex. The fire attracted the attention of authorities, forcing Yousef and Khalid Sheikh Mohammed to flee to Pakistan. Pakistani authorities eventually caught Yousef and extradited him to the United States, but his uncle remained at large.

Dramatic flair and theater are what make terrorist attacks so successful, and al-Qaeda began to realize this. Though the number of deaths caused by this bombing was relatively small, the immense fear that was generated by an attack on one of the most symbolic skyscrapers in the busiest city in America surely served as an indication to al-Qaeda that even without large casualties, an attack could be economically and politically devastating to its superpower enemy if conducted on the right target with enough intensity, complexity, and sophistication.

Despite assurances by then-President George H.W. Bush to King Fahd of Saudi Arabia in 1990 that the U.S. would withdraw all its forces from Saudi Arabia once the Iraqi threat had been resolved, American troops were still on Saudi soil in 1996. While this was not drawing any Saudi protests, bin Laden used their presence as his justification to declare war on America. He claimed that "the 'evils' of the Middle East arose from America's attempt to take over the region and from its support for Israel. Saudi Arabia had been turned into an American colony."[28]

In August 1996, Osama bin Laden issued his first call for *jihad* against the U.S. in the form of a *fatwa* (religious decree). Called the "Declaration of Jihad on the Americans Occupying the Country of the Two Sacred Places," the *fatwa* lambasted Washington's continued military occupation in Saudi Arabia and urged all able Muslims to engage in *jihad* against the U.S. since it was now their sacred duty: "It should not be hidden from you that the people of Islam had suffered from aggression, iniquity and injustice imposed on them by the Zionist-Crusaders alliance and their collaborators; to the extent that the Muslims blood became the cheapest and their wealth as loot in the hands of the enemies. Their blood was spilled in Palestine and Iraq. The horrifying pictures of the massacre of Qana, in Lebanon are still fresh in our memory. Massacres in Tajikistan, Burma, Kashmir,

---

[28] Robert Fisk, *The Great War for Civilisation: The Conquest of the Middle East* (New York: Vintage House, 2005), 22.

Assam, Philippines, Pattani, Ogaden, Somalia, Eritrea, Chechnya, and in Bosnia-Herzegovina took place, massacres that send shivers in the body and shake the conscience. All of this and the world watch and hear, and not only didn't respond to these atrocities, but also with a clear conspiracy between the USA and its' allies and under the cover of the iniquitous United Nations, the dispossessed people were even prevented from obtaining arms to defend themselves. The people of Islam awakened and realized that they are the main target for the aggression of the Zionist-Crusaders alliance. All false claims and propaganda about 'Human Rights' were hammered down and exposed by the massacres that took place against the Muslims in every part of the world."

Though the *fatwa* had limited immediate impact on the world in general, it did have a significant effect on bin Laden's outlook, and therefore, on the direction al-Qaeda would take. After seeing his homeland "desecrated" by the presence of foreign infidels, bin Laden felt he must first cut off the head of the snake in order to save the Muslim world, and this head was none other than the United States.

On August 7, 1998, simultaneous bombs exploded at the U.S. embassies in Dar es Salaam, Tanzania and Nairobi, Kenya, which led to the deaths of hundreds of civilians and embassy personnel and the destruction of two American embassies. The two operations were extremely well planned, which became a trademark of future al-Qaeda operations. As far back as 1993, al-Qaeda operatives began to relocate to Kenya and Tanzania, and around December 1993, al-Qaeda operatives reportedly began casing potential targets in Nairobi for future attacks. Initial planning was suspected to have begun sometime in early 1998, when great numbers of key operatives began their move into East Africa. Surveillance reports were created and delivered to bin Laden, who along with his top advisers decided on the U.S. Embassy in Nairobi as one of the targets. Operatives divided into cells in Nairobi and Dar es Salaam, and members of the cells rented residences and purchased bomb-making materials, as well as transport vehicles and big trucks to carry the bombs.[29] Extended periods of reconnaissance were conducted, placements of the truck bombs were discussed and decided, and detonators and explosives were manufactured.

In total, 224 people, including 12 Americans, were killed, and more than 4,500 were wounded. The attacks were again claimed by al-Qaeda, and they triggered a harsh response from President Bill Clinton, who initiated Operation Infinite Reach and ordered cruise missiles launched against Osama bin Laden's suspected training camps in Afghanistan and Sudan. An indictment was swiftly issued against bin Laden and 20 other al-Qaeda operatives, and bin Laden was placed on the FBI's 10 most-wanted fugitives list, finally bringing al-Qaeda to the attention of not only the U.S. government but also the American public.

Together with the December 1992 Aden bombings, the U.S. Embassy bombings marked a dramatic and undeniable shift from local to global jihad. Al-Qaeda was no longer restricted by state boundaries, and it

---

[29] *The 9/11 Commission Report*, 69.

demonstrated its ability to smoothly operate across borders and continents. Additionally, the twin bombings also showed al-Qaeda's capacity to plan and conduct simultaneous operations, as well as its expertise in explosives manufacturing. The attack brought into sharp focus the immediate danger posed by al-Qaeda and transnational jihadists of its ilk.

The embassy bombings also made clear bin Laden and al-Qaeda's ruthlessness, and just how far they were willing to go to achieve their goals. When interviewed some time later about the deaths of civilians in the bombings, particularly Kenyan citizens, bin Laden replied, "When it becomes apparent that it would be impossible to repel these Americans without assaulting them, even if this involved the killing of Muslims, this is permissible under Islam."[30] Bin Laden effectively dismissed the deaths as justifiable collateral damage on the path of *jihad.*

Aden became the stage for another major al-Qaeda operation on October 12, 2000, when two al-Qaeda operatives on a small ship filled with explosives approached the U.S. Navy guided-missile destroyer USS *Cole,* which had been harbored at the port of Aden for refueling. Without warning, a deafening explosion rocked the waters and blew a hole 40-feet wide in the side of the ship, killing 17 American sailors and injuring more than three dozen. [31] Al-Qaeda swiftly claimed responsibility for the deadly attack, eulogizing the suicide bombers who

[30] Ibid., 70.

[31] U.S. Library of Congress, Congressional Research Service, *Terrorist Attack on USS Cole: Background and Issues for Congress,* by Raphael Perl and Ronald O'Rourke, CRS Report RL20721 (Washington, DC: Office of Congressional Information and Publishing, January 30, 2001).

triggered the explosions as martyrs. After extensive investigation by the FBI, in conjunction with assistance from local Yemeni law enforcement officials, it was concluded that the *Cole* bombing was a full-fledged al-Qaeda operation supervised directly by bin Laden. The 9/11 Commission Report noted the extent of bin Laden's involvement, stating that he "chose the target and location of the attack, selected the suicide operatives, and provided the money needed to purchase explosives and equipment."[32]

The USS *Cole* being towed by another ship after the attack

The USS *Cole* bombing was obviously well planned and meticulously executed, and it was now abundantly clear that the world was dealing with an organized, patient, and

---

[32] *The 9/11 Commission Report*, 190.

well-armed group with an unprecedented global outlook. Al-Qaeda learned a lot from this attack as well. The immense frenzy and political blame game that followed (Sudan was accused by the U.S. of being complicit in the bombing) showed that a small, non-state organization waging a low-intensity conflict could still rouse entire governments and dominate global media. The success of this attack galvanized al-Qaeda's recruitment efforts as well; propaganda videos were released by al-Qaeda's media arm and were widely disseminated, emboldening many young men with extremist thoughts to travel to Afghanistan for training and *jihad*.

Some believe that the successful bombing of the USS *Cole* served as the impetus for 9/11. The 9/11 Commission Report, which was prepared as the official report of the events leading up to the 9/11 attacks, asserted, "Bin Laden anticipated U.S. military retaliation [following the attack on USS *Cole*]…but a source reported that…[bin Laden] complained frequently that the United States had not yet attacked." According to this cited source, "bin Laden wanted the United States to attack, and if it did not, he would launch something bigger."[33] A congressional report released in January 2001 warned that any U.S. retaliation for the attacks must be "adequately planned," and that "[i]f it is determined that the attack was linked to Bin Ladin, a major issue is how the U.S. responds and prevents further attacks from a network that is believed responsible for several anti-U.S. attacks since 1992. The U.S. retaliatory attack on Afghanistan in August 1998, a response to the East Africa

---

[33] *The 9/11 Commission Report*, 191.

Embassy bombings, did little to damage Bin Ladin's network or his ability to plan attacks.[34]

Ultimately, the U.S. did little to retaliate, in part because of ongoing presidential elections and the transition of power from the Clinton Administration to the Bush Administration. Condoleezza Rice, who was then Bush's National Security Advisor, stated at a Senate hearing that the President "made clear to us that he did not want to respond to al Qaeda one attack at a time. He told me he was 'tired of swatting flies.'" Rice recalled that Bush said he was "tired of playing defense," and that he wanted to "take the fight to the terrorists," as catching terrorists one by one was not an approach he thought would be successful. According to Rice, this conversation took place in May 2001, just four months before September 11.[35]

9/11

"America has been hit by Allah at its most vulnerable point, destroying, thank God, its most prestigious buildings." – Osama bin Laden

With Operation Bojinka in shambles, Khalid Sheikh Mohammed began thinking of even more creative ways to target planes. After escaping the Philippines, he changed the plot to involve hijacking the planes and crashing them into targets. Experts believe he met bin Laden and presented the idea to him as early as the mid-90's, likely around the time al-Qaeda was forced to relocate to Afghanistan. Although bin Laden didn't immediately accept the plot, intelligence reports in 1998 began warning against potential airplane hijackings.

---

[34] Congressional Research Service, *Terrorist Attack on USS Cole.*
[35] *The 9/11 Commission Report*, 202.

Originally, the attacks were much more integrate and were planned at a much larger scale. Having already conceived of a plot to bomb a dozen jets, the initial plan Khalid Sheikh Mohammed proposed to bin Laden and Atef involved hijacking up to 10 planes, which would then be used to hit targets on both the East and West coasts, including FBI and CIA headquarters, buildings in California and Washington D.C., and nuclear power plants.

Furthermore, Khalid Sheikh Mohammed also proposed to bin Laden that he could fly the tenth plane, kill all the male passengers, land the plane in a United States Airport, and contact the media. At that point, Khalid Sheikh Mohammed would then denounce the U.S. policies in the Middle East and release all of the women and children. Perhaps not surprisingly, bin Laden felt the plan was too complex and rejected the public statement portion of the plan. It is also unclear whether Bin Laden's initial approval provided for more than four planes, as he only provided Khalid Sheikh Mohammed with four operatives upon approving of the plan.

Intelligence experts now believe that al-Qaeda began to put the plot into motion around 1999, following a series of meetings in 1999 between bin Laden and Khalid Sheikh Mohammad that likely discussed the attacks. Another member of Al-Qaeda, Mohammed Atef, began planning the logistics of the attack, including coordinating travel for the hijackers. Some leaders from al-Qaeda reported that bin Laden himself chose the targets for the attack. It's believed that some of the initial targets were the U.S. Capitol, the White House, and the World Trade Center.

At the early stages, bin Laden already had a few members in mind for the plot and offered them up to Khalid Sheikh Mohammed. Al-Qaeda selected Nawaf al-Hazmi and Khalid al-Mihdhar to hijack the planes, and the two arrived in the United States as early as 2000 to take flying lessons in San Diego. Al-Qaeda leaders later explained that California was ideal because it was an easy entry point from Asia and far from the intended targets. Both men had planned to learn English and learn to fly, possibly to receive pilot licenses, but neither of them were successful, and Mihdhar left the United States after less than one year. Hani Hanjour replaced Mihdhar in San Diego. Hanjour had an American pilot's license, but he continued to receive additional flying lessons.

In the early summer of 2000, an additional group of terrorists from Hamburg arrived in the United States to begin flight training. The men included Mohamed Atta, Marwan al-Shehhi, and Ziad Jarrah. This group of men, along with Hanjour, would operate the airplanes after hijacking them. In conjunction with these pilots, al-Qaeda began to select muscle hijackers around the summer of 2000. This second group of terrorists would force the cockpit and airplane crew to rescind power of the airplanes can control passengers. Despite the fact the phrase "muscle hijackers" was widely used to describe these men and their roles in the attacks, most of them were only between 5' 5" and 5' 7" tall.

When al-Hazmi and al-Mihdhar arrived in the U.S. in early 2000, it quickly became clear to al-Qaeda just how difficult an operation 9/11 was going to be. After landing in Los Angeles, the two men began taking flying lessons in San Diego, with al-Qaeda intentionally choosing locations in California because it was an an easy entry point from Asia and far removed from the intended targets on the East Coast. Both men had planned to learn English and learn to fly, possibly to receive pilot licenses, but they quickly set off red flags with their flight instructors. The two men started flight school completely inexperienced with piloting, but they immediately explained to their flight instructors that they were interested in flying jets and did not want to train on small planes. Neither of the men were successful in obtaining pilot licenses, and al-Mihdhar left the United States after less than one year in the country.

Before al-Mihdhar's had even left the country, al-Qaeda leaders had determined that additional operatives were needed in the United States and began to plan for the possibility that one or both of the operatives currently in the United States would fail. As a result, al-Qaeda recruited four more men who would go to Afghanistan and undergo the same intensive training that the first four had received. The new operatives, consisting of Atta, Ramzi Binalshibh, Marwan al-Shehhi, and Ziad Jarrah, hailed from Egypt, United Arab Emirates, Lebanon and Yemen, but they had studied together in Hamburg, Germany, and all four had planned to use their skills to commit jihad in other parts of the world before being selected for the 9/11 attacks. These men were likely selected because they were educated, had experience living in Western society, were proficient in English, and would be more likely to obtain visas. In essence, they were likely to avoid the pitfalls that al-Qaeda believed would plague or had already plagued al-Mihdhar and al-Hazmi.

During the summer of 2001 the pilots kept busy by assisting the muscle hijackers and taking additional flight training, including cross-country flights. During training, two of the pilots requested that they be allowed to fly the Hudson Corridor, a low altitude flight along the Hudson River that passed by the World Trade Center. Al-Shehhi took a cross-country trip from New York to San Francisco on May 24, and others took similar flights following Shehhi. The purpose of the cross-country flights was to determine what obstacles the men might encounter on the day of the attacks, with each man flying first class in the same type of plane he would later pilot.

At this point, there were two groups of terrorists spilt between Florida and New Jersey. Atta was considered the leader of the groups and relied on al-Hazmi when he needed to communicate with the group in New Jersey. In mid-July, Atta met with Binalshibh in Spain. Binalshibh was the Hamburg operative who was not able to obtain a visa and had thus stayed behind to help coordinate the attacks. Atta provided a status update, which included informing Binalshibh that the group of terrorists needed five or six more weeks of preparation before an attack could be scheduled. Atta also stated that he and other men were successful in bringing box cutters onto flights and had determined the best time to storm the cockpit. After the meeting, Binalshibh headed to Afghanistan to update al-Qaeda's leaders, and Atta returned to Florida.

One of the muscle hijackers had failed to enter the United States, so al-Qaeda sent another man to replace him. In August, the 20th man arrived in Florida at the Orlando airport. In August, Atta, Hazmi and Hanjour flew to Las Vegas to meet in person and update each other on progress in person. But that same month, Moussaoui was arrested. Although there are still some doubts as to whether Moussaoui was going to participate in 9/11, al-Qaeda now had 19 hijackers staying in New Jersey and Florida in the weeks leading up to 9/11.

Immediately preceding the attacks, top Al-Qaeda officials met in Spain to plan the final details of the attack. Some reports indicate that there was some disagreement between al-Qaeda and the Taliban about how the attacks should be implemented. Regardless, by early 2001, United States officials were beginning to receive frequent reports about threats from Al-Qaeda, and during the summer of 2001, more and more threats poured in. Many officials recognized the summer of 2001 as unprecedented for the number of threat reports, which suggested an imminent attack. However, many reports were fragmented or unclear, and intelligence officials were unprepared for the type of attack al-Qaeda was planning, as it had never been attempted by a terrorist group before.

The influx of threats declined significantly in August, and the threats were all but non-existent in early September, signifying the calm before the storm. After 9/11, the 9/11 Commission Report demonstrated the disturbing ease with which the hijackers entered the country and freely moved around, as well as other clues about their intentions while at flight school. For example, all of the 9/11 hijackers entered the country legally using their real names, and even though all of the hijackers had likely traveled to Afghanistan at one time or another for training, the hijackers were easily able to conceal this by traveling through Iran (which did not stamp Saudi passports) or by having their passports doctored by al-Qaeda experts. Furthermore, the eventual hijacker pilots attended flight school under their real names, and some of them had demonstrated no interest in learning how to land or take off. The 9/11 Commission's Report also stated that the Mossad, Israel's intelligence agency, gave Atta's name to the CIA on August 23, 2001 as part of a list of names believed to be planning an imminent attack. Al-Shehhi, al-Mihdhar and al-Hazmi were also on the list.

In the weeks before 9/11, the 19 terrorists began making their last minute preparations inside the U.S. Some of the men continued to practice flying rented planes, while others trained at gyms in hotels where they were staying. The operatives also purchased multiple knives, which they likely planned to use during the attacks. During the last week of August, one of the men purchased a GPS unit from a pilot shop in Miami, along with aeronautical charts. However, none of these activities or purchases raised any suspicions. Unlike other terrorist attacks, where the men would have to buy bomb-making materials, these purchases were seen as typical.

Approximately two weeks before the attacks, the men began purchasing plane tickets on the planes they would eventually hijack. The training provided by KSM was put to use, as the operatives purchased the tickets at airports, on the phone and by Internet. They then wired their excess funds back to al-Qaeda, totaling about $26,000. Experts estimate that in all, al-Qaeda spent approximately

$500,000 on the attacks, with approximately half of that money being spent in the United States.

Finally, the terrorists traveled to the departure points where they would board planes on 9/11. The men who eventually hijacked American Airlines Flight 77 grouped in Laurel, Maryland, staying at a motel there during the first week of September and even spending time at a neighboring gym. The night before the attacks, they stayed at a hotel in Herndon, Virginia, closer to the airport. Meanwhile, the men who would hijack United Airlines Flight 93 stayed in Newark. The group that hijacked United Airlines Flight 175 arrived in Boston. Only Atta and another member of his group would take a connecting flight on 9/11 itself, traveling from Portland, Maine before boarding American Airlines Flight 11.

The successful attacks, which destroyed the entire World Trade Center complex and killed about 3,000 people, were unlike anything the world had ever seen before, and it was carried out on a scale that had been unmatched by previous terrorist attacks with a plot that was practically undreamed of by Western intelligence. Just months before 9/11, convicted Oklahoma City bomber Timothy McVeigh had been executed, marking the demise of the man who had been responsible for the deadliest terrorist attack on American soil. McVeigh's attack had killed about 170 people, less than six percent of the casualties inflicted by al-Qaeda on 9/11. At the same time, Western intelligence was caught by surprise just as badly as the American public. Although a few FBI agents had theorized that terrorists were training in flight schools for the potential purpose of flying into targets, the intelligence community had continued to focus on preventing the kinds of attacks terrorists had been using for decades, such as car bombs and truck bombs, suicide attacks by individuals wearing bombs, and taking hostages for political ransom.

Although al-Qaeda initially denied involvement in 9/11, Bush Administration officials and intelligence officials immediately suspected al-Qaeda was to blame. The almost simultaneous hijackings and suicide attacks bore al-Qaeda's hallmarks and required a level of sophistication and planning that few terrorist groups could muster. 9/11 demonstrated the incredibly deadly capabilities of the group, as well as the extent to which it was a highly trained, tightly managed, and well coordinated network with strong financing.

No one knows what Osama bin Laden's true expectations were following 9/11, but some have speculated that he had believed the U.S. would collapse, as the Soviet Union had after the war in Afghanistan, while others theorize that he had anticipated that the U.S. would not immediately retaliate, as was the case with the USS *Cole* bombing.[36] Regardless, there is no doubt that he was taken off guard by the speed and intensity with which the U.S. responded in the post-9/11 worldwide manhunt for al-Qaeda and the forcible toppling of the Taliban regime.

Much has been written about the significant and lasting impacts 9/11 had on the U.S., the world, and global security. However, beyond tightened airport security, the creation of an entire homeland security apparatus in the

---

[36] Thomas R. McCabe, "The Strategic Failures of Al Qaeda," *Parameters* (Spring 2010): 63.

U.S., the passage of a slew of rigid anti-terrorism laws in dozens of countries across the world, and the U.S.-led war against al-Qaeda and the Taliban in Afghanistan, the 9/11 attacks had a great impact on al-Qaeda itself. Although 9/11 was a grand victory for al-Qaeda, it was a watershed event for the group in the years that followed. In fact, it was perhaps too great of a success, as it triggered an international response that was so furious and far-reaching that it completely altered the environment in which al-Qaeda operated. Al-Qaeda militants, including Osama bin Laden, were forced into hiding in the caves of Tora Bora, Afghanistan, as American drones flew overhead day and night and tribal Afghan leaders who were once al-Qaeda's allies were one by one bought off by the U.S. "We are about three hundred mujahideen," bin Laden recounted as he and Ayman al-Zawahiri struggled to convince their fellow militants to stay and hold ground.[37]

In short order, the Taliban fell in Afghanistan, and al-Qaeda was forced to relocate to far more dangerous territories of Pakistan in search of a new safe haven. Hundreds of operatives were killed and captured, training camps and havens were utterly destroyed, and the core leadership was forced into hiding. Nonetheless, bin Laden remained defiant in the years that followed. Three years after the attacks, in October of 2004, bin Laden publicly and officially claimed responsibility for the 9/11 attacks in an 18-minute message released just four days before the U.S. presidential election: "Is defending oneself and punishing the aggressor in kind, objectionable terrorism? If it is such, then it is unavoidable for us."[38]

---

[37] Wright, *The Looming Tower*, 371.

Al-Qaeda Franchises

"You, gracious brothers, are the leaders, guides, and symbolic figures of jihad and battle. We do not see ourselves as fit to challenge you, and we have never striven to achieve glory for ourselves. All that we hope is that we will be the spearhead, the enabling vanguard, and the bridge on which the Islamic nation crosses over to the victory that is promised and the tomorrow to which we aspire. This is our vision, and we have explained it. This is our path, and we have made it clear. If you agree with us on it, if you adopt it as a program and road, and if you are convinced of the idea of fighting the sects of apostasy, we will be your readied soldiers, working under your banner, complying with your orders, and indeed swearing fealty to you publicly and in the news media, vexing the infidels and gladdening those who preach the oneness of Allah. On that day, the believers will rejoice in Allah's victory. If things appear otherwise to you, we are brothers, and the disagreement will not spoil our friendship. This is a cause in which we are cooperating for the good and supporting jihad. Awaiting your response, may Allah preserve you as keys to good and reserves for Islam and its people." – Abu Musab al-Zarqawi

The post-9/11 years marked the end of al-Qaeda as a centralized, united group with a clear hierarchy and chain of command. The forcible scattering of al-Qaeda elements across Afghanistan and Pakistan, the region, and the world led to the emergence of a new kind of al-Qaeda,

---

[38] For full transcript of speech, see "Full Transcript of Bin Ladin's Speech," *Al Jazeera*, November 2, 2004,
http://web.archive.org/web/20070613014620/http://english.aljazeera.net/English/archive/archive?ArchiveId=7403.

one that was decentralized and diffused. With that, al-Qaeda transformed from a group into more of a network, and the al-Qaeda franchise came into existence.

It is crucial to distinguish between the "al-Qaeda core" – the central group of al-Qaeda that originally gathered around bin Laden and is today led by al-Zawahiri – and the affiliate organizations operating outside Afghanistan and Pakistan. Bin Laden envisioned from the outset that al-Qaeda would be a global organization uninhibited by state boundaries, and the al-Qaeda franchise became just that: a network of militant groups, independent in their day-to-day operations but still adhering to the ideology, tactics, and overall strategy of the al-Qaeda core.

While dozens of different radical Islamist groups have been identified as being part of the al-Qaeda franchise, only a few have shown consistent compliance with al-Qaeda core. In other cases, al-Qaeda has also co-opted or formed alliances with existing militant groups and networks across the Middle East and Eastern Europe, and these alliances have been quickly severed if the allying organization did not operate according to al-Qaeda's directives, such as Abu Sayyaf in the Philippines, or the Islamic State in Iraq and the Levant (ISIL) in Syria. However, there remains dozens of al-Qaeda associates who are either inspired by or adhere to al-Qaeda's tenets and tactics, so the al-Qaeda franchise continues to hold sway over dozens of organizations that are ideologically aligned to al-Qaeda core.

The backbone of today's al-Qaeda remains the core group in Afghanistan and Pakistan, and the various affiliates have all sworn formal *bayat* (oath of allegiance) to al-Qaeda core's senior leadership and seemingly continue to operate under the core's directives. The official, established affiliates include al-Qaeda in Iraq, al-Qaeda in the Arabian Peninsula, al-Qaeda in the Islamic Maghreb and al-Shabaab in Somalia, while al-Nusrah Front in Syria has emerged as the most nascent affiliate.

Jam'at al Tawhid wa'al-Jihad, or the Organization of Monotheism and Jihad, was founded in the early 2000s by Jordanian jihadist Abu Musab al-Zarqawi with the aim of establishing an Islamic state in Iraq. Though originally a small and loosely organized group of fighters, it grew into a sophisticated network during the early years of the Iraq War, and Al-Zarqawi's groups became a key opponent of U.S. and coalition forces in Iraq, claiming responsibility for dozens of lethal attacks against coalition troops and bases.

Abu Musab al-Zarqawi

In 2004, after numerous name changes, al-Zarqawi's group officially pledged allegiance to the al-Qaeda core, issuing an online statement dedicated to Osama bin Laden.[39] It has since become commonly referred to as al-Qaeda in Iraq (AQI) and has executed a number of high-profile suicide attacks, kidnappings, and bombings. In October 2004, AQI penetrated the Green Zone and successfully detonated an explosive in a popular café and market, and AQI also taped and published the grisly video of the beheading of American Nicholas Berg, who was allegedly executed by al-Zarqawi himself. AQI also publicized the beheadings of Americans Jack Armstrong and Jack Hensley in September 2004. In 2005, AQI showed its global reach when it claimed responsibility for three attacks outside Iraq: suicide bombings in Amman, Jordan, a rocket attack against a U.S. Navy ship in Aqaba, Jordan, and rocket attacks into Israel from Lebanon.[40]

Since al-Zarqawi's death in June 2006, the group has been led by several men, including Abu Ayyub al-Masri, Abu Omar al-Baghdadi, and its current leader, Abu Bakr al-Baghdadi. It has been analyzed that AQI reached its operational apex in 2006-2007, after which its militants were forced to flee many of their strongholds due to targeted and intensive military offensives conducted by Iraqi government-backed local militias and coalition forces. By 2008, AQI's operational capacity was severely weakened, and by early 2010, U.S. and Iraqi forces

---

[39] For full statement, see Jeffrey Pool, "Zarqawi's Pledge of Allegiance to Al-Qaeda: From Mu'asker Al-Battar, Issue 21," *The Jamestown Foundation Terrorism Monitor 2*, no. 24 (Dec 2004): 4-6.

[40] U.S. State Department, Office of the Coordinator for Counterterrorism, *Country Reports on Terrorism*, April 28, 2006,
http://web.archive.org/web/20070711072535/http://www.state.gov/s/ct/rls/crt/2005/65275.htm.

concluded that they had "either picked up or killed 34 out of the top 42 al-Qaeda in Iraq leaders". In June 2010, it was asserted that the organization had "lost connection with [al-Qaeda core] in Pakistan and Afghanistan."[41]

AQI was no longer viewed as an immediate or significant threat, and though the organization continued to conduct attacks throughout 2010-2011, it was deemed too isolated, disorganized, and disrupted to pose a threat to Iraqi or coalition forces. Although many Western leaders assumed that AQI had been completely destroyed, remnants of it still lingered.

As such, after the U.S. withdrawal of forces from Iraq in December 2011, the organization steadily began to gain strength again. The resurgence of AQI was caused by several factors, most prominently the political instability caused by the U.S. withdrawal, the radicalization of the region following the Arab Spring, and the start of the Syrian civil war in 2011. The number of attacks surged, and fatalities in Iraq sharply increased by approximately 500 in January 2012, just one month after the withdrawal of U.S. forces. In July 2012, AQI leader Abu Bakr al-Baghdadi announced the start of what he called the "Breaking the Walls" campaign, which triggered a massive launch of suicide attacks, simultaneous bombings, jail breaks, and assassination attempts.[42] The reboot of AQI was complete, and the world soon realized that the group had come back with even greater manpower and willpower than it ever had before.

[41] Jessica D. Lewis, "Al-Qaeda in Iraq Resurgent: The Breaking the Walls Campaign, Part I," *Middle East Security Report* 14 (September 2013): 9.
[42] Ibid., 10.

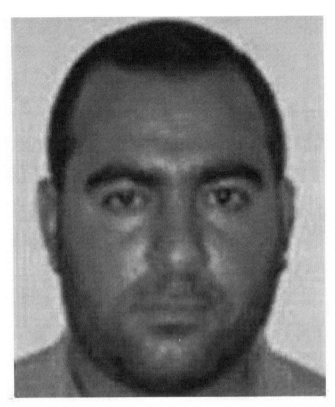

Abu Bakr al-Baghdadi

The strength of the AQI's insurgency has perhaps reached its apex in early 2014. In April 2013, AQI leader Abu Bakr al-Baghdadi released an audio statement announcing the birth of the Islamic State in Iraq and the Levant (ISIL), a symbolic move that represented the group's intentions to expand its operations into the Levant[43], and particularly, into Syria. ISIL has since become one of the most ruthless and influential rebel groups on the Syrian battlefield, and by June 2014, the organization has grown in such strength that it succeeded seizing control of multiple key cities in Iraq, including Samara, Tikrit, and Iraq's second largest city, Mosul.

AQI has experienced its highs and lows, but it remains

---

[43] The Levant is a geographic and cultural term most commonly describing the land occupied by Israel, Jordan, Lebanon ,Syria, Palestine, southern Turkey, and Cyprus. Alternatively, this group name has also been reported as the Islamic State in Iraq and Syria (ISIS), or Islamic State in Iraq and al-Sham. *Al-Sham* is the Arabic word for Levant.

one of the most dangerous al-Qaeda franchises, particularly because it is so well established, experienced, and connected. At the same time, however, it's unclear whether there are any actual ties between the ISIL and al-Zawahiri's al-Qaeda core. Often described as al-Qaeda's first franchise, AQI has nonetheless maintained its own structure, operations, and tactics independent of the al-Qaeda core, especially after rebranding itself as ISIL.

Al-Qaeda has been operating in North Africa for over 20 years, and in the 1990s, the Armed Islamic Group (GIA) was formed in Algeria as a militant opposition group fighting the secular leadership in Algiers. The group was excessively brutal in its tactics, and beheadings, mutilations, and torture were common. In 1998, a group of GIA commanders who realized their barbaric ways were alienating the population and depleting them of their support base left the GIA to form the Salafist Group for Preaching and Combat (GSPC). The GSPC disavowed the harming of civilians and vowed to continue to fight for the toppling of the secular government, which helped it draw wide support from the Algerian population, but by the early 2000s, a government amnesty campaign and intensive counterterrorism efforts by Algerian forces drove the group underground and into disarray.[44]

In 2006, the GSPC swore allegiance to the al-Qaeda core and rebranded itself as al-Qaeda in the Islamic Maghreb (AQIM). This was a move to regain its relevance and strength by siding with an already established, well-

---

[44] Zachary Laub and Jonathan Masters, "Al-Qaeda in the Islamic Maghreb (AQIM)," *Council on Foreign Relations,* January 8, 2011, http://www.cfr.org/terrorist-organizations-and-networks/al-qaeda-islamic-maghreb-aqim/p12717.

known organization, showing the strength and symbolic potency of the al-Qaeda brand. The union was announced by Ayman al-Zawahiri himself on September 11, 2006. This move was significant because it led to a shift in the goals and strategies of the AQIM; the group's target was no longer limited to the secular government of Algeria but now included the West at large. Adopting the al-Qaeda name also gave the group legitimacy and credibility among extremists in the region, while at the other end, al-Qaeda core was able to boast its international credentials and far reach.

Following this alliance with al-Qaeda, AQIM expanded its operations and aims. In 2006-2007, the group conducted several improvised explosive device (IED) attacks and ambushes against foreign nationals in Algeria. In December 2007, AQIM detonated a car bomb at the United Nations offices in Algiers and crossed the border to launch an attack on the Israeli Embassy in Nouakchott, Mauritania. In November 2013, AQIM shocked the world when it abducted and brutally executed two French journalists, Ghislaine Dupont and Claude Verlon, in Mali.[45]

AQIM's tactics are more based on guerilla-style raids, but it still conducts kidnappings, assassinations, and al-Qaeda's hallmark tactic: suicide bombings. AQIM has definitively defied its earlier pledge to not harm civilians, as the group has frequently targeted aid workers, tourists, and employees of multinational corporations. It is also suspected to be heavily involved in the local narcotics

[45] Kerry A. Dolan, "The Secret Of Al Qaeda In Islamic Maghreb Inc.: A Resilient (And Highly Illegal) Business Model," *Forbes,* December 16, 2013, http://www.forbes.com/sites/kerryadolan/2013/12/16/the-secret-of-al-qaeda-in-islamic-maghreb-inc-a-resilient-and-highly-illegal-business-model/.

trade, which is likely how the group funds its activities.[46]

Though the number of attacks launched by AQIM has dwindled in recent months, the group still continues to be a major threat to the security and stability of the region. AQIM still operates across North Africa, the Sahel, and West Africa despite intensive efforts by regional governments to eradicate its operations. The 2011 Arab Spring in Libya and the subsequent fall of the once powerful Muammar Gaddafi led to a security crisis in Libya that continues to deteriorate and destabilize the region, and the Libyan armed conflict has provided AQIM with an opportunity to augment its threat by dispatching armed convoys to Libya to acquire arms and higher-grade weaponry from unsecured Libyan arms depots.

The transformation of the group from a localized entity concerned with mostly national issues in Algeria into a full-blown transnational terrorist organization is a perfect example of the trajectory that groups who obtain the al-Qaeda seal follow. AQIM today is an amorphous and adaptive group that has shown great resilience in the face of stringent counterterrorism campaigns conducted by African and Western forces. As a result, AQIM has demonstrated that perhaps the greatest advantage a group attains when they pledge allegiance to al-Qaeda core and attain the al-Qaeda brand is not operational advice or resources but intangible things like the confidence, the credentials, and the capacity to expand beyond boundaries and overseas. Aside from this, AQIM has shown little if any indication that it is a full-fledged al-Qaeda affiliate; it has increasingly dipped into the realms of organized

---

[46] Laub and Masters, "Al-Qaeda in the Islamic Maghreb (AQIM)."

transnational crime by resorting to kidnapping, extortion, and participation in the regional narcotics trade. It has also displayed few of the political characteristics of al-Qaeda core, and in the wake of bin Laden's death, it's believed the group will continue to operate with growing independence.

Further to the east, Al-Qaeda in the Arabian Peninsula (AQAP) was formed in January 2009 through a merger of al-Qaeda's Saudi and Yemeni branches, which were mostly composed of senior *mujahideen* who had fought in Afghanistan during the Soviet occupation and subsequently returned to their homelands of Yemen or Saudi Arabia. AQAP has frequently been described as the most dangerous of the al-Qaeda affiliates, possibly because it is the branch that is most attached to the al-Qaeda core and frequently communicates with al-Qaeda leadership in Afghanistan and Pakistan. Moreover, as the al-Qaeda core's influence and ranks continue to thin, there have been talks of the core leadership relocating to Yemen and reestablishing the core base there.[47]

The environment in Yemen was conducive to the formation of AQAP from the very beginning. Historically, Yemen is a country rooted in tribalism, and though state laws are recognized in the country, tribal arbitration conducted by sheikhs continue to be the most effective and widely-used means of conflict resolution. This tribalism has been one of the main sources of instability in Yemen's political transition, particularly after the Arab

---

[47] Eric Schmitt, "As Al Qaeda Loses a Leader, Its Power Shifts From Pakistan," *The New York Times,* June 7, 2012, http://www.nytimes.com/2012/06/08/world/asia/al-qaeda-power-shifting-away-from-pakistan.html?_r=3&partner=rss&emc=rss.

Spring-inspired revolution in 2011 and the subsequent abdication of long-time ruler Ali Abdallah Saleh. Since tribalism acts as a powerful check and a possible impediment to effective state-building, the political transition process in Yemen has staggered and stalled in recent years, giving AQAP an even greater opportunity to flourish with impunity.

President Saleh

AQAP was initially focused on launching small-scale attacks, but the group gradually began to expand its operations by focusing on external targets. In August 2009, AQAP conducted its first major external operation when Ibrahim al-Asiri, the group's senior explosives expert, designed a concealable explosive device that was worn by an AQAP operative who tried to detonate the bomb as he was meeting with the Saudi Deputy Interior Minister. Two months later, AQAP attempted to launch a second plot, which was foiled when its operatives were killed trying to smuggle explosives across the Saudi border.[48]

AQAP has been perhaps the most noteworthy franchise because it has focused on targeting the U.S. more than any of the other al-Qaeda franchises over the past several years, and it may be the closest to the al-Qaeda core in terms of ideology and tactics. In December 2009, AQAP became the first al-Qaeda affiliate to target the U.S. homeland when master bombmaker Ibrahim al-Asiri designed an explosive device for Umar Farouk Abdulmutallab – the now-famed "underwear bomber" – who attempted to conceal the bomb in his undergarments and detonate it on board a Detroit-bound plane.[49] Fortunately, the plot was foiled because the bomb failed to detonate, but the event demonstrated al-Qaeda's continued dedication to harm the U.S. on its soil. The U.S. swiftly sanctioned and designated AQAP and its leaders, Said al-Shihri and Nasser al-Wahayshi, as foreign terrorists, but AQAP continued its efforts to target the U.S. In October 2010, two packaged containing plastic explosives and detonators were found on separate cargo planes bound for the U.S., and a week after the bombs were discovered, AQAP claimed responsibility.

---

[48] Katherine Zimmerman, "Testimony: AQAP's Role in the al Qaeda Network," *Critical Threats*, September 18, 2013, http://www.criticalthreats.org/al-qaeda/zimmerman-testimony-aqaps-role-al-qaeda-network-september-18-2013.

[49] Ibid.

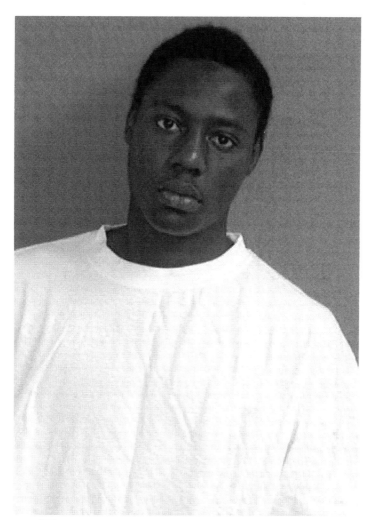

Umar Farouk Abdulmutallab

As a result, AQAP has been singled out by many analysts as the al-Qaeda affiliate that poses the most direct threat to the U.S. homeland. Whereas AQI/ISIL has been focused mainly on foreign targets in Iraq and Syria, and AQIM has focused its efforts in Africa, AQAP has repeatedly attempted to launch lethal attacks on American soil. It is also possibly the most innovative al-Qaeda affiliate, and it likely has the greatest number of militants who have combat experience fighting during the Soviet occupation of Afghanistan.

Additionally, AQAP is well known for being particularly active in forming alliances and relations with other branches of al-Qaeda. It has an established relationship with al-Shabaab, the al-Qaeda affiliate in Somalia, and it has provided explosives and military training to al-Shabaab operatives in the past. It is also believed that AQAP facilitated al-Shabaab's initial communications with al-Qaeda core,[50] and two letters written in May 2012 and August 2012 were made out by AQAP leader Nasser al-Wahayshi and addressed to Abdelmalek Droukdel, the leader of AQIM. In the letters, al-Wahayshi advises Droukdel on operations and provides guidance, further indicating AQAP's close ties to other branches of al-Qaeda.[51]

Before his death, American cleric Anwar al-Awlaki arguably became al-Qaeda's chief propagandist, and it was believed he managed to become a leader of AQAP. He was tied to Abdulmutallab's plot and the cargo plane plot, and when a drone strike killed him, it raised constitutional questions about the federal government's ability to target and assassinate American citizens without affording regular due process rights.

Thanks to al-Awlaki's participation, AQAP has been extremely active in propaganda dissemination and establishing links with other militant groups, particularly other al-Qaeda branches. As Yemen faces ongoing political, economic, and security challenges, how its government responds to the AQAP threat, as well as how world powers like the U.S. assist in counterterrorism efforts, will play a major role in destroying not only

---

[50] Ibid.

[51] Bill Roggio, "Wuhayshi Imparted Lessons of AQAP Operations in Yemen to AQIM," *The Long War Journal*, August 12, 2013,
http://www.longwarjournal.org/archives/2013/08/wuhayshi_imparts_les.php.

AQAP but the al-Qaeda franchise as a whole.

Anwar al-Awlaki

The Harakat Shabaab al-Mujahidin, more commonly known as al-Shabaab (literally meaning "the youth"), was originally the militant arm of the Somali Islamic Courts Union (ICMU), a loose collective of Islamic judicial systems (*sharia* courts) that governed and controlled most of southern Somalia, including its capital, Mogadishu. The ICMU is often compared to the Taliban in Afghanistan in that it served as the ad hoc government of the regions it controlled, and its fall also mirrored that of the Taliban. In 2006, the ICMU was forced to divide into smaller factions after a successful military offensive by Somali and Ethiopian forces, and al-Shabaab was one of the factions that resulted from the dispersal of ICMU. Since then, it has continued its violent insurgency in Somalia purportedly aimed at waging *jihad* against all enemies of Islam.

Since its founding, al-Shabaab has claimed responsibility for many attacks, including suicide bombings, across Somalia, and the main targets have thus far been Somali government officials, armed forces, and perceived allies of the Somali government. There have been no active attempts to attack the U.S., but in 2012, al-Shabaab pledged loyalty to al-Zawahiri, cementing its relationship with al-Qaeda core.

Al-Shabaab is perhaps the least organized of the al-Qaeda affiliates, and part of this has to do with the clan-based society of Somalia and much of East Africa. Similar to Yemeni tribalism, the Somali clan system is highly politicized and an important component of the Somali culture. Clans usually follow their own deeply ingrained customary laws instead of state laws, thereby making them completely ignorant of modern state structures, perhaps even more so than the tribes of Yemen. [52] Furthermore, not many al-Shabaab members have the common link of fighting the *jihad* against the Soviets in Afghanistan.

Al-Shabaab is thus much more decentralized and

---

[52] Austrian Centre for Country of Origin and Asylum Research and Documentation (ACCORD), *Clans in Somalia*, December 2009, http://www.refworld.org/docid/4b29f5e82.html.

nebulous in structure than the other al-Qaeda branches, with individual warlords often leading factions within it. Recent high levels of infighting among the leadership have also demonstrated that al-Shabaab is not unified in its goals, and furthermore, its rank-and-file come from different clans. Thus, the group is extremely vulnerable to internal divisions.

Compared to the other branches, much of the al-Shabaab membership has no concern for global *jihad* and instead focus entirely on the nationalistic battle against the Somali government. Though the group has conducted external operations outside Somalia, such as the July 2010 suicide bombing in Kampala, Uganda, small-scale grenade attacks in Nairobi, Kenya, and the infamous September 2013 attack on the Westgate shopping mall in Kenya (which resulted in at least 67 deaths and 175 wounded), the main target has been and appears to still be the Somali government.[53]

Ayman al-Zawahiri, when announcing the merger of the two groups, said in a video that "the jihadi movement is growing...despite the fiercest Crusader campaign in history launched by the West against Muslims." He then continued, "Today, I have pleasing glad tidings for the Muslim Ummah that will please the believers and disturb the disbelievers, which is the joining of the Shabaab al Mujahideen Movement in Somalia to Qaedat al Jihad [al-Qaeda], to support the jihadi unity against the Zio-Crusader campaign and their assistants amongst the treacherous agent rulers who let the invading Crusader

[53] Scott Stewart, "Al Shabaab's Threat to Kenya," *Stratfor Global Intelligence,* April 26, 2012, http://www.stratfor.com/weekly/al-shabaabs-threat-kenya.

forces enter their countries.[54]

It is curious that al-Zawahiri decided to accept al-Shabaab into the al-Qaeda fold, given that al-Shabaab is fighting for a much more nationalistic goal than that of the other branches and it is disorganized and disunited. The one certain thing that al-Qaeda core did gain from the union with al-Shabaab was the ability to say that al-Qaeda is still continuing to grow, even to another continent and to a non-Arab country.

The most recently formed al-Qaeda franchise is one of the most active today. Al-Nusrah Front (also known as Jabhat al-Nusrah or Support Front for the People of the Levant) was formed in January 2012, and what started as a group barely distinguishable from the hundreds of other militant opposition groups fighting the Bashar Assad regime in Syria catapulted into the spotlight when it pledged loyalty to the al-Qaeda core in 2013. Today, al-Nusrah Front is al-Qaeda's official branch in Syria.

As with the other al-Qaeda affiliates, al-Nusrah Front's ultimate goal is to establish an Islamist state, but unlike AQIM or AQI/ISIL, which have fought against or attacked Western targets, and certainly unlike AQAP, which has attempted multiple attacks against the U.S. homeland, al-Nusrah Front is purely focused on fighting the Alawite Assad regime and establishing an Islamist state in Syria. Al-Nusrah Front has been significant for the al-Qaeda franchise because it played a significant role in radicalizing the Syrian conflict, and as one of the most active Islamist groups operating in Syria, al-Nusrah Front

---

[54] Thomas Joscelyn and Bill Roggio, "Shabaab Formally Joins Al Qaeda," *The Long War Journal,* February 9, 2012, http://www.longwarjournal.org/archives/2012/02/shabaab_formally_joi.php.

took the relatively moderate and secular war that began in 2011 and turned it into a full-fledged *jihad*. Analysts have voiced concerns that should al-Nusrah Front continue to gain territory and popularity while expanding its membership, Syria will likely become a hotspot for al-Qaeda activity.

Of course, this does not mean al-Nusrah Front accepts the West, but the group does not actively call for its downfall either. In fact, there have been numerous reports suggesting that the U.S. may even be equipping, training, and/or supplying al-Nusrah Front in its fight against the Assad regime, which has never been a friend of Washington. Alternatively, there have been indications that U.S. arms supplied to the Syrian rebels have inadvertently ended up in the hands of al-Nusrah Front fighters. Either way, it appears that al-Nusrah Front is concerned primarily about the conflict in Syria, at least for now.

When the Syrian conflict started, al-Qaeda initially had two affiliates operating in Syria: al-Nusrah Front and the Islamic State in Iraq and the Levant (ISIL). In fact, it is believed that al-Nusrah Front originated as a branch of ISIL, as many cadres of al-Nusrah came from the jihadist network of AQI's al-Zarqawi. ISIL asserted that back in the early 2000s, when it was still operating only in Iraq as AQI, it had sent a group of jihadists to Syria to establish networks there. One such jihadist was Abu Mohammad al-Joulani, al-Nusrah Front's current leader.[55]

---

[55] Noman Benotman and Roisin Blake, "Jabhat al-Nusra," *Quillam Foundation*, http://www.quilliamfoundation.org/wp/wp-content/uploads/publications/free/jabhat-al-nusra-a-strategic-briefing.pdf.

When the Syrian revolution began, more and more members of AQI relocated to Syria to participate in the fighting, and AQI eventually expanded its operation as ISIL. It remains unclear whether al-Nusrah Front emerged at this time as a branch of ISIL or as an entity separate from it, but nonetheless, al-Nusrah Front began to define itself as an independent entity, even as ISIL continued to profess that al-Nusrah Front was merely a sub-battalion of ISIL. The disagreement mounted into multiple clashes between the two groups that should have ideologically been on the same side.

Ayman al-Zawahiri and other notable al-Qaeda-linked jihadist ideologues such as Abu Muhammad al-Maqdisi attempted to mediate between the two groups, but to no avail. Eventually, in a surprising announcement made on February 2, 2014, al-Zawahiri published a statement online that announced al-Qaeda had disowned the ISIL and expelled it from the al-Qaeda franchise. With that, al-Nusrah Front was designated the official al-Qaeda branch in Syria. The statement read, "Al-Qaeda al-Jihad announces that it has no link to the Islamic State of Iraq and the Levant. It did not create it, did not invest it with authority, did not consult with it, and did not express approval of it. Rather, al-Qaeda ordered it to stop its actions. Therefore, it is not an al-Qaeda affiliate, no organizational relationship binds the two, and al-Qaeda is not responsible for its behavior."[56]

There are several likely reasons that explain why al-Zawahiri chose to back one group and disown the other.

---

[56] Juan Cole, "'Too Extreme for Al Qaeda': Al Zawahiri Disowns ISIL," *Mideast Posts,* May 2, 2014, http://mideastposts.com/middle-east-politics-analysis/extreme-al-qaeda-al-zawahiri-disowns-isil/.

First, there could only be one al-Qaeda representative in Syria, and it was difficult as it was for al-Qaeda core to keep tabs on its affiliate thousands of miles away. Obviously, it reflected poorly on al-Qaeda to have two affiliated groups fighting each other. But perhaps more importantly, ISIL was becoming too extremist in its ideology and especially in its tactics, even for al-Qaeda's standards. ISIL massacred, looted, tortured, and killed civilians and soldiers alike, conducted mock trials and brutal executions, and published grisly videos and photographs online of beheaded bodies, crucifixions of alleged thieves, dead children, and mass graves of executed Syrian soldiers. Additionally, ISIL began attacking other Syrian rebel groups, regardless of whether they were Islamist or moderate, including al-Nusrah Front. The infighting was costly for the opposition, as it led to the deaths of hundreds of opposition fighters and gave Assad's forces time to regroup, reorganize, and attack.

As the division between the ISIL and al-Nusrah Front suggest, it is difficult to determine how many of these organizations are ideologically and operationally fully committed and loyal to al-Qaeda core, or whether they are just paying lip service as a means to operate under the al-Qaeda flag. It is equally hard to assess exactly how frequently the affiliates are in contact with the core command, since al-Qaeda must maintain a substantial clandestine apparatus and work hard to conceal much of its operational ties and relationships among affiliates.

However, the important point to take from the existence and operations of these various affiliates is that collectively, the al-Qaeda core and its affiliates form a substantial, transnational, and well-connected terrorist network that is intent on acquiring territory, establishing an Islamist state, and executing terrorist attacks against the West and its allies. Though the affiliates seem to enjoy a large degree to latitude in running daily operations to achieve short-term goals, there is evidence showing that the al-Qaeda core still commands the overall strategy pursued by the affiliates, as seen by al-Qaeda core's abrupt disavowal of ISIL.

The dismissal of ISIL from the al-Qaeda franchise also showed how important the *bayat* (oath of allegiance) is. The affiliates have sworn loyalty to the al-Qaeda core and recognized Ayman al-Zawahiri as their ultimate leader, and even when they disagree with al-Zawahiri's decisions, as was the case when al-Zawahiri ordered al-Nusrah Front and ISIL to stop the infighting and enter into mediation, representatives of both al-Nusrah Front and ISIL at least nominally accepted al-Zawahiri's orders. Al-Nusrah Front temporarily halted its attacks against ISIL, and ISIL followed suit, but when ISIL leader Abu Bakr al-Baghdadi decided to reignite his war against fellow jihadist groups again, al-Zawahiri was quick to run him out of the herd. All the while, despite ISIL's rancor and the drama that ensued, al-Nusrah Front still remained deferential to the al-Qaeda core leadership.

The Future of Al-Qaeda

"In today's wars, there are no morals." – Osama bin Laden

Over 20 years after bin Laden founded the organization out of a few dozen members, al-Qaeda is a franchised organization with branches operating largely independently across the Middle East and Africa. The fact that bin Laden's death has had little impact on the spread of al-Qaeda or the strength of its affiliates is a clear indication of the highly decentralized, amorphous, and diffused nature of the al-Qaeda network. As Brookings Institution scholar William McCants aptly put it, "Al Qaeda is kind of a ready-made kit now. It is a portable ideology that is entirely fleshed out, with its own symbols and ways of mobilizing people and money to the cause. In many ways, you don't have to join the actual organization anymore to get those benefits."[57]

Events like the Arab Spring of 2011 and the subsequent toppling of leaders in Tunisia, Yemen, Libya, and Egypt have weakened Arab governments and created an unstable environment in the region that is even more conducive to al-Qaeda operations. Furthermore, with the advent of technology and advances in communications and transportation, the impact this has on al-Qaeda's recruitment and propaganda efforts, and the blurring of state lines due to increasing globalization, the al-Qaeda network itself become more diffuse and amorphous, and its membership has also become highly varied in terms of ethnicity, social status, and experience. No longer is the typical al-Qaeda member a battle-scarred Arab man with memories of fighting on the battlefronts of Afghanistan, because the Syrian conflict has triggered yet another foreign fighter phenomenon. In the past few years, hundreds of young men and women from different

[57] Ben Hubbard, "The Franchising of Al Qaeda," *The New York Times,* Jan 25, 2014, http://www.nytimes.com/2014/01/26/sunday-review/the-franchising-of-al-qaeda.html.

countries – including the United Kingdom, France, Germany, Spain, Turkey, Russia, and the U.S. – and with varied backgrounds – including teenage students, young professionals, doctors, and lawyers – have traveled to Syria to join one of the many jihadist groups and fight.

Equally worrying is the rising numbers of al-Qaeda-inspired groups. These groups may not officially belong to the al-Qaeda franchise, but they have studied it, learned from it, and have attempted to emulate its tactics and strategies. An example is the emergence of a militant group calling itself Ansar Bayt al-Maqdis (literally, "Supporters of the Holy House") in Egypt, which has claimed responsibility for dozens of deadly attacks in Egypt since its formation in 2011. Though there has been no definitive indication that Ansar Bayt al-Maqdis declared allegiance to al-Zawahiri and al-Qaeda, it is clear that it has received some significant arms, weapons, and explosives training judging by the sophistication of its attacks. Moreover, in its propaganda videos, Ansar Bayt al-Maqdis frequently displays al-Qaeda flags and quotes al-Qaeda leaders, and in his January 2014 audio statement, al-Zawahiri mentioned "our people in the Sinai," strengthening the speculation that there is some connection between the two groups.[58]

Similarly, Boko Haram (meaning "Western education is Sin") in Nigeria is not formally considered part of the al-Qaeda franchise, but according to Western intelligence agencies, the leadership of the group has ties to several al-

[58] Patrick Kingsley, "Egypt Faces New Threat in Al-Qaida-Linked Group Ansar Beyt Al-Maqdis," *The Guardian,* January 31, 2014, http://www.theguardian.com/world/2014/jan/31/egypt-alqaida-terrorist-threat-ansar-beyt-almaqdis.

Qaeda affiliates. Known for attacking churches, schools, tourists, and police stations, and most infamously known for kidnapping hundreds of schoolgirls to force them into marriage, Boko Haram is believed to have strong ties to AQIM, al-Shabaab, and AQAP. The exact nature of these ties are speculative at best, but it has been reported that leaders of Boko Haram have admired and received inspiration from Osama bin Laden and al-Qaeda and have attempted to pledge allegiance and establish communication.[59]

There are dozens of other groups in various regions of the world – from the Caucasus to Southeast Asia – that may not be considered full-fledged al-Qaeda affiliates but have been inspired and possibly guided or supported by al-Qaeda. Such a development makes the global security situation even more unpredictable and murky, because as al-Qaeda grows increasingly diffuse, it becomes more and more difficult to pinpoint where exactly its most important cells and operatives are located. Describing al-Qaeda of today as a "syndicate" more than a uniform organization, former U.S. Secretary of Defense Robert Gates stated in a 2010 press conference, "What we see is that the success of any one of these groups leads to new capabilities and a new reputation for all…A victory for one is a victory for all."[60] This "syndicate" description of al-Qaeda remains appropriate today, particularly evidenced by the fact that al-Qaeda seems to have been barely disrupted by the death of bin Laden.

---

[59] Jacob Zenn, "Leadership Analysis of Boko Haram," *CTC Sentinel* 7, no. 2 (February 2014): 23-24.

[60] Craig Whitlock, "Gates: Al-Qaeda Has Assembled a 'Syndicate' of Terror Groups," *The Washington Post,* January 20, 2010, http://www.washingtonpost.com/wp-dyn/content/article/2010/01/20/AR2010012001575.html.

The deteriorating security environment in the region, the expanding and diffusive nature of al-Qaeda, and the development of the al-Qaeda franchise have all made it extremely difficult for policy makers and counterterrorism efforts around the world to gauge and combat threats. Though al-Qaeda in its original form may have weakened somewhat, at least operationally speaking, it has been made abundantly clear that the franchise that formed from it is equally if not more dangerous to global security. Today, the al-Qaeda franchise is more geographically and operationally diverse than ever, and al-Qaeda members are operating in more countries now than at any other time before or after 9/11. The network has shown its endurance and resiliency as it has overcome numerous hurdles and challenges – from massive counterterrorism operations to infighting – and it has shown an ability to deftly adapt to the changing circumstances of the post-9/11 times.

It was always Osama bin Laden's ultimate goal to dispatch al-Qaeda members around the world and have them establish foreign cells and branches, and al-Qaeda has continued to pursue this policy of global expansion. In the post-9/11 world, the terrorists' ability to instill fear and paranoia has increased substantially, even as the world's capabilities to respond to such threats have immensely improved as well. It's clear the fight will continue indefinitely, because over a decade after the deadliest terrorist attacks in history, Al-Qaeda has demonstrated its capacity to challenge and seize territory across parts of Africa, the Middle East, regions of Eastern Europe, and into Central and Southeast Asia. And through it all, the al-Qaeda core that bin Laden initially developed over two decades ago has still been able to maintain safe havens in provinces of Afghanistan and Pakistan.

Abu Musab Al-Zarqawi

Abu Musab al-Zarqawi

"You, gracious brothers, are the leaders, guides, and symbolic figures of jihad and battle. We do not see ourselves as fit to challenge you, and we have never striven to achieve glory for ourselves. All that we hope is that we will be the spearhead, the enabling vanguard, and the bridge on which the Islamic nation crosses over to the victory that is promised and the tomorrow to which we aspire. This is our vision, and we have explained it. This is our path, and we have made it clear. If you agree with us on it, if you adopt it as a program and road, and if you are convinced of the idea of fighting the sects of apostasy, we will be your readied soldiers, working under your banner, complying with your orders, and indeed swearing fealty to you publicly and in the news media, vexing the infidels and gladdening those who preach the oneness of Allah. On that day, the believers will rejoice in Allah's victory. If things appear otherwise to you, we are brothers, and the disagreement will not spoil our friendship. This is a cause in which we are cooperating for the good and supporting jihad. Awaiting your response, may Allah preserve you as keys to good and reserves for Islam and its people." – Abu Musab al-Zarqawi

As of February 2014, ISIS is officially no longer part of the al-Qaeda franchise, but it was still a product of al-Qaeda's expansionist efforts to globalize and export its brand. In order to understand why al-Qaeda's core leadership in Pakistan and Afghanistan took an interest in a small band of insurgents in Iraq, it's necessary to understand the context of the times, and particularly the Iraq War. The post-9/11 years marked the end of al-Qaeda as a centralized, united group with a clear hierarchy and chain of command, but the forcible scattering of al-Qaeda elements across Afghanistan and Pakistan led to the emergence of a decentralized and diffused group. With that, al-Qaeda transformed from a group into more of a network, and the al-Qaeda franchise came into existence. Even today, it is still crucial to distinguish between the "al-Qaeda core" – the central group of al-Qaeda that originally gathered around Osama bin Laden and is today led by Ayman al-Zawahiri, and the affiliate organizations that sprung up.

Just hours after the terrorist attacks on 9/11, President George W. Bush stood before a shocked and devastated nation and vowed that the U.S. would respond to the terrorist attacks that occurred that day, and that Washington would make "no distinction between those who planned these acts and those who harbor them." His intention was clear – the American government will not only punish those who perpetrated the attacks, but also anyone and everyone who harbored, aided, or abetted the terrorists.[61]

On the morning of September 17, 2001, President Bush agreed with his core advisors that Afghanistan would be the singular focus of the initial U.S. response to the 9/11 attacks. Bush had been intent on attacking Iraq at first, but the lack of evidence of Saddam Hussein's involvement led many of his advisors to push for an invasion of Afghanistan instead of Iraq. However, less than two months later, Bush again shifted his focus back to Hussein and secretly ordered the Joint Chiefs of Staff to initiate plans to depose him.[62] In his State of the Union address on January 29, 2002, Bush began to publicly push for the nation's attention to shift to Iraq, which he famously labeled as one of the countries making up the "axis of evil" that was allegedly supporting terrorism and posing a grave danger to U.S. national security. He followed this with what is now notoriously known as an utterly unsubstantiated claim and one of the Bush administration's biggest blunders: that Iraq was in possession of weapons of mass destruction (WMDs).[63] Thus emerged what has popularly become known as the

---

[61] Jon Western, *Selling Intervention and War: The Presidency, the Media, and the American Public* (Baltimore: The John Hopkins University Press, 2005), 175.

[62] Tommy Franks, *American Soldier General Tommy Franks* (New York: Regan Books, 2004), 315.

[63] George W. Bush, "The President's State of the Union Address" (speech, Washington DC, January 29, 2002), The White House Archives, http://georgewbush-whitehouse.archives.gov/news/releases/2002/01/20020129-11.html.

Bush Doctrine, a term first coined by Charles Krauthammer to describe the Bush administration's unilateral foreign policy centered on the idea that "either you are with us or you are with the terrorists."[64]

In October of 20o2, just over a year after 9/11, Bush received the support of nearly three-fourths of the Congress for a resolution authorizing him to use any means necessary against Iraq – an amendment called the Join Resolution to Authorize the Use of United States Armed Forces against Iraq. Six months after that, in March 2003, Bush ordered the launch of what was being called a preventive war to unseat Hussein. Polls taken during this time show that Bush enjoyed widespread public support, partly due to the administration's elaborate domestic public relations campaign to market the war to its people. It was shown that in February 2003, a staggering 64% of Americans supported military action to remove Saddam Hussein from power.[65]

There was still no evidence of Saddam Hussein's complicity in the events of September 11, but the Bush administration led a coalition of forces that invaded Iraq in March 2003 and deposed Saddam Hussein at lightning speed. On March 18 2003, shrugging off fierce condemnation by the United Nations (UN), the U.S. began its bombing campaign in Iraq, joined by forces from the U.K., Spain, Italy, Poland, Australia, and Denmark. Eventually, some 30 countries joined in what the Bush administration was calling the "coalition of the willing."[66]

---

[64] Charles Krauthammer, "Charlie Gibson's Gaffe," *The Washington Post,* September 13, 2008, http://www.washingtonpost.com/wp-dyn/content/article/2008/09/12/AR2008091202457.html.

[65] Bootie Cosgrove-Mather, "Poll: Talk First, Fight Later," *CBS News,* January 23, 2003, http://www.cbsnews.com/news/poll-talk-first-fight-later/.

Three weeks into the invasion, on April 10, 2003, Coalition forces entered the Iraqi capital of Baghdad. Children ran alongside U.S. tanks, screaming Bush's name in glee, and the iconic statue of Saddam Hussein was pulled down. Back in the U.S., the American media ran videos of Iraqi citizens thanking U.S. soldiers in broken English, shaking their hands and giving them gifts.

However, the fall of Baghdad also triggered the outbreak of regional and sectarian violence throughout the country. It was the single biggest indication that Saddam's reign was over, a signal to the dozens of various independent militant groups across the country that now that Saddam was in hiding, they were now free to carve out their own territories and amass power. Old grudges and new ambitions made way for fresh fighting, and the U.S. and Coalition forces quickly found themselves in the midst of a potential civil war. U.S. forces swiftly ordered the immediate cessation of hostilities and announced that Baghdad was to remain the capital, but while militant groups temporarily halted their fighting, tensions had already risen to the point of no return.

Eventually, Hussein was captured on December 13, 2003, by the U.S. Army's 4th Infantry Division and members of Task Force 121 in a massive raid called Operation Red Dawn. The former dictator had been hiding in a hole under a farmhouse in rural Adwar, Iraq. Saddam Hussein was convicted of crimes against humanity by a special tribunal and subsequently executed on December 30, 2006.[67] That said, former Secretary of State Lawrence

---

[66] Steve Schifferes, "US Names 'Coalition of the Willing," *BBC News,* March 18, 2003, http://news.bbc.co.uk/2/hi/americas/2862343.stm.

Eagleburger's now famed quote rings true today: "I am scared to death that they [the war hawks in Washington] are going to convince the president that they can do this overthrow of Saddam on the cheap, and we'll find ourselves in the middle of a swamp because we didn't plan to do it the right way."[68]

Eagleburger's statements proved ominously prophetic, because the war in Iraq also gave militants in Iraq the ability to regroup and unite to fight the foreign boots on their soil. Furthermore, instead of going after al-Qaeda elements in Iraq or focusing more on counterterrorism efforts in Afghanistan, where al-Qaeda's core leaders actually were, the U.S. ultimately spent millions in military funding and deployed thousands of troops to topple an enemy that was not connected to 9/11.

The U.S. easily toppled Hussein's regime, but there were already people ready to utilize the chaos in Iraq to establish the original form of what eventually became known as the Islamic State of Iraq and the Levant, most prominently Abu Musab al-Zarqawi. Al-Zarqawi was a Jordanian Sunni militant born Ahmed Fadil Nazzal al-Khalayleh in October 1966, and he was raised in a mining town in Jordan called Zarqa, which is where his nom de guerre (al-Zarqawi) came from.[69] The world first learned about al-Zarqawi on February 5, 2003, when U.S. Secretary of State Colin Powell appealed to the UN for

[67] "Saddam Hussein Captured 'Like a Rat' in Iraq Ten Years Ago Today," *Fox News,* December 13, 2013, http://www.foxnews.com/world/2013/12/13/saddam-hussein-captured-like-rat-in-iraq-ten-years-ago-today/.

[68] "Transcript: Lawrence Eagleburger on FNS," *Fox News,* August 19, 2002, http://www.foxnews.com/story/2002/08/19/transcript-lawrence-eagleburger-on-fns/.

[69] Adel Darwish, "Abu Musab Al-Zarqawi," *The Independent,* June 9, 2006, http://www.independent.co.uk/news/obituaries/abu-musab-alzarqawi-481622.html.

the authorization of the U.S. invasion of Iraq and cited al-Zarqawi to make the case; Powell stated to the UN Security Council: "Iraq today harbors a deadly terrorist network headed by Abu Musab Al-Zarqawi, an associate and collaborator of Osama bin Laden and his Al Qaeda lieutenants. When our coalition ousted the Taliban, the Zarqawi network helped establish another poison and explosive training center camp. And this camp is located in northeastern Iraq. He traveled to Baghdad in May 2002 for medical treatment, staying in the capital of Iraq for two months while he recuperated to fight another day. During this stay, nearly two dozen extremists converged on Baghdad and established a base of operations there. These Al Qaeda affiliates, based in Baghdad, now coordinate the movement of people, money and supplies into and throughout Iraq for his network, and they've now been operating freely in the capital for more than eight months. We asked a friendly security service to approach Baghdad about extraditing Zarqawi and providing information about him and his close associates. This service contacted Iraqi officials twice, and we passed details that should have made it easy to find Zarqawi. The network remains in Baghdad."[70]

Analysts have since concluded that the statement made by Powell was false, because at the time of this statement in February of 2003, there were no significant ties between bin Laden and al-Zarqawi that indicated an extensive relationship, nor was there any evidence that

[70] Loretta Napoleoni, "Profile of a Killer," *Foreign Policy,* November 9, 2005, http://www.foreignpolicy.com/articles/2005/11/09/profile_of_a_killer?page=0,2&hidecomments=yes
.

Powell presented that proved al-Zarqawi to be one of bin Laden's top commanders. It was only over a year later, in December 2004, that bin Laden named al-Zarqawi the *emir* (commander or leader) of an al-Qaeda branch in Iraq. A 2006 Senate Report on the intelligence gathered about Iraq before the war also concluded, "Postwar information indicates that Saddam Hussein attempted, unsuccessfully, to locate and capture al-Zarqawi and that the regime did not have a relationship with, harbor, or turn a blind eye toward Zarqawi."

In fact, Abu Musab al-Zarqawi and Osama bin Laden could not have differed much more than they did. Bin Laden grew up the son of a wealthy and successful construction magnate with ties to the Saudi royal family, whereas al-Zarqawi was born and raised in one of the poorest quarters of Zarqa in Jordan. Bin Laden attended an elite secondary school in Jeddah[71], while al-Zarqawi was heavily involved in crime during his teenage years, including dealing drugs in a dilapidated town cemetery that his house overlooked.[72] Bin Laden attended King Abdulaziz University in Jeddah to study economics, where he began studying religion fervently, but al-Zarqawi dropped out of secondary school, drank heavily, and covered his body with tattoos, earning him the nickname "Green Man," as both alcohol and tattoos are considered *haram* (sinful) in orthodox Sunni Islam.[73] Though bin Laden first decided to take up arms and wage violent *jihad* while participating in the fight against the

[71] Lawrence Wright, *The Looming Tower: Al-Qaeda and the Road to 9/11* (New York: Random House, 2006), 78.

[72] Darwish, "Abu Musab Al-Zarqawi."

[73] Ibid.

Soviets in Afghanistan, al-Zarqawi had been arrested numerous times for shoplifting, mugging, drug dealing, sexual assaults, and drunken fights since his teenage years.

Bin Laden

As in many countries of the Middle East, the worlds of petty crime and radical Islam often overlapped, especially in prison, and it was while he was in captivity that al-Zarqawi met revolutionary Islamists and received his first jihadist indoctrination. The dedication that al-Zarqawi eventually developed for Islam and *jihad* was perhaps the only thing comparable to bin Laden. In 1988, al-Zarqawi enrolled in a Salafist mosque in Amman, Jordan for religious instruction. The al-Hussein bin Ali mosque that al-Zarqawi attended was well known for its radical leaning and was considered an essential stage in preparing young men for the Afghan *jihad*. After months of studying there, al-Zarqawi became engrossed; he gave up alcohol and even threw acid on his skin to remove his tattoos. In 1989, he traveled to Afghanistan with recruits from the same mosque to take up arms in the holy war against the ungodly Soviets.

As it turned out, al-Zarqawi was too late, because by the time he arrived at the camps of the Afghan and Arab *mujahideen*, the Soviet army had already left. Disappointed, al-Zarqawi decided to continue to study Islam at several mosques in Afghanistan and Pakistan, but he felt out of place as an inexperienced fighter among the groups of hardened *mujahideen*, so he eventually returned to Zarqa in 1993. However, from 1993-1994, al-Zarqawi became increasingly involved in militant activities, and had plotted an attack and was preparing explosives in his home when he was arrested in 1994. He was sentenced to 15 years in prison in 1996, but he was pardoned in May 1999 after Jordan's King Abdullah acted on bad advice and gave presidential pardons to dozens of prisoners who had been imprisoned on terrorism charges, including al-Zarqawi.[74]

As a result of that decision, in August 1999, al-Zarqawi left for Afghanistan yet again, and this time he eventually ended up at an al-Qaeda camp in Herat. This is where he first had extended interactions with bin Laden, and after spending several months proving his trustworthiness to

---

[74] Ibid.

the al-Qaeda leader, al-Zarqawi was granted the honor of managing the Herat training camp and even got approval to receive funds from al-Qaeda to set up a network of his own in various countries across the region and beyond, including a cell in Germany.

However, it soon became clear that the wealthy Saudi and the Jordanian ex-delinquent were too different, not just in affluence or social status but also in their views toward *jihad* and the ideal Islamic state. Though the two agreed that the ultimate aim should be the complete deliverance of Muslims, problems arose when they discussed strategies for achieving this. Bin Laden, with his ties to Arabia's political elite and his seemingly unlimited source of funds, had a global, expansionist, and anti-imperialist vision in mind, so he was focused on enemies as grand as the United States and had no interest in containing his *jihad* to just one country or region. Al-Zarqawi, on the other hand, a working-class jihadist who grew up in the slums of Zarqa amid crime and violence, who was tortured and beaten in Jordan's dark prisons, was more focused on local *jihad*. Al-Zarqawi wanted to return to his home country, or infiltrate another country run by an apostate regime, and take over the government there. Furthermore, whereas bin Laden believed the enemy "non-believers" to be non-Muslims (and primarily Western powers), al-Zarqawi interpreted the term to represent all those who did not share his Salafi ideology, which would later lead to his attacks against Iraqi Shiite shrines.

This disagreement over strategies is why al-Zarqawi did not pledge allegiance to bin Laden at this meeting, contrary to popular belief. Though he enjoyed the support of and funds from bin Laden and continued to manage the Herat camp, he did not consider himself an al-Qaeda member; he followed no orders, and he set up the Herat camp so that he could prepare people to go back to Jordan to carry out suicide missions.

The 9/11 attacks dramatically changed the course of al-Zarqawi's militancy, and rumors about a U.S. attack on Iraq spurred al-Zarqawi to leave Afghanistan and head for Iraqi Kurdistan. By the summer of 2002, he was in Baghdad and already preparing for battle with the United States. However, Powell's presentation before the UN Security Council in February of 2003 brought al-Zarqawi under the international media spotlight, and seemingly overnight, al-Zarqawi's name was known to governments, intelligence agencies, and militaries across the world. He was linked to dozens of bombings, attacks, and militant cells across the globe, from Spain to Germany, Turkey to Morocco. Whether al-Zarqawi truly had a hand in any of the attacks and militant activities he was accused of having involvement in is unknown, but he was indeed preparing for *jihad* in Iraq, and as Coalition forces began their invasion of Iraq in March 2003, al-Zarqawi worked in the shadows of Iraq's mountains, establishing networks, mapping out supply routes, and setting up training camps and recruitment centers.

In August 2003, when all preparations were complete, al-Zarqawi announced his presence with two major attacks – a bombing at the UN headquarters in Baghdad, and days later, a car bombing attack on the Imam Ali mosque, an attack executed by the father of al-Zarqawi's second wife. The group continued to launch attacks, but while these attacks were destructive, they weren't always lethal.

Letters that have recently been recovered at a raided al-Qaeda safe house have shown that al-Zarqawi was in frequent contact with bin Laden between 2003 and 2004. Al-Zarqawi was working to secure bin Laden's approval for his actions in Iraq, which demonstrated al-Zarqawi's realization that his network was only one of many different militant groups operating in Iraq – both Shiite and Sunni – and he needed the support and funds of a more powerful organization to give him the backing he needed to emerge as the top player on the Iraqi battlefield. On April 5, 2004, al-Zarqawi wrote in a letter to bin Laden that he had only two options: stay in Iraq and continue fighting U.S. and Coalition forces while also confronting the opposition of some Iraqis to his methods, or leave Iraq in search of another country to wage *jihad*. Days later, on April 9, 2004, he and his supporters kidnapped and beheaded U.S. national Nicholas Berg and then broadcasted the brutal execution on the Internet, and analysis of the video suggests it was al-Zarqawi himself who conducted the beheading.

This was only the beginning of a series of brutal beheadings and executions that al-Zarqawi and his group conducted from April to November 2004, and it was a clear sign to Osama bin Laden that al-Zarqawi had decided to stay in Iraq.[75] On December 27, 2004, al-Zarqawi's group officially pledged allegiance to al-Qaeda's core group in Afghanistan and Pakistan, issuing

---

[75] Napoleoni, "Profile of a Killer."

an online statement dedicated to bin Laden.[76] Bin Laden accepted the pledge and welcomed al-Zarqawi and his network into the folds of al-Qaeda. A message posted on a website around that time announced, "Numerous messages were passed between 'Abu Musab' (Allah protect him) and the al-Qaeda brotherhood over the past eight months, establishing a dialogue between them. No sooner had the calls been cut off than Allah chose to restore them, and our most generous brothers in al-Qaeda came to understand the strategy of the Tawhid wal-Jihad organization in Iraq, the land of the two rivers and of the Caliphs, and their hearts warmed to its methods and overall mission. Let it be known that al-Tawhid wal-Jihad pledges both its leaders and its soldiers to the mujahid commander, Sheikh 'Osama bin Laden' (in word and in deed) and to jihad for the sake of Allah until there is no more discord and all of the religion turns toward Allah...By Allah, O sheikh of the mujahideen, if you bid us plunge into the ocean, we would follow you. If you ordered it so, we would obey. If you forbade us something, we would abide by your wishes. For what a fine commander you are to the armies of Islam, against the inveterate infidels and apostates!"

In his biography of al-Zarqawi, Jean-Charles Brisard noted, "Zarqawi might almost be said to represent the antithesis of Osama bin Laden in that their origins, careers, education, and worldviews are very different. Yet it must be noted that, thanks to the second war in Iraq, what Bin Laden had been able to win on the ideological

---

[76] For full statement, see Jeffrey Pool, "Zarqawi's Pledge of Allegiance to Al-Qaeda: From Mu'asker Al-Battar, Issue 21," *The Jamestown Foundation Terrorism Monitor 2,* no. 24 (Dec 2004): 4-6.

terrain Zarqawi has reshaped through the use of weapons, so much so that today, and perhaps permanently, he has eclipsed Bin Laden's leadership of the partisans of a radical and aggressive Islam."[77] As Brisard asserts, the sheer violence and brutality of his tactics and methods are what boosted al-Zarqawi's status and position among Islamist militants, not just in Iraq but across the world. This enabled him to become the face of a new kind of *jihad,* and it ultimately allowed him to consolidate his networks and unite the various disparate tribes, militant groups, and cells that were operational in Iraq.

In other words, instead of al-Zarqawi and his initial band of fighters being an al-Qaeda group, it was the U.S. invasion of Iraq that gave al-Zarqawi the opportunity to consolidate his network, amass his power, and establish formal ties with al-Qaeda. The war gave him the chance to confront not just the near enemy, but also the far enemy simultaneously. Just like the Soviet occupation of Afghanistan gave bin Laden and his early supporters the perfect battleground to gain popularity and gather strength, the Iraq War was key in the development of al-Zarqawi's group from a loosely structured network of militant fighters into an organized, well-funded, and well-equipped army that fought not just Coalition forces but rival militants, particularly those from Shiite brigades.

The connection with al-Qaeda further empowered al-Zarqawi. He now enjoyed greater credibility and legitimacy that came with being part of the al-Qaeda band, and his group's increasing popularity led to a steady

---

[77] Jean-Charles Brisard and Damien Martinez, *Zarqawi: The New Face of Al-Qaeda* (Cambridge: Polity Press, 2005), 203.

flow of funds, arms, and fresh recruits. In turn, bin Laden gained as well; al-Qaeda had been suffering operationally following its ejection from Afghanistan after 9/11, so al-Zarqawi represented the fighting figurehead bin Laden needed to regain al-Qaeda's momentum.

In May 2007, President Bush declassified a U.S. intelligence report revealing that bin Laden had enlisted Zarqawi to plan strikes inside the U.S., and the report also warned that in January 2005, bin Laden had tasked Zarqawi with setting up a militant cell inside Iraq that would be used to plan and carry out attacks against the U.S. [78] Whether al-Zarqawi actually followed orders and established such a cell is unknown, but fortunately, he never came close to conducting attacks on U.S. soil because he was killed by an airstrike on June 7, 2006 in Baquba, Iraq. Nonetheless, his legacy still resonates in Iraq, because his "martyrdom" skyrocketed his reputation; radical clerics cite al-Zarqawi's words and past actions to this day, and new militant groups have formed in his honor, such as the al-Zarqawi Brigades in Mauritania[79] and the al-Zarqawi group in Bajuar, Pakistan.[80] The living legacy of one of the darkest figures of the region's history is now very deeply rooted in the jihadist movements that are exploiting the breakdown in law and order across the Islamic and Arabic world today.

The Evolution of ISIL

Today, many still hold the misconception that ISIS/ISIL,

---

[78] Dan Froomkin, "Failing to Reassure," *The Washington Post,* May 24, 2007, http://busharchive.froomkin.com/BL2007052401145_pf.htm.

[79] "Morocco's Militants," *The Economist,* Feb 21, 2008, http://www.economist.com/node/10733039.

[80] "Another Militant Group Opposes BISP," *The News,* April 10, 2009, http://www.thenews.com.pk/TodaysPrintDetail.aspx?ID=171651&Cat=7&dt=4/9/2009.

and its preceding form as al-Qaeda in Iraq, was created and developed by al-Qaeda. This is absolutely not the case, because even though al-Zarqawi's group and al-Qaeda did eventually merge to establish al-Qaeda in Iraq, this was more of a merger of convenience, and the alliance eventually broke down in 2014. Thus, while ISIS/ISIL's history and evolution most certainly were influenced by al-Qaeda, the group was in no way actually a product of the more notorious terror group. In fact, there were distinct stages in the evolution of al-Zarqawi's loose network of militant fighters into the highly organized and disciplined group of today.

At the beginning, al-Zarqawi is believed to have formed Jam'at al-Tawhid wa'al-Jihad[81] (JTJ) in Afghanistan at some point in 2000, likely around the time he was managing the al-Qaeda-linked training camp in Herat. At this time, JTJ was more of a network than an organized group, made up of local Islamist sympathizers and militants along with some foreign fighters. Thus, it was initially transnational in nature and organized the movement of fighters, funds, and arms across borders.

Using personal funds received from bin Laden, al-Zarqawi slowly built up this small group into a mobile army, which was his original aim, as he sought to create a force that could take action anywhere in the world where *jihad* was to be waged. Drawing on contacts he had slowly developed in Peshawar, Afghanistan, and back home in Jordan, al-Zarqawi attracted a steady stream of

---

[81] Also commonly referred to as Tawhid and Jihad, Tawhid wal-Jihad, Tawhid al-Jihad, or even just Tawhid or al-Tawhid. Alternatively, it is known as the Monotheism and Jihad Group and the al-Zarqawi Network.

recruits mainly from the exiled Jordanian, Palestinian, and Syrian Islamist populations in Europe.[82] A Center for Strategic and International Studies report on al-Zarqawi's network wrote of the reaction Seif al-Adel (al-Qaeda's security chief and close associate to Osama bin Laden) had when he visited al-Zarqawi's camp to see his progress: "In his monthly visits to the camp, Adel was consistently impressed with the growth and progress Zarqawi achieved with his recruits, who arrived first by the dozens, then by the hundreds. By the October 2001 U.S. air strikes against Afghanistan, the population of the Herat camp had reached 2,000-3,000 and included the only Levantine recruits in Afghanistan. In Herat, Zarqawi became a full-fledged terrorist commander."[83]

Seif al-Adel

[82] Gary Gambill, "Abu Musab al-Zarqawi: A Biographical Sketch," *The Jamestown Foundation,* December 15, 2004, http://www.jamestown.org/single/?tx_ttnews%5Btt_news%5D=27304.

[83] M. J. Kirdar, "Al Qaeda in Iraq," *Center for Strategic and International Studies* (June 2011): 3.

Al-Zarqawi had initially established his network with the purpose of returning to Jordan and overthrowing the monarchy to establish an Islamic state there, but what had started as an endeavor to cleanse his home country of what he deemed an apostate regime became much more as his network grew and developed. Al-Zarqawi eventually abandoned his exclusive focus on Jordan, no doubt in part because many of his fighters were not Jordanian, and also because his Jordanian fighters didn't want to return anyway.

At this point, JTJ enjoyed the support and funding of al-Qaeda, but it was still not an al-Qaeda group, or even an affiliate. Al-Zarqawi and his men "refused to march under the banner of another individual or group," recalled one Libyan Islamist leader who was in contact with al-Zarqawi at the time.[84] The distinct separation of JTJ from al-Qaeda demonstrates al-Zarqawi's personality; he was intensely committed to his cause and his cause only.

In the aftermath of 9/11, al-Zarqawi and his operatives decided to relocate, and using al-Zarqawi's Iranian connections, crossed overland into Iran. From there, al-Zarqawi planned to set up camp and launch JTJ's operations, but the capture of Europe-based JTJ operatives in early 2002 alerted Western authorities to al-Zarqawi's presence in Iran. Al-Zarqawi was forced to leave his base in Iran as the pressure on Tehran to expel al-Zarqawi intensified. After briefly traveling to Syria and Lebanon, al-Zarqawi and JTJ eventually relocated to what is modern-day Iraqi Kurdistan in northern Iraq. A number of Arab Islamists had already set up camp there, including

---

[84] Gary Gambill, "Abu Musab al-Zarqawi: A Biographical Sketch."

the Kurdish Islamist group Ansar al-Islam, and al-Zarqawi saw the advantages of joining forces with them. At this time, U.S. calls for an invasion of Iraq were mounting, and when al-Zarqawi realized that an American invasion was imminent, he began preparing for war with the Americans.

Seif al-Adel, al-Qaeda's military and security chief, is believed to have provided al-Zarqawi considerable funds and support during JTJ's relocation to northern Iraq. In turn, al-Adel requested that al-Zarqawi coordinate the entry of al-Qaeda operatives into Iraq through Syria in anticipation of a war in Iraq. Al-Zarqawi agreed, and by the end of 2003, hundreds of Islamist foreign fighters were being funneled into Iraq via Syria. Though many of these militants were not JTJ members, nor did they have any intention of joining JTJ prior to infiltrating Iraq, they became more or less dependent on the influential al-Zarqawi's network of contacts, boosting al-Zarqawi's position as the default *emir* of Islamist militants in Iraq.[85]

Following the invasion of Iraq, JTJ developed and grew even more, and al-Zarqawi began mobilizing his now massive network of safe houses, weapon caches, militant networks, and local support. Once the invasion began, al-Zarqawi launched a four-pronged strategy to drive out U.S. and Coalition forces from Iraq, topple the Iraqi government, and establish a pure Islamic state (as he envisioned one). First, al-Zarqawi aimed to politically ostracize the U.S. by pressuring international actors into rescinding their support for an invasion that was not authorized by the UN in the first place. The tactics JTJ

---

[85] Ibid.

used to implement this strategy involved repeatedly targeting Coalition and U.S. forces to make them reassess the value of fighting a war on foreign soil. In this endeavor, JTJ enjoyed mild successes, and the August 2003 truck bombing of the UN headquarters in Baghdad was an achievement for him in this regard because it effectively ended the UN's direct involvement on the ground in Iraq. Other examples of al-Zarqawi's pursuit of this strategy include the attacks against the Jordanian Embassy in Baghdad in August 2003 and the headquarters of Italy's paramilitary police headquarters in Nasiriyah.[86]

The second strategy al-Zarqawi employed was designed to deter local Iraqi militants and civilians from supporting the U.S. and Coalition forces, particularly after the toppling of Saddam Hussein in April 2003 and the subsequent U.S.-led transition process for a democratized Iraq. To achieve effective deterrence, JTJ targeted and attacked various police stations and recruitment centers, killing hundreds of both Iraqi military personnel and civilians, and the group also assassinated several leading pro-U.S. Iraqi politicians.

In addition to that, al-Zarqawi aimed to obstruct Iraq's reconstruction process by targeting civilian contractors, humanitarian aid workers, and other foreigners who were in Iraq with the expressed purpose of helping rebuild the war-torn country. JTJ abducted and gruesomely beheaded foreign nationals such as Nicholas Berg in May 2004, then subsequently distributed the grisly videos of the executions online. The CIA has since verified that al-

[86] "Bomb at Italian Police HQ in Iraq Kills 26," *Fox News,* November 12, 2003, http://www.foxnews.com/story/2003/11/12/bomb-at-italian-police-hq-in-iraq-kills-26/.

Zarqawi himself had personally beheaded Berg.[87] The aim was to further deter foreigners from coming into Iraq while also discouraging local Iraqis from supporting the U.S.-led reconstruction process.

Finally, al-Zarqawi's fourth strategy was designed to target the Shiite population of Iraq and provoke a Shiite-Sunni war. With that, al-Zarqawi also aimed to entrap U.S. and Coalition forces in a sectarian conflict so severe, so religiously motivated, and so foreign that U.S. and Coalition forces would have no choice but to leave. The cold-blooded attack against prominent Shiite leader Sayyid Muhammad al-Hakim in the holy city of Najaf is a prime example of this strategy. In a letter to Osama bin Laden dated January 2004, al-Zarqawi explained this tactic: "Targeting and striking their [the Shiite population's] religious, political, and military symbols will make them show their rage against the Sunnis and bear their inner vengeance. If we succeed in dragging them into a sectarian war, this will awaken the sleepy Sunnis who are fearful of destruction and death."[88]

Though al-Zarqawi and JTJ's brutal methods – particularly the published videos of the beheading of foreign civilians – horrified and appalled many Muslims, these inhumane and violent tactics did resonate with the anger of many Sunni Islamists in Iraq and elsewhere. Though a large majority of Iraqis condemned JTJ, the group appealed to a small minority of extremist fighters who wanted a chance to fight foreign soldiers, so JTJ

[87] Robert S. Leiken, "Who Is Abu Zarqawi?" *CBS News,* May 18, 2004, http://www.cbsnews.com/news/who-is-abu-zarqawi/.
[88] Gary Gambill, "Abu Musab al-Zarqawi: A Biographical Sketch."

enjoyed a steady flow of recruits and rapidly began to grow its membership and support base.

JTJ continued to conduct numerous attacks throughout 2004, including bold attacks inside the high-security Green Zone perimeter in Baghdad, further bolstering its reputation as a vicious and highly effective group. On March 2, 2004, JTJ executed a series of bombings against Shiites celebrating the *Ashura* holiday, killing at least 185 civilians and wounding more. A Shiite mosque was the target of a suicide attack in July 2004, killing 98 people, and a suicide truck bombing against Shiite workers in August 2004 killed more than 100 civilians.[89]

Throughout JTJ's campaign of terror, amid the assassinations, the bombings, the kidnappings, and suicide attacks, al-Zarqawi began to realize that he needed a plan bigger than his four-pronged strategy. Though his group was gaining notoriety, there were still other influential militant groups on the Iraqi battleground, including the forces of prominent Shiite cleric Moqtada al-Sadr, who also had Iranian backing.

---

[89] Emily Hunt, "Zarqawi's 'Total War' on Iraqi Shiites Exposes a Divide among Sunni Jihadists," *The Washington Institute,* November 15, 2005, http://www.washingtoninstitute.org/policy-analysis/view/zarqawis-total-war-on-iraqi-shiites-exposes-a-divide-among-sunni-jihadists.

Moqtada al-Sadr

In December 2004, JTJ officially pledged allegiance to al-Qaeda, and bin Laden formally named al-Zarqawi as the *emir* of the al-Qaeda branch in Iraq. The group renamed itself Tanzim Qaidat al-Jihad fi Bilad al-Rafidayn ("al-Qaeda in the Land of Two Rivers"), but it was more commonly known as al-Qaeda in Iraq (AQI).[90] A translated transcript of al-Zarqawi's pledge to bin Laden read, "We will listen to your orders. If you ask us to join the war, we will do it and we will listen to your instructions. If you stop us from doing something, we will abide by your instructions."[91]

The JTJ-al-Qaeda merger was a mutually beneficial deal. In the overpopulated world of militant Islamists in Iraq, AQI was able to stand out as a credible, legitimate branch

---

[90] "Tanzim Qaidat al-Jihad fi Bilad al-Rafidayn (QJBR)," *Terrorism Research and Analysis Consortium (TRAC),* http://www.trackingterrorism.org/group/tanzim-qaidat-al-jihad-fi-bilad-al-rafidayn-qjbr-al-qaeda-land-two-rivers-see-separate-entry.

[91] Caroline Faraj, "Al-Zarqawi Group Claims Allegiance to Bin Laden," *CNN,* October 18, 2004, http://www.cnn.com/2004/WORLD/meast/10/17/al.zarqawi.statement/.

of an organization that was known across the world. Not only this, AQI now enjoyed the funding, expertise, networks, and connections of the al-Qaeda core, giving it the boost it needed to continue fighting for an Islamic state in Iraq. At the other end of the deal, al-Qaeda also benefited greatly from this merger, because the post-9/11 U.S. invasion of Afghanistan hurt al-Qaeda greatly, and bin Laden and al-Qaeda's senior leadership were forced into hiding in Pakistan and elsewhere. Al-Qaeda's central leadership was scattered, and the situation was too dangerous for them to come back together and attempt another attack. With al-Zarqawi and AQI in Iraq, however, there was a surrogate figurehead that would propel the waning al-Qaeda momentum forward again.

CSIS, in its analysis of the transformation of JTJ into AQI, described the al-Qaeda-al-Zarqawi merger as such: "The foreign intervention of the U.S.-led invasion in March 2003 and the subsequent occupation was the chief factor that led to Zarqawi's formal allegiance to al Qaeda core and the creation of AQI. It served as a driving factor in three ways: it fed the al Qaeda narrative of the West's war against Islam; it attracted and provided sanctuary for terrorist organizational and operational activities; and it served as a common enemy framework that encouraged marriages of convenience between groups that had previously formed distinct, more manageable threats."[92]

To al-Qaeda's delight, the number of AQI's signature high-profile suicide attacks steadily rose throughout 2005. However, following the 2005 national elections in Iraq and the subsequent drafting of the new Iraqi constitution,

---

[92] Kirdar, "Al Qaeda in Iraq," 6.

tensions among the competing factions of the Iraqi insurgency finally boiled over and led to significant and deep fractures, resulting in widespread condemnation of al-Zarqawi's high-profile, heinous, and increasingly unpopular tactics of random killings, beheadings, and assassinations. Al-Zarqawi's agenda was proving to be even more radical than that of the al-Qaeda leadership in Afghanistan and Pakistan, but in May 2005, under the al-Qaeda banner, al-Zarqawi released a statement declaring that collateral killing of Muslims is justified in Islam.[93] He had unleashed a new level of terror that was ferociously brutal, even by al-Qaeda's standards.

In addition to the appalling tactics that turned off many in Iraq, it's important to remember that al-Zarqawi was not an Iraqi by birth or by upbringing, so it was not lost on some that a foreign leader seemed so passionate about ridding Iraqi land of foreign influence and returning Islam to Iraq. With widening dissatisfaction against al-Zarqawi and his tactics, the fact that he was a foreigner became a prominent point of contention, and nationalist elements of the Iraqi insurgency began to distance themselves and publicly condemn the presence of foreign fighters in Iraq, especially those like al-Zarqawi who were engaging in divisive tactics that were aimed at fueling sectarian strife. As early as July 2005, al-Qaeda's core leadership in Afghanistan and Pakistan called upon al-Zarqawi to mend ties with other groups and conveyed to him the importance of maintaining popular support, minimizing collateral damage and civilian deaths, and promoting

---

[93] Abdel Bari Atwan, *The Secret History of Al Qaeda* (Berkeley: University of California Press, 2006), 205.

AQI's image by stressing the presence of Iraqi members in the group.

Nonetheless, on November 9, 2005, AQI launched coordinated bombings against three hotels in Amman, Jordan. The attacks killed 60 people, most of them Muslims attending a wedding party, and following the brutal attacks, thousands of Jordanians took to the streets shouting for the downfall of al-Zarqawi. This was the last straw for al-Qaeda's core, and in January 2006, al-Qaeda ordered AQI and five other affiliated Iraqi groups to merge with the Mujahideen Shura Council (MSC), an umbrella organization aimed at unifying all the Sunni groups in Iraq and led by a council of group leaders (from which al-Zarqawi was excluded).[94]

Subsequent attempts by al-Zarqawi to regain his standing and influence ultimately failed, and on June 7, 2006, he was killed in a U.S. airstrike. Despite al-Zarqawi's death, however, AQI's attacks continued, and the void left by al-Zarqawi was swiftly replaced by a senior AQI leader named Abu Ayyub al-Masri (also known as Abu Hamza al-Muhajir), whose ascension as *emir* of AQI was officially announced on June 7, 2006.[95]

[94] Kirdar, "Al Qaeda in Iraq," 5.

[95] Mathieu Guidère, *Historical Dictionary of Islamic Fundamentalism* (Plymouth: Scarecrow Press, 2012), 222.

Al-Masri

Also known as Abu Hamza al-Muhajir, Abu Ayyub al-Masri was an Egyptian-born al-Qaeda affiliate, close associate of al-Qaeda leader Ayman al-Zawahiri, and an explosives expert. Al-Masri was also al-Qaeda's ideal leader for AQI/ISI. Al-Zarqawi had proved so reckless, brutal, uncompromising, and ignorant of the importance of local support that plenty of al-Qaeda leaders were no doubt somewhat relieved that al-Zarqawi was killed. In contrast to the rogue al-Zarqawi, al-Masri was a former top confidante and aide to al-Zawahiri, so he was reliable, had close ties to al-Qaeda and its leadership, and was also a master bomb maker and explosives expert.[96]

Al-Masri reportedly began his militant career in 1982, when he became involved with the Egyptian Islamic Jihad

[96] Bill Roggio, "US and Iraqi Forces Kill Al Masri and Baghdadi, Al Qaeda in Iraq's Top Two Leaders," *The Long War Journal,* April 19, 2010,
http://www.longwarjournal.org/archives/2010/04/al_qaeda_in_iraqs_to.php.

(EIJ), a militant group led by al-Zawahiri that eventually merged with al-Qaeda, and al-Masri subsequently travelled to Afghanistan to train in explosives and weapons.[97] After the fall of the Taliban, it is believed al-Masri made his way to Iraq and began to make contact with insurgent groups there on behalf of al-Qaeda. Once the invasion in Iraq took place, al-Masri became increasingly active and claimed involvement in multiple attacks and killings.

In June 2006, al-Masri was named the new leader in al-Zarqawi's place, but it is not clear whether he fully filled the role left vacant by al-Zarqawi's death or whether his leadership was more limited. U.S. Central Command spokesman Jamie Graybeal said of al-Masri in May 2008 that "the current assessment, based on a number of factors, shows that he is not an effective leader of al Qaeda in Iraq as he was last year." The U.S. government subsequently reduced the bounty placed on al-Masri's head from $5 million to $1 million in 2007, then to $100,000 in February 2008.[98]

As AQI continued its attacks throughout 2006 and 2007, backlash against its continued brutal tactics culminated in the formation of the National Council for the Salvation of Iraq, or the *Sahwa* (Awakening) Movement[99], established as a coalition of prominent Iraqi tribes that united to maintain security in their communities with the aid and support of the U.S. and Iraqi governments. *Sahwa* was

---

[97] Scott Peterson, "Picture of a Weakened Iraqi Insurgency," *The Christian Science Monitor,* June 16, 2006, http://www.csmonitor.com/2006/0616/p01s04-woiq.html.

[98] Mike Mount, "Reward for Wanted Terrorist Drops," *CNN,* May 13, 2008, http://edition.cnn.com/2008/WORLD/meast/05/13/pentagon.masri.value/index.html.

[99] Sahwa Movement is also known as the Sunni Salvation Movement, Anbar's Salvation Movement, or the Sons of Iraq program.

particularly aimed at combating the terrorist insurgency in parts of Anbar province, and by early 2009, over 100,000 Sunni tribesmen had joined the *Sahwa* forces and were funded by the U.S. to fight AQI.[100]

The formation of the *Sahwa* Movement was a severe blow to the AQI. It had never truly had local support prior to this, but there had been no outright backlash or confrontation until now. AQI members were actively being hunted down by *Sahwa* members, and on top of that, the U.S. "surge" in Iraq led to the deployment of 20,000 additional U.S. troops in June 2007. Thousands of AQI militants were killed or captured, greatly depleting AQI's forces, and the deteriorating conditions also led to the withering of the flow of foreign recruits; AQI had garnered hundreds of foreign fighters per month at one point, but by 2009, only five or six entered Iraq each month.[101]

Thus, AQI had reached its operational apex in 2006-2007, after which its militants were forced to flee many of their strongholds due to targeted and intensive military offensives conducted by the Iraqi government-backed local militias and Coalition forces. By 2008, AQI's operational capacity was severely weakened, and by early 2010, U.S. and Iraqi forces concluded that they had "either picked up or killed 34 out of the top 42 al-Qaeda in Iraq leaders." By June of 2010, the organization had "lost connection with [al-Qaeda core] in Pakistan and Afghanistan."[102] AQI was no longer viewed as an

---

[100] Kirdar, "Al Qaeda in Iraq," 5.

[101] Ibid., 5.

[102] Jessica D. Lewis, "Al-Qaeda in Iraq Resurgent: The Breaking the Walls Campaign, Part I," *Middle East Security Report* 14 (September 2013): 9.

immediate or significant threat, and though the organization continued to conduct attacks throughout 2010-2011, it was too isolated, disorganized, and disrupted to pose a serious threat to Iraqi or coalition forces.

Unfortunately, the U.S. incorrectly assumed that AQI had been completely destroyed, but it had only briefly been defeated, and remnants of the group still lingered. On October 15, 2006, the creation of the Islamic State of Iraq (ISI) was announced after neither the AQI nor the MSC was able to gain popular support. Abu Ayyub al-Masri was renamed ISI's war minister, while a new figure named Abu Omar al-Baghdadi was named ISI leader. ISI based itself primarily in Anbar province, but it also had a strong presence in southern Baghdad and the provinces of Diyala, Salah ad-Din, Niveneh, and parts of Babil.

Even as the group was being decimated, great mystery continued to surround the group's leader, Abu Omar al-Baghdadi, whose leadership, death, and even existence have been questioned by numerous analysts and intelligence agencies. The identity of Abu Omar was called into question in July 2007 when the U.S. military announced that Abu Omar did not exist and was actually a fictitious character created by al-Masri to make an Iraqi face the representative of an increasingly non-Iraqi AQI. The leadership and membership of AQI were becoming dominated by foreign figures and fighters, and this image of AQI as a puppet of foreign powers like al-Qaeda was ostracizing the group on the ground. According to senior U.S. military officials, al-Masri therefore hired an actor named Abu Abdullah al-Naima to play the part of a fictional Iraqi-born leader named Abu Omar al-Baghdadi. Al-Masri then played his own part as War Minister of ISI and swore allegiance to this contrived leader Abu Omar al-Baghdadi, "which was essentially swearing allegiance to himself, since he knew that Baghdadi was fictitious and totally his own creation," according to U.S. Brigadier General Kevin Bergner in a press briefing.[103]

The U.S. based these allegations on information gleaned through the interrogations of Khalid Abdul Fatah Da'ud Mahmud al-Mashadani, a senior ISI leader and close associate of al-Masri who was captured on July 4, 2007 by Coalition forces in Mosul. Reportedly, during these interrogations, al-Mashadani confessed that AQI/ISI was merely a front organization established by senior al-Qaeda leaders in order to put an Iraqi face on the insurgency. According to the U.S., the rank and file of AQI/ISI were completely unaware that al-Baghdadi was a fictional figurehead whose creation and image were controlled by al-Qaeda leaders in Pakistan and Afghanistan, and that all the while, they had been following the orders of the Egyptian al-Masri.

This has remained a theory based on little concrete evidence, but the fictitious identity of Abu Omar al-Baghdadi would help explain why there had been so many false reports and rumors of al-Baghdadi's capture and death over the years. Eventually, this speculation of a fictional al-Baghdadi died down as the man purporting to be Abu Omar al-Baghdadi continued to release videos and audiotapes of his sermons and speeches. It must be noted,

[103] Bill Roggio, "Islamic State of Iraq – An AL Qaeda Front," *The Long War Journal,* July 18, 2007, http://www.longwarjournal.org/archives/2007/07/islamic_state_of_ira.php.

however, that al-Baghdadi's face was always blurred, and his voice continued to match that of the alleged actor Abu Abdullah al-Naima, according to U.S. officials.

Even more confusion over the true identity of Abu Omar al-Baghdadi arose in May 2008 after the police chief of the city of Haditha in Iraq stated in an interview that the true name of Abu Omar al-Baghdadi was Hamed Dawood al-Zawy, and that al-Zawy was a former officer in the Iraqi army who was ultimately dismissed from the service because of his extremism.[104] The police chief also released photographs of al-Zawy, which remain one of the very few possible photographs of Abu Omar al-Baghdadi to date.

The situation grew even more complex after the U.S. military released a series of communications between Ayman al-Zawahiri of al-Qaeda, Abu Ayyub al-Masri, and Abu Omar al-Baghdadi, which had been intercepted by Coalition forces in April 2008.[105] Al-Baghdadi was referred to many times in the letters, and al-Zawahiri personally wrote advice and recommendations to al-Baghdadi. After being challenged by claims that al-Baghdadi is actually al-Zawy, a former member of the Iraq security forces, the U.S. military responded by stating that al-Qaeda must have filled the position of al-Baghdadi with an actual person and not just an actor after the Naima charade was disclosed. A senior U.S. military official reportedly disclosed to *The Long War Journal* that "Al

---

[104] "Report: True Identity of 'Islamic State of Iraq' Leader Revealed, Photos Aired," *CBS News,* May 7, 2008, http://www.cbsnews.com/news/report-true-identity-of-islamic-state-of-iraq-leader-revealed-photos-aired/.

[105] Bill Roggio, "Letters from Al Qaeda Leaders Show Iraqi Effort Is in Disarray," *The Long War Journal,* September 11, 2008,
http://www.longwarjournal.org/archives/2008/09/letters_from_al_qaed.php.

Qaeda in Iraq filled in the position with a real individual after Multinational Forces Iraq revealed that Abdullah al Naima was a hired actor." Furthermore, according to this anonymous source, this new figure, al-Zawy, was one of the few senior AQI leaders who could "meet the criteria of being descended from Hussein that was a key part of Baghdadi's biography." Tracing lineage back to Hussein Ali, the grandson of Prophet Mohammad and revered as a martyr in Islam, was reportedly a requirement for leadership of ISI.[106]

Despite questions over the nature of the group's leader, it's apparent that ISI was meant to have a looser structure than its predecessors and function more like an umbrella grouping of different tribal groups and Islamist brigades, including AQI and MSC. It resembled an embryonic state of its own, and in this way, it was much like the Taliban in Afghanistan. It had a full cabinet and ministry positions, as well as a draft constitution for a post-invasion Islamist Iraq. Therefore, in this way, ISI was more forward-thinking than JTJ or AQI were. Al-Zarqawi had been primarily focused on consolidating power and defeating his immediate enemies, while ISI showed organizational maturity by placing a great focus on the future of the war, the group, and Iraq.[107]

At the same time, this is not to say that there was a definitive lack of continuity in the transformation of JTJ to AQI and subsequently to ISI. The goals and strategies of ISI were still in line with the early objectives of al-

[106] Bill Roggio, "Who Is Abu Omar Al Baghdadi?" *The Long War Journal,* September 14, 2008, http://www.longwarjournal.org/archives/2008/09/who_is_abu_omar_al_b.php.

[107] Atwan, *The Secret History of Al Qaeda,* 203.

Zarqawi, and the group's main aims continued to be to oust foreign influence from Iraqi territory, topple the current government, and establish in its stead a pure Islamic state.

It has been claimed by some that AQI and the subsequent ISI's presence and strength in Iraq was exaggerated, particularly by the Bush administration. For example, a July 2007 National Intelligence Estimate and a Defense Intelligence Agency (DIA) report stated that AQI accounted for 15% of the total attacks in Iraq, but the Congressional Research Service noted in a September 2007 report that AQI's actual attacks accounted for less than 2% of the total number of violent incidents in Iraq.[108] The 2008 U.S. State Department report on terrorism indicated that AIQ was "the largest terrorist group in Iraq" and that the group's operations were predominantly Iraq-based, but "maintains an extensive logistical network throughout the Middle East, North Africa, Iran, South East, and Europe."[109]

Of course, the lower numbers indicated that while AQI's strength in Iraq was overly exaggerated. AQI's image and reputation had suffered greatly as a result of the indiscriminate attacks and massive civilian deaths it had caused in previous years, thus isolating the group. The surge also led to dozens of high-level AQI members being captured or killed, and by late 2008, it appeared AQI was completely driven out of its former territories.

On April 23, 2009, the Iraqi government proudly

---

[108] Andrew Tilghman, "The Myth of AQI," *Washington Monthly,* October 2007, http://www.washingtonmonthly.com/features/2007/0710.tilghman.html.

[109] U.S. State Department, Office of the Coordinator for Counterterrorism, Country Reports on Terrorism, April 30, 2007, http://www.state.gov/j/ct/rls/crt/2006/82738.htm.

declared that it had finally captured the elusive Abu Omar al-Baghdadi, and videos and photographs of a handcuffed al-Baghdadi being taken into custody were shown in Iraq and across the world. In early May 2009, the Iraqi news stations broadcasted confessions of the alleged terrorist leader, who stated his real name to be Ahmed Abed Ahmed Khamees al-Mujamaie and admitted that he joined AQI in 2005 and became the emir of the ISI in 2006.[110] However, ISI soon fired back with a media statement of its own, and militant websites in May 2008 published an audio message purportedly recorded by Abu Omar al-Baghdadi, denying reports of his arrest and berating the Iraqi government for failing to capture the "real" al-Baghdadi. "Everyone was surprised by the lies of the Green Zone leaders who claimed again that they detained me," the voice on the audio said. The U.S.-based SITE Intelligence Group, which monitors jihadist online activity and media, stated that the voice in the audio appeared to be close to al-Baghdadi's purported statements in the past.[111]

This was not the first time the Iraqi government erroneously announced al-Baghdadi's demise. When al-Baghdadi was reported as killed in May 2005, a spokesman at the Iraqi Interior Ministry stated that authorities had somehow brought in people who knew al-Baghdadi "for 20 years," and they had identified his body.[112] However, the Iraqi government later acknowledged that

[110] Yousif Bassil, Mohammed Tawfeeq and Cal Perry, "Iraq TV Airs Alleged Confession of Terrorist Leader," *CNN,* May 18, 2009, http://www.cnn.com/2009/WORLD/meast/05/18/iraq.alleged.terror.confession/index.html?iref=24hours.

[111] Paul Schemm, "Iraqi Al Qaeda Group Leader Still In Custody: Iraqi FM," *Huffington Post,* May 13, 2009, http://www.huffingtonpost.com/2009/05/13/iraqi-al-qaeda-group-lead_n_202995.html.

[112] "Who Was the Real Abu Omar Al-Baghdadi?" *Asharq Al-Aqsat,* April 20, 2010, http://www.aawsat.net/2010/04/article55251030.

the body they had was not al-Baghdadi's. Again in 2007, the Iraqi government announced that al-Baghdadi had been killed in a raid and subsequently released photographs of what it said was his body. Later in 2007, after it was revealed that the body was not that of al-Baghdadi, authorities stated they had arrested al-Baghdadi. Again, this turned out to be untrue. Naturally, al-Baghdadi and the ISI were quick to use the Iraqi government's mistakes to their advantage. "Sunnis, the Shi'ites are your enemies," al-Baghdadi declared in an audio message released denying his capture. "Their history is full of treacheries and plotting against you. Don't trust them or let their honeyed words fool you."[113]

On April 18, 2010, Abu Omar was reported to have been killed in a joint U.S. and Iraqi raid near Tikrit – the same raid that killed Abu Ayyub al-Masri. Iraqi Prime Minister Nouri al-Maliki at a news conference in Baghdad announced their deaths and presented photographs of the two leaders' bloody corpses.[114] Though analysts and jihadists alike were doubtful about the Iraqi government's claims after years of false death and arrest reports, final confirmation came a week later on April 25, 2010, when ISI released a statement eulogizing the deaths of its two leaders. "After a long journey filled with sacrifices and fighting falsehood and its representatives, two knights have dismounted to join the group of martyrs," the statement said, referring to Abu Omar al-Baghdadi and

---

[113] Lin Noueihed, "Qaeda-Linked Group in Iraq Denies Head Captured," *Reuters,* May 12, 2009, http://www.reuters.com/article/2009/05/12/us-iraq-baghdadi-idUSTRE54B4WI20090512.

[114] "2 Most Wanted Al Qaeda Leaders in Iraq Killed by U.S., Iraqi Forces," *Fox News,* April 19, 2010, http://www.foxnews.com/world/2010/04/19/iraqi-al-qaeda-leader-killed-countrys-intelligence-team-pm-maliki-says/.

Abu Ayyub al-Masri. "We announce that the Muslim nation has lost two of the leaders of jihad, and two if its men, who are only known as heroes on the path of jihad."[115]

Regardless of whether he actually existed, Abu Omar al-Baghdadi was and remains a significant and symbolic figure who served as the uniting force behind ISI's regaining of strength. The Iraqi government's fixation on him and their numerous failed attempts to kill and capture him bolstered al-Baghdadi's reputation in the eyes of jihadists, further boosting ISIL's credibility and recruitment efforts. Furthermore, the deaths of al-Masri and al-Baghdadi were swiftly followed by the announcement of a new leader named Abu Bakr al-Baghdadi, even though 80% of ISI's leaders had been killed or captured by this point.[116]

[115] "Al-Qaeda Confirms Iraq Leaders' Deaths," *The Telegraph,* April 25, 2010, http://www.telegraph.co.uk/news/worldnews/middleeast/iraq/7632630/Al-Qaeda-confirms-Iraq-leaders-deaths.html.

[116] Guidère, *Historical Dictionary of Islamic Fundamentalism*, 288.

Abu Bakr al-Baghdadi

With a $10 million bounty on his head, Abu Bakr al-Baghdadi is likely the most prominent and influential figure in ISIL history since Abu Musab al-Zarqawi; he has been described as "the world's most dangerous man" by TIME magazine and "the new bin Laden" by Le Monde.[117-118] Biographies released by ISIL identify Abu Bakr as a scholar and a pious imam from a religious family descended from noble tribes who enjoys writing poetry and has a PhD from Baghdad's Islamic University. He is said to hold many other degrees in Islamic studies, history, and Arabic linguistics, and his brothers and uncles include preachers and professors of Arabic, rhetoric, and logic.[119] Though Abu Bakr al-Baghdadi is in fact often addressed as "Doctor" instead of "Sheikh," how much of this purported biography is propaganda is unknown, making it impossible to distinguish between fact and myth. However, intelligence agencies claim that Abu Bakr's true name is Ibrahim Awwad Ibrahim Ali al-Badri.

According to U.S. intelligence agencies, al-Badri was born in 1971, meaning he is in his 40s today. Al-Badri is believed to be from Samarra, a majority Sunni city that was once the capital of the Abbasid Caliphate, and he was reportedly active in the Iraq War, including fighting in Fallujah during the war and reportedly founding his own armed group. After gaining some territory in Rawa close

[117] Frank Kearney, "Abu Du'a," *TIME,* April 23, 2014, http://time.com/70832/abu-dua-2014-time-100/.

[118] Christophe Ayad, "Abou Bakr Al-Baghdadi, Le Nouveau Ben Laden," *Le Monde,* May 29, 2014, http://www.lemonde.fr/proche-orient/article/2014/05/29/abou-bakr-al-baghdadi-le-nouveau-ben-laden_4428636_3218.html.

[119] Terrence McCoy, "How ISIS Leader Abu Bakr Al-Baghdadi Became the World's Most Powerful Jihadist Leader," *The Washington Post,* June 11, 2014, http://www.washingtonpost.com/news/morning-mix/wp/2014/06/11/how-isis-leader-abu-bakr-al-baghdadi-became-the-worlds-most-powerful-jihadi-leader/.

to the border with Syria, he named himself governor of the town and imposed a strict and brutally conservative form of sharia that became the hallmark of ISIL, but in 2005, he was captured by U.S. forces and detained at Camp Bucca for close to five years. Those who oversaw the camp recalled that al-Badri was "savvy" and manipulative, both toward his fellow inmates and his guards.[120] However, he was hardly a troublesome inmate that required constant supervision by the guards, as one might imagine from the eventual leader of one of the most brutal groups in jihadist history. Al-Badri was only one of over 25,000 Iraqi prisoners, and in 2009, he was released on a presidential pardon.[121]

Following the deaths of al-Masri and Abu Omar al-Baghdadi, al-Badri became leader of ISIL, but it's unclear how he rose up to this position, or whether he was appointed by al-Qaeda or self-appointed. Either way, he gained enough respect by 2010 that al-Qaeda swiftly gave its blessing to the new leader. Like Abu Omar al-Baghdadi before him, al-Badri did not flaunt his influence or release grandiose videos and statements like many other leading jihadists in the region. Instead, he kept a relatively low profile, and for years, very little was known of the man.

What is known is that al-Badri is a strategist and opportunist. When the fighting began in Syria in March 2011, he saw his chance and almost immediately opened a

[120] Tracy Connor, "The Secret Life of ISIS Leader Abu Bakr Al-Baghdadi," *NBC News,* June 17, 2014, http://www.nbcnews.com/storyline/iraq-turmoil/secret-life-isis-leader-abu-bakr-al-baghdadi-n132311.

[121] Shashank Joshi, "Abu Bakr Al-Baghdadi: The World's Most Wanted Man," *The Telegraph,* July 1, 2014, http://www.telegraph.co.uk/news/worldnews/middleeast/10935790/Abu-Bakr-al-Baghdadi-The-worlds-most-wanted-man.html.

branch there and renamed ISI to ISIL. Instead of blindly attacking, he made strategic gains in key territories, taking over border crossings, supply routes, and oil fields. It is his shrewdness as a tactician and his ruthlessness as a military leader that has helped his reputation skyrocket among jihadists in the region, and it's altogether possible that he has surpassed even al-Qaeda leader Ayman al-Zawahiri in clout and prestige among Islamist jihadists. He has shown a high level of charisma, leadership, intelligence, and aggressiveness not seen since bin Laden's early years as al-Qaeda leader.

Another significant point is that it appears al-Badri's popularity is not so much about a cult of personality, as eventually became the case with Osama bin Laden, but more about his proven strength as a strategist and aggressiveness as a fighter. His prowess and leadership skills became abundantly clear in 2013 when he began to openly defy the orders issued to him by Ayman al-Zawahiri, and while leaders like al-Zawahiri are hiding in caves and safe houses in the mountains of Pakistan and can only able to speak to their followers through audio tapes and videos, al-Badri is presumably on the ground and in the thick of the fight. This is where the difference lies between the two leaders, and this is why more and more militants have been pledging allegiance to ISIL instead of al-Qaeda.

Along with the new leader's ascension, after the U.S. withdrawal from Iraq in December 2011, the organization steadily began to gain strength again. The resurgence was caused by several factors, most prominently the political instability caused by the U.S. withdrawal, the radicalization of the region following the Arab Spring, and the start of the Syrian civil war in 2011. An additional reason why ISI regained its power can be found in the disbanding of *Sahwa* forces. Though Iraqi Prime Minister Nouri al-Maliki had promised to integrate the now militia-less *Sahwa* fighters into the regular army upon the U.S. withdrawal, this promise was not fulfilled. Instead, al-Maliki purged Sunnis from the government[122] and prominent public positions and heavily cracked down on Sunni protests and activism.[123] As a result, he gave the disbanded militants neither a legitimate army to fight for nor a peaceful outlet through which they could voice their grievances. It is highly likely that with nowhere to go, many *Sahwa* fighters joined ISI and other militant Islamist groups, feeling that al-Maliki would never offer them a fair deal.

---

[122] Sunnis are a minority (around 20%) in Iraq, but for a long time, the minority Sunnis held power, and Shiites were often persecuted – despite their being the majority. Saddam Hussein was a Sunni.

[123] "Two Arab Countries Fall Apart," *The Economist,* June 12, 2014, http://www.economist.com/news/middle-east-and-africa/21604230-extreme-islamist-group-seeks-create-caliphate-and-spread-jihad-across.

Nouri al-Maliki

It may not have been just the *Sahwa* remnants that joined ISI either, because ordinary Sunnis were also growing tired of the repression and persecution of the al-Maliki government. Al-Maliki went after senior Sunni officials, including his own Vice President, Tariq al-Hashimi, and he also arrested thousands of ordinary citizens on flimsy terrorism charges. Tensions and anger rose in April 2013 after Iraqi troops shot at least 50 protesters dead at a peaceful sit-in protest in the Sunni city of Hawija.[124] Undoubtedly, al-Maliki's openly antagonistic and hostile views and actions toward Sunni Iraqis boosted the recruitment efforts of ISI.

---

[124] "How Did It Come to This?" *The Economist,* June 19, 2014, http://www.economist.com/news/middle-east-and-africa/21604627-crisis-iraq-has-roots-going-far-back-history-recently-folly.

Tariq al-Hashimi

The number of attacks surged, and fatalities in Iraq sharply increased by approximately 500 in January 2012, just one month after the withdrawal of U.S. forces. In July 2012, Abu Bakr al-Baghdadi announced the start of what he called the "Breaking the Walls" campaign, which triggered a massive launch of suicide attacks, simultaneous bombings, jail breaks, and assassination attempts.[125] The reboot of the group was complete, and the world soon realized that ISI had come back with even greater manpower and willpower than it ever had before.

It is interesting to note that relations between the ISI and al-Qaeda at this point were weak if not altogether non-existent. Documents discovered in bin Laden's compound in Abbottabad, Pakistan highlighted the lack of communication between the two groups. In January 2011, al-Qaeda's U.S. spokesperson Adam Gadahn confirmed

---

[125] Lewis, "Al-Qaeda in Iraq Resurgent: The Breaking the Walls Campaign, Part I," 10.

that relations between ISI and al-Qaeda were "cut off for a number of years." [126] Bin Laden himself reportedly regretted the "scarcity of communications from Iraq" in a letter dated April 26, 2011, a week before his death in a targeted U.S. Special Forces raid.[127]

In April 2013, Abu Bakr al-Baghdadi released an audio statement announcing the birth of the Islamic State in Iraq and the Levant (ISIL). Adding the words "and the Levant" to the group's name was a symbolic move that signified the group's intentions to expand its operations into the Levant, especially Syria. ISIL has since become one of the most ruthless and influential rebel groups on the Syrian battlefield, and it has morphed into a truly transnational organization that has thousands of members on both sides of the Iraqi-Syrian border.

In January 2014, ISIL claimed full control of Fallujah, one of the key cities the U.S. focused on reclaiming during the Iraq War, and throughout 2014, the group has taken various parts of Aleppo. By June 2014, the organization has grown in such strength that it has successfully seized control of multiple key cities in Iraq, including parts of Samara, Tikrit, and Mosul, Iraq's second largest city. It goes without saying that this was a significant feat for a group much smaller than the Iraqi army, and in Mosul, when less than 1,000 ISIL fighters advanced against the city on June 10, 2014, they forced two Iraqi army divisions of nearly 30,000 equipped,

[126] Robin Simcox, "The 'Islamic State of Iraq'," *The Wall Street Journal,* July 31, 2012, http://online.wsj.com/news/articles/SB10000872396390443477104577550500445383554.

[127] "Description of the Abbottabad Documents Provided to the CTC," *The Washington Post,* http://www.washingtonpost.com/r/2010-2019/WashingtonPost/2012/05/03/Foreign/Graphics/osama-bin-laden-documents-combined.pdf.

trained, and battle-ready soldiers into a chaotic retreat.[128] The seizure of Iraq's second largest city was not just a significant military advantage either, because ISIL looted banks in Mosul and is believed to have stolen somewhere between $450 million to a staggering $1.5 billion, making it one of the most cash-rich militant groups not just in Syria but also in the world.[129]

Despite the fact that ISIL may be small and still only has an estimated several thousand fighters in Iraq and a few thousand more in Syria, it is by no means a ragtag group of poorly trained, poorly equipped radical thugs. Instead, it is well-equipped, enjoys support and funds from a wide range of private donors and state sponsors in the region, and has used its long years of experience on the battlefield to establish numerous training camps steadily producing well-prepared fighters. Abu Muhammad al-Adnani, a primary spokesperson for ISIL, attributed the group's current success to God's will, stating, "The state has not prevailed by numbers, nor equipment, nor weapons, nor wealth, rather it prevails by Allah's bounty alone, through its creed."[130]

In retrospect, it's shocking how swiftly ISIL was able to adapt, transform, and rebrand itself within the rapidly changing political and security contexts in Iraq and the region. When it was facing heavy competition with rival brigades and was in need of funds, resources, and status, JTJ turned to al-Qaeda and formed an alliance. When AQI

[128] Ramzy Baroud, "ISIL and Iraq's Pandora's Box," *Middle East Eye,* June 15, 2014, http://www.middleeasteye.net/columns/isil-and-iraq-s-pandora-s-box/817321027.

[129] "Profile: Islamic State in Iraq and the Levant (ISIS)," *BBC News,* June 16, 2014, http://www.bbc.com/news/world-middle-east-24179084.

[130] "All You Need to Know about ISIS and What Is Happening in Iraq," *RT News,* June 20, 2014, http://rt.com/news/166836-isis-isil-al-qaeda-iraq/.

experienced significant backlash from *Sahwa* forces and other anti-Islamist tribal groups on the U.S. payroll, it rebranded and restructured itself as ISI, a looser umbrella organization composed of a number of different brigades, each with different constituencies and support bases. And when the Syrian conflict began in 2011 and the group saw an opportunity to expand its operations across the border, it quickly changed its name once more and ventured into Syria to join the civil war.

Though it has been difficult to uncover the precise structure and internal organization of AQI, ISI, and ISIL, there have been records and documents recently declassified that hint at the changes in the leadership's management style as the group transitioned from AQI to ISI. One such document was the Sinjar Records, documents uncovered by U.S. and Coalition troops in October 2007 that contained the biographical sketches of nearly 700 foreign fighters in Iraq, many of whom were affiliated with AQI, MSC, or both. The biographies of the fighters were detailed and the records were well organized, which seemed to indicate that following al-Zarqawi's death, AQI's organizational structure became more bureaucratic, organized, and institutionalized. Other documents dated after al-Zarqawi's death included a standardized application form for recruits to fill out and detailed records of AQI's spending and revenues. It appears al-Zarqawi's death and the subsequent rebranding as ISI also signified a shift from an autonomous, leader-centric, top-down organizational structure into an institutionalized and bureaucratized structure.

There are some analysts who contend that ISIL was

ultimately a U.S. creation. Though it cannot be said that ISIL was directly created by the U.S., it is also apparent that the invasion into Iraq, the subsequent occupation, and the hurried and abrupt departure of U.S. forces from Iraq in December 2011 all played a significant role in fostering the growth and development of ISIL. Indeed, the current ISIL leader, Abu Bakr al-Baghdadi, was something of a product of the U.S. occupation of Iraq; Abu Bakr fought against U.S. forces and was held (and allegedly tortured) at Camp Bucca – the largest U.S. prison in Iraq – for five years. Abu Bakr al-Baghdadi was only one of thousands of Iraqis who were held in the dungeons of a U.S. prison, likely furthering their radicalization.

The Ideology of ISIL

"Islam is different from any other religion; it's a way of life. We were trying to understand what Islam has to say about how we eat, who we marry, how we talk. We read Sayyid Qutb. He was the one who most affected our generation." - Mohammed Jamal Khalifa, a college friend of bin Laden's

"While the leadership's own theological platform is essentially Salafi, the organization's umbrella is sufficiently wide to encompass various schools of thought and political leanings. Al-Qaeda counts among its members and supporters people associated with Wahhabism, Shafi'ism, Malikism, and Hanafism. There are even some whose beliefs and practices are directly at odds with Salafism, such as Yunis Khalis, one of the leaders of the Afghan mujahedin. He is a mystic who visits tombs of saints and seeks their blessings—practices inimical to bin Laden's Wahhabi-Salafi school of thought.

The only exception to this pan-Islamic policy is Shi'ism. Al-Qaeda seems implacably opposed to it, as it holds Shi'ism to be heresy. In Iraq it has openly declared war on the Badr Brigades, who have fully cooperated with the US, and now considers even Shi'i civilians to be legitimate targets for acts of violence." – Abdel Bari Atwan

As a movement advocating the return of Muslims to the fundamental tenets of Islam, Islamic fundamentalism emerged in the 1920s, but it was only in the late 1970s to 1980s that the movement began to gain significant political traction in the Middle East. Starting from this period, fundamentalism swept across the region to fill the ideological void felt by many Muslims, thereby providing what was largely deemed as a much needed blueprint for the role of Islam, of Muslims, and of the Middle East in the future of the world.

Several factors can be attributed to why Islamic fundamentalism blossomed in this era, but there were three key events that decidedly contributed to this phenomenon, and ultimately to the emergence of such radical ideologies like that of al-Qaeda. These events were the 1973 oil boom and the rise of Saudi Arabia, the Iranian Revolution of 1979, and the Soviet War in Afghanistan from 1979-1989. In a period that featured an increasing realization that the secular state had failed and Muslims were in a state of political crisis and decline, these three events created a region-wide social and political environment in which Muslims brought to light new fundamentalist ideological interpretations of their religion, their countries, their politics, and their existence.

In October 1973, the Organization of the Petroleum Exporting Countries (OPEC), a Saudi-led economic cartel formed by oil-producing countries, initiated an oil embargo against the U.S. and other countries in protest of Western support of Israel against Arab nations in the Yom Kippur War of 1973. The embargo and the subsequent quadrupling of oil prices had devastating effects on U.S. and world economies, while also exposing the sheer severity of Western dependency on oil. As a result, the oil-rich monarchies, particularly Saudi Arabia, gained much notoriety and prestige among Arabs. People in the region could look to conservative Saudi Arabia – for decades branded as "American-made" and historically shunned to the fringes of Middle Eastern politics that was, at this time, overflowing with Nasserites and Arab socialism – suddenly bringing major countries to bend to its will. King Faysal was touted as the victorious hero, and Saudi Arabia the epitome of oil wealth and power, an Arab nation that stood apart from the rest not only in terms of unprecedented political sway but also in economic power. Whereas affluence and nobility were associated with Westernized suits and uncovered heads a decade ago, the rise of Saudi Arabia made devotion to Islamic practices a mark of prestige.

Meanwhile, oil money flooded into Saudi Arabia and was subsequently used to finance a campaign for its own Saudi brand of Islam: Wahhabism, the same branch of Islam Osama bin Laden practiced. The Saudis extended a sympathetic hand to fundamentalists, who inherently shared Wahhabism's anti-secular, puritanical streak, and from the 1970s onward, Saudi Arabia began to fund the activities and proliferation of Islamic educational institutions called *madrasas*, bankrolling its Wahhabism across the region and giving it basis in these religious schools. Saudi Arabia invested not so much in roads or bridges but more in the building of mosques and other Islamic causes, and the Saudis' mass distribution of radical Islamic texts across the region fell into the hands of many, particularly the youth. These efforts transformed the region into one rife with religious conservatism, which further made it more receptive to fundamentalism.

The explosive growth of Saudi-funded *madrasas* continued and became increasingly important during the Soviet occupation of Afghanistan, as extremist *madrasas* emerged in the Pakistan-Afghanistan region that focused more on *jihad* against the infidels than on Islamic scholarship. Saudi oil wealth was therefore used to give birth to a certain regional milieu, and equally important, it provided an institutional base that allowed for and encouraged fundamentalist interpretations of Islam.

The second key event was the 1979 Iranian Revolution, which led to the toppling of the Western backed Pahlavi dynasty in Iran and its replacement with a purely Islamic republic under Ayatollah Khomeini. The revolution was an event that enhanced Islamic fundamentalism as a viable alternative ideology for opposition against and overthrow of long-established secular regime, and its success in Iran confirmed the failure of the secular state model and proved the power of Islam. Fundamentalists could now point to Iran as proof that Islam could overthrow an entire system that was backed by the West, achieving what all other ideologies like Marxism and

Leninism failed miserably to do. Iran thus became the concrete example of progress and independence as achieved through Islam, and from Lebanon to Palestine, Senegal to Malaysia, and even in Muslim communities in Europe, there was an identifiable surge in Islamist enthusiasm. Even Osama bin Laden was heavily inspired by this revolution, despite the fact that it was a Shi'a victory; there is evidence that bin Laden was so impressed with Shi'a radicalism and the Iranian Revolution that he gladly received assistance from Iranian backed militant groups like Hezbollah despite being a Sunni fundamentalist.[131]

[131] *The 9/11 Commission Report: Final Report of the National Commission on Terrorist Attacks Upon the United States*, official government edition (Washington, DC: U.S. Government Printing Office, 2004), 240.

Ayatollah Khomeini

In general, people do not personally and privately adopt a certain ideology or belief system simply and solely because an authority, or the state, or certain scriptures tell them to; they do so because it offers an efficient solution and a realistic chance of success. Islamic fundamentalism at its core is about the creation of an Islamic state, and before Iran's revolution, this seemed a desperately intangible figment of imagination. The emergence of the Islamic state of Iran served as the much-needed success story, bringing the fundamentalist argument out of the realm of theories. The fact that the revolution was led by an exiled cleric was further proof that Islam can overcome seemingly impossible odds and bring about regime change, making the concept of the Islamic state actually viable in the minds of many. This realization and resurgence of a new kind of optimism resonated throughout the region.

The Soviet War in Afghanistan was the third significant event that precipitated the resurgence of political Islam and Islamic fundamentalism. The Afghan *jihad* and the subsequent Soviet withdrawal showed that Islam was capable of defeating a superpower, and it was the watershed event that took Islamic fundamentalism to an even higher level. Its impact went beyond the realm of Sunnis versus Shiites, or Iran versus Saudi Arabia, because the Afghan *jihad* transformed into an Islamic *jihad*, a holy war won by all Muslims of the world.

The significance of this event lay in the fact that Muslims came to Afghanistan to fight from all over the world and then returned to their respective home countries all across the world. Legions of young men traveled to Afghanistan, received military training, fought side-by-side, and eventually returned home, but their minds remained in Afghanistan. Throughout the 1980s, these young guerillas gathered, exchanged ideas, and created a community in which the Afghan war became a universal Islamic *jihad* that was neither particular to Afghanistan nor to any other single Muslim country, as it pertained to any and all Muslims as one united struggle. Once the notion of the Afghan war as an Islamic *jihad* spread, more and more Islamists travelled to Afghanistan, including Osama bin Laden, Abdullah Azzam, and the early founders of al-Qaeda.

As an Islamist and al-Qaeda-linked group, ISIL follows the Islamic fundamentalist trend, as many militant Islamist groups in the region do, and like al-Qaeda, ISIL adheres to a radical and political form of Islam; it holds certain beliefs that are common among Islamic fundamentalist groups, the most important of them being the idea that Islam is the comprehensive and exclusive solution for all political, economic, and social problems of the world. It must be noted that groups like ISIL are not nationalist groups operating under the cloak of religion but are jihadist groups committed to the liberation of Muslims across the world. Its aim is not forming a Salafist or Sunni state system in Iraq but an Islamic Caliphate encompassing the entire region of the Levant, from Iraq and across Syria to Lebanon and beyond. Thus, Islam is therefore interpreted as a political ideology rather than as a purely theological construct, and it is taken outside of the religious realm it has historically occupied and into the secular domain of politics. As such, what groups like ISIL call for is the establishment of an Islamic Caliphate in the country or region they are fighting in, and once this local Caliphate is established, then a global Caliphate is pursued.

ISIL's ideology has been labeled "extreme," even in comparison to hardliners like al-Qaeda, and it is this potent and explosive combination of extremist ideology with guerilla experience, professional military expertise, steady flow of funds and recruits, and a large collection of arms and weaponry, that makes ISIL such a powerful and dangerous force.

In cities like Raqqa, Syria, where ISIL has near complete control, citizens are murdered and oppressed in the name of Islam. Black flags hang from everywhere, earning the city the name "Black Province," and multiple checkpoints manned by ISIL militants stop cars and check if women are veiled and dressed according to ISIL's interpretation of Islamic attire. If they are not, then both the women and the men who are accompanying them are punished. Students, doctors, teachers, children, and anyone believed to be violating ISIL laws are punished by the various ISIL policing units that patrol the city. Anyone who smokes or sells cigarettes gets lashed publicly, while those deemed traitors for favoring Assad's regime in Syria are executed.[132]

The justified killing of Muslims is one of the key components of the distorted ideology of both al-Qaeda and ISIL. According to the Qur'an, he who murders one innocent is judged "as if he had murdered all of mankind," and the killing of fellow Muslims is an even more punishable act. The Qur'an then concludes that those who do engage in the killing of Muslims will find that their "repayment is Hell, remaining in it timelessly, forever."[133] Yet, both al-Qaeda and ISIL use distorted and perverse interpretations of Islam to justify and legitimize the killing of fellow Muslims. In fact, ISIL takes it one step further, and this is perhaps one of the biggest differing points between the ideology of ISIL and that of al-Qaeda. ISIL openly and aggressively attacks Shiite targets, not just mosques and shrines but civilians as well. Al-Zarqawi

---

[132] Hadil Aarja, "ISIS Enforces Strict Religious Law in Raqqa," *Al-Monitor,* March 21, 2014, http://www.al-monitor.com/pulse/security/2014/03/isis-enforces-islamic-law-raqqa-syria.html.

[133] Wright, *The Looming Tower*, 124.

ordered dozens and dozens of attacks against Shiite civilians, and this targeted slaughter of a specific religious sect and this severe sectarianism this strategy was based on are what differentiates al-Qaeda and ISIL, and specifically, Osama bin Laden and Abu Musab al-Zarqawi. While both men followed the strict Salafi code of Islam that deems Shiites to be apostates, bin Laden decided to take the middle ground and called for unity between Shiites and Sunnis. In fact, he frequently and openly collaborated and received support from many Shiite militant groups, such as Hezbollah, and from Shiite-dominated governments like Iran. Al-Zarqawi himself held refuge many times in the safe havens of the mountains of Iran; yet he was in favor of attacking Shiites, calling them "the most evil of mankind...the lurking snake, the crafty and malicious scorpion, the spying enemy, and the penetrating venom."[134] He subsequently ordered assassinations of senior Shiite government officials and religious leaders in Iraq, as well as bombings of Shiite festivals and weddings.

The Start of the Syrian Civil War

"First of all, you're talking about the president of the United States, not the president of Syria -- so he can only talk about his country. It is not legitimate for him to judge Syria. He doesn't have the right to tell the Syrian people who their president will be. Second, what he says doesn't have anything to do with the reality. He's been talking about the same thing -- that the president has to quit -- for a year and a half now. Has anything happened? Nothing has happened." – Bashar al-Assad

---

[134] Leiken, "Who Is Abu Zarqawi?"

Late 2010 and early 2011 was a very tumultuous time in the Middle East. Waves of protesters took to the streets for days on end in Tunisia, Egypt, Bahrain, and Yemen. Syria was also one of these countries to suffer from a long period of instability, and of course it has since become the focal point of the multi-faceted conflicts roiling the region.

The primary grievance for most protesters in the region, during what has come to be known as the "Arab Spring," was a call for social justice and reforms which eventually turned into demands for regime change against long-standing dictatorships. While some of these Arab countries underwent rapid and immense changes in leadership, in most cases, the clashes among protesters and police were mostly infrequent during this time and did not amount to large-scale violence between the military and civilians.

Syrian President Bashar Assad, on the other hand, did not respond with as much restraint as other leaders in the region. As protester demands changed from a desire for social reforms to regime change, Assad began to blame foreign entities for the ensuing chaos. The theme of blaming foreigners for all internal problems is fairly common throughout the Middle East, particularly in dictatorship, since it attempts to absolve the country's leader from any guilt or wrongdoing. This notion of blaming foreign enemies eventually played well into Jabhat Al-Nusra's plan for localizing its activities, as it claims to be a native movement.

Assad

The Arab Spring officially began in December 2010 in Tunisia when a student and fruit vendor named Muhammad Bouazizi had his fruit cart confiscated by police who probably wanted a bribe (Lesch 2012, 45). Bouazizi reacted with the extreme form of protest of self-immolation, a suicide that led to protests fuelled by social media. The protests reached the capital of Tunis on January 13, 2011, and they ultimately forced Tunisia's dictator, Ben Ali, to flee to Saudi Arabia (Lesch 2012, 47).

The scene of angry street protests directed at a despotic

leader was replayed in Egypt, and as the protests continued, Western pressure induced Egyptian dictator Hosni Mubarak to step down from the presidency just weeks after the events in Tunisia (Lesch 2012, 48). It seemed that no dictator in the Arabic speaking world was immune, and protests sprouted from the Gulf States to Morocco. Despots who had ruled for decades, including Ali, Mubarak, and Qaddafi in Libya, were eventually overthrown.

Although Syria witnessed anti-government protests similar to those in other countries during the Arab Spring, they were initially much smaller and not very organized (Lesch 2012, 53). The lack of large-scale protests initially in Syria can be attributed to its uniqueness as a nation among its Arabic speaking neighbors. The complex intelligence and police state apparatus in Syria no doubt contributed to stamping out many of the protests before they could grow into something much larger, but the personality and public perception of Bashar al-Assad is another factor that mitigated protests in Syria. Bashar was much less hated by his people than the other dictators who were toppled during the Arab Spring (Lesch 2012, 52). For example, Ali and Mubarak were viewed by many of their peoples as American stooges, while Qaddafi had rightly earned his reputation as an eccentric tyrant.

One of the more important and unique aspects of Syria that reduced the amount and intensity of initial protests there was its demographic composition. In the 21st century, Syria is a country comprised of many different religious sects and tribes; the Sunni Muslims are the majority, but the minority Shia and Christian sects form about 30% of the population, and they have traditionally been loyal to the al-Assad family, who they view as protectors (Lesch 2012, 51-52).

As the last two years have made clear, far worse has happened in Syria than mere protests. If the early Arab Spring protests never took hold in Syria, how did the country devolve into the current situation? The answer is a combination of Assad's hubris and his inability to understand tide of change in the Middle East. It is unknown whether or not if the protests would have been suppressed or fizzled out, but in March 2011, several schoolboys from the southwestern Syrian city of Deraa scribbled the words "down with the regime" in Arabic on a wall in their school (Lesch 2012, 55). In any other time the boys would have probably just been punished by the school authorities, but in the shadow of the Arab Spring the kids were arrested and tortured (Lesch 2012, 56). As a result of the children's incarceration and torture, their families protested in central Deraa on March 15, 2011, which then spread across Syria via social networking websites (Lesch 2012, 56). Ironically, these repressive tactics were being used the very same month *Vogue*'s puff piece on Asma was published, making clear the extent of the Assad family's propaganda attempts with the West and humiliating the magazine so badly that the article on Asma was quickly removed from their website. As Gawker's editor, John Cook, put it, "I think it's important that people are aware of how Vogue…felt about the Assads, and characterized the Assads. It came out almost exactly as the regime embarked on its campaign of murdering women and children…And now in the context of the United States possibly going to war with Syria, it's important for people to see how the magazine portrayed them... "

Bashar might have been able to stem the tide of the protests with conciliatory gestures, but his pride and ego got the best of him. Instead of admitting the mistakes his police agents made in the Deraa situation, Assad chose to blame outside sources and "conspiracies" for the protests and unrest. Bashar said in a speech to the Syrian People's Assembly on March 30, 2011: "Our enemies work every day in an organized, systemic and scientific manner in order to undermine Syria's stability. We acknowledge that they had been smart in choosing very sophisticated tools in what they have done, but at the same time we realize that they have been stupid in choosing this country and this people, for such conspiracies do not work with our country or our people." (Lesch 2012, 76-77) Even late in 2012, with the civil war raging, Assad remained defiant when *Der Spiegel* asked if he was sorry about the way his supporters handled Deraa: "There were personal mistakes made by individuals. We all make mistakes. Even a president makes mistakes. But even if there were mistakes in the implementation, our decisions were still fundamentally the right ones."

Bashar's obstinate attitude toward the protesters took a violent turn when he gave his brother, Maher, a free hand to deal with them. Maher filled a role similar to his uncle Rifaat before he was exiled from Syria, as he was head of the Fourth Armored Division and the Republican Guard, which served to protect the regime (Lesch 2012, 105). Just as Bashar's father Hafez called in Rifaat to put down the

Muslim Brotherhood insurgency in the late 1970's and early 1980s, Bashar appealed to Maher to suppress protests in Syria 30 years later, which he gladly did with equally brutal methods, often carried out personally (Lesch 2012, 105). The primary difference between the two situations was that the methods employed by Hafez and Rifaat ultimately proved to be successful, while those used by Bashar and Maher have apparently thrown Syria into a state of sectarian warfare.

Hafez al-Assad

Maher al-Assad

Rifaat al-Assad

One of the primary strengths of the Assad dynasty, the backing of the Alawite sect, also became one of the major reasons why Syria devolved into sectarian warfare. Most of the government and police forces who participated in the violent crackdowns against protesters were Alawites, while the majority of the opposition was from the Sunni community, which was portrayed by the Assad regime as fundamentalists (Lesch 2012, 106). Assad has used the fragmented sectarian demographic background of Syria to his advantage by arguing that if fundamentalist Sunnis came to power in Syria, it would mean bloodshed for the

Alawites, Ishmailis, Druze, and Christians whom his family protected. After all, the Syrian minorities only needed to look at the persecution the Christian Copts of Egypt were experiencing in the wake of their Arab Spring (Lesch 2012, 107).

In April of 2011, Assad's regime commanded the Syrian Army to begin firing upon neighborhoods in Damascus and around Syria[135] to combat what they told the world were "terrorists" trying to bring the country down. This narrative of blaming Syria's instability on foreign-backed terrorists would come to shape the international conversation among states who believed that intervention in the civil war would be seen as an attack on sovereignty rather than support of revolutionary forces against a brutal dictator. As the attacks raged around the country, soldiers in the military began to defect from the army and form the Free Syrian Army.

Although Assad's tactic of dividing Syria's population may have initially helped him stay in power, it had the effect of deepening the sectarian conflict. Furthermore, as defectors from the Syrian army began to form the Free Syrian Army, Islamic militant jihadists also began to enter the war (Lesch 2012, 174-75). Although the Free Syrian Army is comprised of a lot of secular elements (British Broadcasting Company 2013, October 17), Assad's propaganda campaign has tirelessly depicted his enemies as Al-Qaeda connected terrorists, and he has portrayed a potential Free Syrian Army victory as genocide for Syria's Shia and Christian communities. The fear has

---

[135] Gattas, K. (2011, May 24). *US policy on Syria 'depends on success in Libya'*. Retrieved from BBC News: http://www.bbc.com/news/world-middle-east-13529923

prompted paramilitary Alawite gangs, known as *Shabihas* (ghosts in Arabic), to kill members of the opposition and Sunnis indiscriminately (Lesch 2012, 177). The situation in Syria has effectively evolved over the last nearly three years from one of protest to revolution and now finally to a sectarian civil war that shows no signs of ending. Perhaps not surprisingly, Assad has denied the Shabihas exist, even while justifying their existence: "There is nothing called 'Shabiha' in Syria. In many remote areas where there is no possibility for the army and police to go and rescue the people and defend them, people have bought arms and set up their own small forces to defend themselves against attacks by militants. Some of them have fought with the army, that's true. But they are not militias that have been created to support the president. At issue is their country, which they want to defend from al-Qaida."

Assad's branding of his enemies as foreign agents and terrorists has greatly helped him. In response to questions from *Der Spiegel* about the Syrian people wanting him gone, Assad said of his enemies, "Again, when you talk about factions, whether they are opposition or supporters, you have to ask yourself the question: Whom do they represent? Themselves or the country that made them? Are they speaking for the United States, the United Kingdom, France, Saudi Arabia and Qatar? My answer here has to be frank and straight to the point. This conflict has been brought to our country from abroad. These people are located abroad, they live in five-star hotels and they say and do what those countries tell them to do. But they have no grassroots in Syria." At the same time, he has cast his opponents as the very Al-Qaeda terrorists the West despises: "The whole problem wasn't about the president. What do killing innocents, explosions and the terrorism that al-Qaida is bringing to the country have to do with me being in office?"

Either way, resistance against the Syrian government and the instability continued to gradually grow and explode not only in Syria but along the borders in the neighboring countries of Iraq, Israel, Jordan, Lebanon, and Turkey. Like in many countries around world, the borders of Syria are porous, which makes it easier for people, weapons, and other resources to pass through. The Syrian Civil War and its resulting consequences have severely impacted the politics, economies, and security of the surrounding states and the world at large due to the enormous amount of refugees fleeing the country. This instability has been most obvious in the development and spread of various armed militias and terrorist groups in Syria and in neighboring countries. The conflict has created a major power vacuum in many parts of Syria, leaving control of the area ripe for the picking.

While many analysts and experts on the region predicted increasing chaos as the violence continued,[136] inaction on the part of the international community allowed for foreign fighters from terrorist groups to set up shop and begin planning attacks against the Assad regime. This was one of a few reasons that Russia and China--both U.N. Security Council members with veto powers and often allied with Syria--vehemently disagreed with Western

---

[136] International Crisis Group. (2011, November 3). *Syria's Tipping Point*. Retrieved from International Crisis Group: https://www.crisisgroup.org/middle-east-north-africa/eastern-mediterranean/syria/syria-s-tipping-poin

interference in the civil war. As conditions continued to deteriorate, many more armed groups joined the fight. These different militias and terrorist groups often claim to have the support of the locals in whose city they occupy in their efforts against the Syrian government forces. The allegiances among these groups have changed often and their tactics have varied as they have taken on the Syrian Army and, at times, each other.

ISIL in Syria

Since renaming itself Islamic State in Iraq and the Levant in April 2013, ISIL has drastically increased its operations in Syria. It is one of the most influential and well-funded groups there, and one of the most brutal. Footages of beheadings and mass executions conducted by ISIL have circulated online, horrifying the world but also radicalizing many youth and compelling plenty to travel to Syria and join the fight. Furthermore, the Syrian conflict served as the perfect opportunity for ISIL to enter a country governed by a regime dominated by the Alawite sect, an offshoot of Shiite Islam.

The Syrian conflict began when small protests began in January 2011 and eventually erupted into full-fledged demonstrations across Syria by March 2011. The government's use of force to crush the demonstrations had the opposite effect of what Syrian President Bashar Assad's regime intended, and by July 2011, hundreds of thousands of Syrians were taking to the streets across the country and demanding Assad's resignation.

Bashar Assad and his wife Asma in Moscow

When it became clear that peaceful means would not deter Assad's use of force or compel him to resign, opposition supporters began to take up arms. Initially, they took up arms to defend themselves, their homes, and their family, but as the rebels grew in strength and numbers, they began to actively attack Assad's forces and attempt to expel them from their towns and cities. The country quickly descended into civil war as these armed citizens began banding together to form ad hoc rebel brigades, and as of 2013, there were as many as 1,000 separate brigades, battalions, and armed groups commanding an estimated 100,000 fighters in Syria.[137]

Although the Syrian civil war started as a purely nationalistic and secular fight over the continued reign of Assad, the war quickly gained religious tones when the secular opposition began suffering from internal fighting and power struggles, thereby significantly weakening its position. Filling its place were nascent Islamist brigades, which took advantage of the secular opposition's failure to organize a united front, and today, even though secular coalitions like the Syrian Military Council still exist, Islamist brigades undoubtedly have the upper hand in the Syria.

The ideology of the group transformed and developed as ISIL entered Syria to join the fighting there. Their ultimate goal continued to be the establishment of an Islamic Caliphate in the Levant, and what was once a faraway dream suddenly seemed entirely feasible as ISIL began conquering town after town and city after city in both Iraq and Syria. The group has released maps depicting what its new state will look like, and how the borders will be rearranged. ISIL's most prominent spokesperson, Abu Mohammed al-Adnani, stated, "The legality of all emirates, groups, states, and organizations

---

[137] David Gritten, Lucy Rodgers and Emily Macguire, "Syria: The Story of the Conflict," *BBC News,* March 14, 2014, http://www.bbc.com/news/world-middle-east-26116868.

becomes null by the expansion of the caliph's authority and the arrival of its troops to their areas."[138]

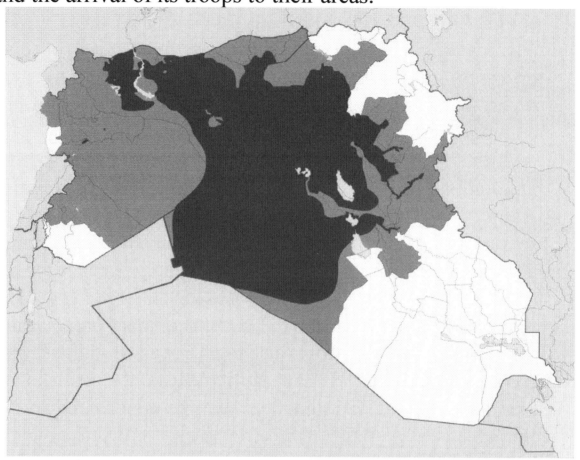

Territory occupied by ISIL in dark red, territory claimed by the group in light red, and the rest of Iraq and Syria in white

Al-Adnani and other ISIL figures define the new Islamic Caliphate controlled by ISIL as spanning from northern Syria to the Diyala province in Iraq, which is an enormous stretch of land, but much of it is already under ISIL control as of June 2014. Furthermore, the group has also published a five-year plan for how it will expand the borders of this newfound Caliphate beyond the region and

---

[138] John Hall, "The ISIS Map of the World," *Daily Mail,* June 30, 2014, http://www.dailymail.co.uk/news/article-2674736/ISIS-militants-declare-formation-caliphate-Syria-Iraq-demand-Muslims-world-swear-allegiance.html.

across the world, to North Africa, to Asia, and to Europe. A *Daily Mail* article summarizes this expansion plan clearly: "Spain, which was ruled by Muslims for 700 years until 1492, is marked out as a territory the caliphate plans to have under its control by 2020. Elsewhere, ISIS plans to take control of the Balkan states - including Greece, Romania and Bulgaria – extending its territories in Eastern Europe as far as Austria, which appears to be based on a pre-First World War borders of the Austro-Hungarian Empire."[139]

In this way, ISIL is perhaps the only al-Qaeda-linked organization in the world to ever come close to obtaining what all al-Qaeda franchises have fought to achieve: the establishment of a purely Islamic state. Most importantly, by controlling a vast swath of territory in the heart of the Arab world, the group has managed to do what the original central al-Qaeda core that was founded by bin Laden has never been close to doing

In addition to this, ISIL is extremely active in the propaganda sphere; in addition to publishing their attacks and campaigns by consolidating them into a full report and releasing it on an annual basis, the ISIL also uses social media tools such as Twitter and Facebook to post attack information, photographs, and videos on a real-time basis. Such dedication to publicity highlights the group's savvy propaganda campaign, which aims not only to attract recruits and raise funds but also to spread terror and fear by posting pictures of crucifixions, beheadings, and mass executions.

---

[139] Ibid.

ISIL's Current Composition and Structure

"We will go to Iraq, Jordan, Lebanon; wherever Sheikh Abu Bakr Al-Baghdadi wants us to go, we will go…the hope of the nation is in your hands, Sheikh."[140] These were the words uttered by an ISIL recruit who left his home, abandoned his studies, and traveled to Syria, where he joined ISIL and appeared in a propaganda video. This recruit was not an Iraqi militant or Syrian fighter but a young Briton of Yemeni origin who was born and raised in the UK. The 17-year-old was planning to go into university to study medicine, but instead, he ended up on the battlefields of Syria declaring an oath of allegiance to Abu Bakr al-Baghdadi.

The foreign fighter phenomenon that occurred during the 1980s war in Afghanistan has replicated itself in Syria, but this time, the phenomenon is more expansive, as fighters have come not just from Arab and Muslim countries but also from Western nations like the UK., U.S., France, Germany, and others. Even more significant is the fact that many of these foreign fighters come from privileged households with a good educational background and a supportive family. The great influx of these fighters into Syria has been a puzzling yet violent and extremely notable aspect of the war.

Furthermore, Chechens are a major fighting force in ISI, to the extent that a red-headed, pale-skinned Chechen named Abu Omar al-Shishani (Abu Omar the Chechen) is one of the leading commanders in ISIL. The foreign component of ISIL is what makes the group unique, and

---

[140] Diana Moukalled, "Opinion: The Western ISIS and Its Second Rebirth," *Asharq Al-Awsat,* July 1, 2014, http://www.aawsat.net/2014/07/article55333827.

this is also why the Syrian conflict has turned into a significant global concern. Youth from countries unrelated to the Syrian war are being radicalized by ISIL propaganda online and traveling to Syria to join the group, but once they have trained and fought with ISIL for several months, they are instructed to go back to their home countries to conduct ISIL-related operations there.

Many countries actually aided in ISIL's recruitment efforts, though in most cases indirectly. Neighboring countries opposed to the Assad regime like Turkey and Saudi Arabia had an interest in supporting the Syrian rebels, so Ankara let a free flow of fighters from all over the world enter Turkey and then cross its borders into Syria. Wealthy and influential Gulf states like Kuwait and Qatar remain lax about the flow of private donations into Syria, and many Gulf-based financiers and "charities" are openly fundraising and sending large sums of money to Islamist groups in Syria, including ISIL. Over the years since 2011, as many as 12,000 militant Islamists entered Syria to join the fight, including approximately 3,000 from Western countries.[141]

Disowned by al-Qaeda

When the Syrian conflict started, al-Qaeda initially had two affiliates operating in Syria: al-Nusrah Front and the Islamic State in Iraq and the Levant (ISIL). Al-Nusrah Front (also known as Jabhat al-Nusrah or Support Front for the People of the Levant) was formed in January 2012, and what started as a group barely distinguishable from the hundreds of other militant opposition groups fighting

---

[141] McCoy, "How ISIS Leader Abu Bakr Al-Baghdadi Became the World's Most Powerful Jihadist Leader."

the Bashar Assad regime in Syria catapulted into the spotlight when it pledged loyalty to the al-Qaeda core in 2013.

As the fighting in Syria spread, more and more members of AQI relocated to Syria to participate in the fighting, and AQI eventually expanded its operation as ISIL. It remains unclear whether al-Nusrah Front emerged at this time as a branch of ISIL or as an entity separate from it, but nonetheless, al-Nusrah Front began to define itself as an independent entity, even as ISIL continued to claim that al-Nusrah Front was merely a sub-battalion of ISIL. The disagreement mounted into multiple clashes between the two groups that should have ideologically been on the same side.

Ayman al-Zawahiri and other notable al-Qaeda-linked jihadist ideologues such as Abu Muhammad al-Maqdisi attempted to mediate between the two groups, but to no avail. Eventually, in a surprising announcement made on February 2, 2014, al-Zawahiri published a statement online that announced al-Qaeda had disowned the ISIL and expelled it from the al-Qaeda franchise, and with that, al-Nusrah Front was designated the official al-Qaeda branch in Syria. The statement read, "Al-Qaeda al-Jihad announces that it has no link to the Islamic State of Iraq and the Levant. It did not create it, did not invest it with authority, did not consult with it, and did not express approval of it. Rather, al-Qaeda ordered it to stop its actions. Therefore, it is not an al-Qaeda affiliate, no organizational relationship binds the two, and al-Qaeda is not responsible for its behavior."[142]

---

[142] Juan Cole, "'Too Extreme for Al Qaeda': Al Zawahiri Disowns ISIL," *Mideast Posts,* May 2, 2014,

There are several likely reasons that explain why al-Zawahiri chose to back one group and disown the other. First, there could only be one al-Qaeda representative in Syria, and it was difficult as it was for al-Qaeda core to keep tabs on its affiliate thousands of miles away. Obviously, it reflected poorly on al-Qaeda to have two affiliated groups fighting each other. But perhaps more importantly, ISIL was becoming too extremist in its ideology and especially in its tactics, even for al-Qaeda's standards. ISIL massacred, looted, tortured, and killed civilians and soldiers alike, conducted mock trials and brutal executions, and published grisly videos and photographs online of beheaded bodies, crucifixions of alleged thieves, dead children, and mass graves of executed Syrian soldiers. Additionally, ISIL began attacking other Syrian rebel groups, regardless of whether they were Islamist or moderate, including al-Nusrah Front. The infighting was costly for the opposition, as it led to the deaths of hundreds of opposition fighters and gave Assad's forces time to regroup, reorganize, and attack.

As the division between the ISIL and al-Nusrah Front suggest, it is difficult to determine how many of these organizations are ideologically and operationally fully committed and loyal to al-Qaeda core, or whether they are just paying lip service as a means to operate under the al-Qaeda flag. It is equally hard to assess exactly how frequently the affiliates are in contact with the core command, since al-Qaeda must maintain a substantial clandestine apparatus and work hard to conceal much of its operational ties and relationships among affiliates.

The Islamic State

On June 28, 2014, ISIL renamed itself yet again, this time as the "Islamic State," and it announced the formation of a Caliphate in the territories it has seized in Iraq and Syria. Abu Bakr al-Baghdadi was declared the first Islamic Caliph, and the group called on all Islamist groups and Muslims to pledge allegiance. ISIL's spokesperson, Abu Mohammed al-Adnani, stated that this new ISIL state will begin imposing all *sharia* duties, such as the execution of prescribed penalties, establishment of Islamic courts, and the levying of *jizya* (taxes). State borders and physical barriers among Islamic countries are now deemed to be moot, as the Islamic State's Caliphate has now established a single economic system and currency for all territories under its control. "The proclamation of the caliphate means that every Muslim has the duty to pledge allegiance to the new caliph of Muslims or otherwise die the death of the time of Jahiliyya. The proclamation of the caliphate invalidates the legitimacy of all other Islamic emirates," al-Adnani professed.[143]

The announcement of the caliphate will have a profound impact on what happens next, and it's controversial among Muslims in the region as well. Historically, caliphates were states governed under Islamic law, with the leadership elected in Sunni practice or appointed from a group of respected Imams in Shia practice. The last

---

[143] Abdallah Suleiman Ali, "ISIS Announces Islamic Caliphate, Changes Name," *Al-Monitor,* June 30, 2014, http://www.al-monitor.com/pulse/security/2014/06/iraq-syria-isis-announcement-islamic-caliphate-name-change.html.

Islamic caliphate was under the Ottoman Empire, which ended with the formation of the secular and non-Islamic Turkish Republic in 1923 by Kemal Ataturk. In the past, the role of caliph, which comes from the Arabic word *khalifa* ("successor"), was largely symbolic, with day-to-day government management delegated to local rulers.

This rebranded Islamic State's claim of the restoration of the caliphate and the establishment of its own state poses an immense challenge to other Islamist groups in the region, especially al-Qaeda. Sheikh Abu Muhammad al-Maqdisi, a prominent Jordanian jihadist ideologue and one of al-Qaeda's spiritual leaders, has already released statements labeling the Islamic State as "a deviant group" and accusing it of going against Islam and *sharia*.[144] That the Islamic State has carved out such a large territory and effectively erased the border between Iraq and Syria will likely trigger a wave of infighting among the various militant factions, and certain groups have already pledged allegiance to the Islamic State. For example, Sunni militant groups in Lebanon have pledged loyalty to Abu Bakr al-Baghdadi, declaring him their caliph, and some factions and cells of the rival al-Nusrah Front have reportedly defected to join the Islamic State as well.

At the same time, there have emerged groups that oppose this declaration. Abu Sulayman al-Muhajir, an Australian preacher and senior *sharia* official of al-Nusrah Front, has released statements via Twitter sharply criticizing the Islamic State's declaration and arguing that the Islamic State's failure to consult jihadist leaders in the region

---

[144] "Al-Qaeda Spiritual Leader Labels Islamic State as 'Deviants,'" *Ammon News,* July 1, 2014, http://en.ammonnews.net/article.aspx?articleno=25875#.U7NcdPmSySo.

before making the announcement is a "clear breach of Islam."[145] Other senior al-Nusrah Front officials, such as Sami al-Uraydi and Gharib al-Muhajir al-Qahtani, have also released statements describing Islamic State's announcement as "a declaration of war against Muslims, rather than [the establishment of] an Islamic Caliphate," and they dismissed the Caliphate as "imaginary" and without the support of "many students of [Islamic] knowledge and leaders."[146] Al-Nusrah Front and 8 other leading rebel groups in Syria have released a statement rejecting the Islamic State's purported establishment of a Caliphate.[147] The statement also warned other groups not to join the Islamic State, while the Islamic State itself has warned of consequences if groups do not pledge allegiance. Therefore, this new move by the Islamic State may spark a massive war among the various militant groups operating not just in Iraq and Syria but across the entire region.

In response to these developments, the region and the entire world have been on alert. The U.S. has sent several hundred troops to Baghdad to act as advisors in containing and defeating this new threat, the first time American boots have stepped on Iraqi soil since the December 2011 withdrawal that had supposedly marked U.S. victory in Iraq.

It has been demonstrated time and time again that this group is more capable, dangerous, and organized than most governments, intelligence agencies, and media

---

[145] Joscelyn, "The Islamic State's Rivals in Syria Reject Announced Caliphate."

[146] Ibid.

[147] Thomas Joscelyn, "The Islamic State's Rivals in Syria Reject Announced Caliphate," *The Long War Journal,* July 1, 2014, http://www.longwarjournal.org/archives/2014/07/the_islamic_states_r.php.

outlets have long believed possible. ISIL has existed in some form or another for over a decade, and though it has undergone many changes since its inception, this has allowed it to develop into an active organization with thick and deep roots in the lands of its operation. What happens next will certainly determine the future of the region.

The Foundations of the Al-Nusra Front

Localized development of terror cells creates a very peculiar and difficult situation for states attempting to counter terrorism and violent extremism. Groups such as Jabhat Al-Nusra do not merely live among populations in the states in which they operate; they are actively recruiting and developing connections and trying to build trust, a very similar model that Hezbollah in Lebanon has taken on over the past 35 years. These groups understand that long-term "success" can only be defined by the willingness of the population to not only surrender to the violent tactics the groups enact, but also feel sympathy and support for those "martyred" by the cause.

ISIL has taken a very different path, defined by its severe brutality and relentlessness to force populations in Syria and Iraq to submit to their control. Some analysts believe, however, that ISIL is not as much of a threat as groups like Jabhat Al-Nusra. According to the Institute for the Study of War: "Jabhat al Nusra draws strength from its intertwinement with Syrian Sunni opposition groups. The slow pace of U.S. strategy and its exclusive prioritization of ISIS are facilitating Jabhat al Nusra's deeper entrenchment within the opposition...Identifying means of separating Jabhat al Nusra from the opposition in order to destroy it is the most difficult intellectual task in developing a strategy for Syria..." [148]

During the mid-2000s, as al-Qaeda experienced a rise and fall of its various occupied territories around Iraq, its leadership declared the establishment of the Islamic State of Iraq (ISI) which included many cities and provinces, such as Anbar and Baghdad. [149] Their control over these areas around Iraq changed frequently over time depending on the actions of the U.S.-led coalition involvement in Iraq and their various surges. ISI/Al-Qaeda ramped up their attacks around Iraq in 2008 and 2009 and when the civil war in Syria broke out in 2011, this was a prime opportunity for the group to spread its propaganda and operations to another state dealing with the chaos left by an ongoing war.

When Abu Muhammad Al-Julani and other top leaders came to Syria, they aimed to create chaos and thereby establish a space "receptive" to their propaganda and actions. These attacks utilize "urban-rural warfare" which focuses on taking over rural periphery locals while slowly flowing into urban city centers.[150] This tactic has led to the capture and hold of Idlib in the northwest and Deir Al-Zour in the eastern part of Syria.

In 2013 and 2014, the term "Khorasan Group" became more prominent in the media. The term, most likely coined by the U.S., referred to a group of about 50 core

[148] Cafarella, J. H. (2016, February). *U.S. GRAND STRATEGY: Destroying ISIS and Al-Qaeda, Report Three.* Retrieved from Institute for the Study of War:
http://www.understandingwar.org/sites/default/files/PLANEX%20Report%203%20FINAL.pdf
[149] Roggio, B. (2006, October 16). *The Rump Islamic Emirate of Iraq.* Retrieved from The Long War Journal: http://www.longwarjournal.org/archives/2006/10/the_rump_islamic_emi.php# (Roggio, 2006)
[150] Benotman, N. a. (n.d.). *Jabhat Al-Nusra: A Strategic Briefing.* Retrieved from Quilliam Foundation: https://web.archive.org/web/20150328080133/http://www.quilliamfoundation.org/wp/wp-content/uploads/publications/free/jabhat-al-nusra-a-strategic-briefing.pdf

leaders in Al-Qaeda primarily from operations in Afghanistan and Pakistan. [151] According to U.S. intelligence reports, this group was sent by Al-Qaeda central leadership to Syria to further recruit and develop a network of fighters and plan attacks against countries from Syria, primarily those thought to be allied with Western states. Many of the individuals in the group were well-acquainted with Bin Laden and worked with him and his organization in past operations, like the terrorist attacks of September 11, 2001. The Khorasan Group worked to continue to lay the foundation for Jabhat Al-Nusra. This group claims to operate in support of the people of Syria against the regime of Bashar Assad and Western encroachment in the civil war.

When Abu Muhammad Al-Julani and his group were sent to Syria in 2011, their mission was to develop operations quickly and effectively throughout the country, ideally leading the linking of several disparate militias and terrorist groups already active in the area. According to the Quilliam Foundation, their goals were 5-fold:

1. to establish a group including many existing jihadists, linking them together into one coherent entity
2. to reinforce and strengthen the consciousness of the Islamist nature of the conflict
3. to build military capacity for the group, seizing opportunities to collect weapons and train recruits,

[151] BBC News. (2014, September 24). *What is the Khorasan Group?* Retrieved from BBC New: http://www.bbc.com/news/world-middle-east-29350271

and to create safe havens by controlling physical places upon which to exercise their power.

    4.   to create an Islamist state in Syria

    5.   to establish a 'Caliphate' in Bilad al-Sham (the Levant) [152]

The group is made up of veteran jihadists from the area who are primarily Syrian but also from outside Syria that have fought in other jihadist ventures with Al-Qaeda, which already sets them apart from the other seemingly rag-tag group of revolutionaries like the Free Syrian Army. For all intents and purposes, AQI/ISI funded Jabhat Al-Nusra's activities in Syria, particularly by building on their previously utilized funding stream of captured oil fields and ransoms from kidnappings. Al-Nusra also supports itself through the weapons it is able to take following battles and with its connections with other militant groups in the country. It has not been uncommon to see Al-Nusra on the battlefield with other groups fighting alongside each other against the Syrian army. There are also reports of the group fighting these very same militants as well, which signifies a larger strategic issue for Al-Nusra's operations in Syria. As much as it needs to ally with the other groups, it cannot risk being subsumed.

The Nusra Front's Ideology and Tactics

Like most Islamic Sunni jihadist organizations, Jabhat Al-Nusra's ultimate goal is to develop a caliphate on Earth, based on their idealized understanding of how life after the Prophet Muhammad was intended to be led and

---

[152] Benotman, N. a. (n.d.). *Jabhat Al-Nusra: A Strategic Briefing.* Retrieved from Quilliam Foundation: https://web.archive.org/web/20150328080133/http://www.quilliamfoundation.org/wp/wp-content/uploads/publications/free/jabhat-al-nusra-a-strategic-briefing.pdf

organized. Al-Nusra's ideology is Salafi--a very conservative form of Islam whose development and prominence in the Islamic world spread during the 19th century. Essentially, Salafists envision a world entirely modeled after the time of the Prophet, where strict adherence to religious law and custom are valued above innovation and convergence with modernity. This world vision sees the time of the Prophet as the most perfect and a time to be desired and emulated.

Al-Nusra is certainly not the first group to attempt to control a society by religious law; in fact, some of their purported supporters (like Qatar) already control society with conservative notions of religious law. The difference, however, is that Al-Nusra and other groups often use extreme violence in their efforts to command the society to behave in a particular way. Reports coming out of ISIL-controlled territory indicate large-scale executions, beheadings, amputations, and other extreme brutality enacted against civilians. In the videos produced by ISIL showing these actions, ISIL fighters indicate the "crime" committed by the civilian in religious terms and will connect the punishment back to Islam using their own interpretation of the religion. These fighters are not religious leaders or scholars by any means, but they have perfected the art of jihadism, essentially drawing connections between parts of the Qu'ran and Hadith (the sayings and actions of the Prophet Muhammad) dictating punishment without any regard for contexts and historical understandings.

While both Jabhat Al-Nusra and ISIL have their roots in Al-Qaeda's jihadist ideology and have recruited fighters from Al-Qaeda's ranks for their respective fights and territories, their leaders have fought over the group's direction and tactics. Both Al-Nusra and ISIL's leaders--Abu Muhammad Al-Julani and Abu Bakr Al-Baghdadi, respectively--have their origins among Al-Qaeda's ranks, and in fact, Al-Baghdadi was the leader of Al-Qaeda in Iraq (AQI) and responsible for sending fighters into Syria to develop Jabhat Al-Nusra. While Al-Julani was taking orders from Al-Baghdadi's leadership team in developing Al-Nusra's operations in Syria, a disagreement among those at the top in Al-Qaeda was taking place. Ayman Al-Zawahiri, the current leader of Al-Qaeda and long-time #2 behind Bin Laden, had encouraged Al-Baghdadi to develop operations in Iraq, but Al-Baghdad's desire for control eventually led to a breakaway from Al-Qaeda and the development of ISIL.[153]

[153] Byman, D. L. (2015, February 24). *ISIS vs. Al Qaeda: Jihadism's global civil war*. Retrieved from Brookings Institution: https://www.brookings.edu/articles/isis-vs-al-qaeda-jihadisms-global-civil-war/

Zawahiri

In order for Al-Baghdadi to further solidify his power in the region as ISIL developed, he made a statement in 2013 indicating that Jabhat Al-Nusra was actually a splinter group of ISIL and operated at their request and under his direction. In response, Abu Muhammad Al-Julani responded that while they had worked with ISIS and received considerable support (particularly when ISIS was still linked with Al-Qaeda), their ultimate loyalty was with Al-Qaeda and Al-Zawahiri.[154] These statements led to many responses among other jihadist groups and Al-Qaeda itself declaring allegiance with one side or the other. According to Mary Habeck, "The early dispute between Jabhat al-Nusra and ISIS was, then, about *power*:

---

[154] Habeck, M. (2014, June 27). *Assessing the ISIS - Al-Qaeda Split: The Origins of the Dispute*. Retrieved from Insite Blog on Terrorism & Extremism: http://news.siteintelgroup.com/blog/index.php/categories/jihad/entry/193-assessing-the-isis-al-qaeda-split-the-origins-of-the-dispute-1

who would swear bay'a to whom and, therefore, which commander was subordinate and which was in charge. It was also about which commander and group would have a closer relationship with Al-Qaeda's leadership, showing how much the favor of Al-Qaeda was prized."[155] As the conflict further inflamed relations among the groups and ISIS took more territory and grew in strength throughout 2013 and 2014, Al-Qaeda formally denounced ISIS' behavior due to its extremely violent approaches to subduing populations (including indiscriminate killing of Muslims) in the areas that it controlled which it considered against Islamic law.

The split and differentiation between ISIS and Al-Qaeda affiliated groups like Jabhat Al-Nusra eventually began to center around a different understanding of ideology and tactics used to create and maintain the Islamic caliphates. Al-Qaeda has generally focused on the West and specifically on the United States as its primary enemy but has understood that in order to continue to be relevant in the context of the post-Arab Spring uprisings, a shift in focus on particular Arab regimes must become a priority. In Iraq, ISIL has focused on bringing down the Iraqi government and, just as its affiliated groups throughout the region, on various Arab and primarily secular regimes such as in Egypt, Tunisia, and Libya while also encouraging lone wolf attacks throughout the West. Jabhat Al-Nusra has also, at Al-Qaeda's command, focused on bringing down Bashar Assad's regime but, as mentioned above, has not strayed away from the "far enemy" idea that the U.S. is responsible for the ills of the

---

[155] Ibid

Muslim world, as espoused by Al-Qaeda.[156]

Just as with other militant groups in and around Syria, Al-Nusra has tried to strike a balance between collaboration and control of the local population. As much as it may agree with ISIL's ideology and many of its tactics, it does not want to be controlled by a group much larger and, seemingly, more powerful than itself, especially since ISIL has decided to strike out on its own and commit many of the same mistakes that Al-Qaeda committed in the past, such as extremely harsh behavior toward civilians and indiscriminate killing. Many experts believe that Al-Nusra is "playing the long game"[157] when it comes to jihadist movements in the region. This is because they have yet to carry out an all-out assault against civilians and different militant groups in the area like ISIL continues to do in its territory. Al-Nusra operates under the assumption that ISIL will burn out as it continues to gain much of the international community's focus and attention. Al-Nusra on the other hand, is operating a little under the radar as it cultivates relationships among the Syrian population.

Thus, while Al-Nusra most definitely interprets religious texts in a similar way and makes those connections in terms of controlling the society they want to develop, their approach has been less harsh and brutal than ISIL's methods. They are intent on developing institutions in order to solidify their rule and commanded behavior. To this end, Jabhat Al-Nusra has developed councils (shuras)

[156] Byman, D. L. (2015, February 24). *ISIS vs. Al Qaeda: Jihadism's global civil war*. Retrieved from Brookings Institution: https://www.brookings.edu/articles/isis-vs-al-qaeda-jihadisms-global-civil-war/

[157] Schatz, B. (2016, August 5). *Meet the Terrorist Group Playing the Long Game in Syria*. Retrieved from MotherJones: http://www.motherjones.com/politics/2016/08/syria-al-qaeda-nusra-battle-aleppo

and courts to administer religious law (shari'a) throughout the areas they control in Syria. According to the Quilliam Foundation, "They and other rebel groups are experiencing a lack of religious scholars to lead prayers and spread their religious message, leading to call for imams to come to Syria from abroad."[158] These imams advise the military leaders and work to resolve disputes in the communities while enacting "God's laws on earth."

As noted earlier, localized cells of Al-Qaeda have shifted their strategy, for the most part, on developing trust and legitimacy among the communities where they launch attacks against the regimes they fight against. Over the past 4 years, Jabhat Al-Nusra has operated in cities and towns on Syria's eastern border with Iraq and around the western borders with Lebanon and Turkey. According to Middle East Institute analyst Charles Lister, "[Jabhat Al-Nusra] has played a methodically implemented long game in Syria, focused on attaining a position of military and social influence and, crucially, establishing a relationship of interdependence with Syria's opposition."[159] Their tactics have been less violent and extreme, according to Lister, "in order to present a friendly face to local communities." This emphasis on building legitimacy continues to impact their operations throughout the country. By emphasizing their intent to support "Syria," they are trying to dispel any idea that they are a foreign group, which has in fact led to disagreement among leadership in Al-Nusra and Al-Qaeda in Iraq.

In order to develop and foster this support, Jabhat Al-

---

[158] Ibid

[159] Schatz, B. (2016, August 5). *Meet the Terrorist Group Playing the Long Game in Syria*. Retrieved from MotherJones: http://www.motherjones.com/politics/2016/08/syria-al-qaeda-nusra-battle-aleppo

Nusra has taken a page right of Hezbollah's book and set up a "Relief Department" focused on distributing goods to the population where they reside.[160] As part of their tactics, Al-Nusra records and distributes videos of this "good behavior," such as distributing food, providing health care, and delivering other services.[161] These activities attempt to further solidify not only the local community's desired perception change toward Al-Nusra, but also increases reliance on the group. On occasions where a city is under siege, goods and services are clearly not going to come from the Syrian government. This is where Jabhat Al-Nusra steps in and begins to develop those relationships with the local community. This strategic positioning helps their public image tremendously.

Such behavior is very common among jihadist and political groups throughout the Middle East, such as the aforementioned Hezbollah in Lebanon and the Muslim Brotherhood in Egypt. When governments are unable or refuse to provide services to poorer communities or those in the periphery of the country, a gap is filled by these groups hoping to sway opinion in their favor. In some cases, the services provided, such as medical care, are better than those provided by the government.[162] This complex reality poses a very unique challenge to not only counter-terrorism but also countering violent extremism in

[160] Benotman, N. a. (n.d.). *Jabhat Al-Nusra: A Strategic Briefing.* Retrieved from Quilliam Foundation: https://web.archive.org/web/20150328080133/http://www.quilliamfoundation.org/wp/wp-content/uploads/publications/free/jabhat-al-nusra-a-strategic-briefing.pdf

[161] Gartenstein-Ross, D. a. (2013, August 22). *How Syria's Jihadists Win Friends and Influence People.* Retrieved from The Atlantic: http://www.theatlantic.com/international/archive/2013/08/how-syrias-jihadists-win-friends-and-influence-people/278942

[162] Farag, N. (2014). *Between Piety and Politics: Social Services and the Muslim Brotherhood.* Retrieved from Frontline - PBS: http://www.pbs.org/wgbh/pages/frontline/revolution-in-cairo/inside-muslim-brotherhood/piety-and-politics.html

a larger way. It is not enough to destroy a terrorist group and prevent recruitment; the very root causes of people joining extremist groups, such as gaps in services and lack of employment, must be addressed as well to lead to long term development.

When it comes to imposing and administering religion in its captured territories, Al-Nusra is taking a different approach than ISIL. Reports from the field indicate that while Al-Nusra most definitely calls people to religion and desires to enforce religion on the area, their tactics change when they encounter resistance. In 2015, there was a report of Al-Nusra fighters shooting Druze in Idlib purportedly because they supported Bashar Assad and, in other instances, they forced Druze to destroy their shrines and to abide by shari'a law.[163] While these actions are obviously repressive and harsh, Al-Nusra tries to make a distinction between itself and the way ISIL treats minorities in its territory, like Christians and Yazidis (e.g., completely slaughter). The leader of Jabhat Al-Nusra, Abu Muhammad Al-Julani, even published a video in 2015 stating that their enemies were not the West, but Bashar Assad.[164]

When people look back and analyze the Arab Spring revolutions during late 2010 and 2011, Twitter and Facebook immediately come to mind as the launch pads where these uprisings appeared to organize. Protesters organized, debated, and reported from the field what was

[163] yalibnan. (2015, March 19). *Al Qaeda forces Druze of Idlib Syria to destory their shrines and convert.* Retrieved from YaLibnan: http://yalibnan.com/2015/03/19/al-qaeda-forces-druze-of-idlib-syria-to-destroy-their-shrines-and-convert

[164] Fanack - Chronicle. (2015, July 1). *Jabhat Al-Nusra Tries to Look Like a Moderate Terrorist Group.* Retrieved from Fanack - Chronicle of the Middle East & North Africa: https://chronicle.fanack.com/specials/extremism/jabhat-al-nusra-tries-to-look-a-moderate-terrorist-group/

happening as they attempted to overturn their governments and work toward real change in the region. In most cases, as the world has come to know, the ultimate reality of social, democratic and regime change has not been completely realized (and in some cases, has only worsened), but Twitter and Facebook are still the primary medium for exchanging information and reporting on events among activists, civil society leaders and journalists.

This has been nowhere near as obvious as in Syria. Activists and civilians have reported the human rights abuses of Assad's military through quick, short tweets and relevant hashtags, which have allowed journalists, policymakers and analysts to keep track of what is happening on the ground, especially since it is too dangerous for the average journalist and the Internet connection has been cut in many areas.

Naturally, the immensely successful ability of Twitter to pass this information on quickly and widely did not go unnoticed by jihadist groups like Jabhat Al-Nusra. According to analysts Nico Prucha and Ali Fisher, "Jihadists...soon adapted that content and the platform for their own propaganda purposes. By rebranding and reframing the content created by civil society activists, jihadists used these grievances to support a key jihadist theme: the obligation to defend and protect the Sunni population in Syria." [165] This grievance is very similar in nature to those used by other jihadist groups around the world: that a particular Muslim population is being

---

[165] Prucha, N. a. (2013, June 25). *Tweeting for the Caliphate: Twitter as the New Frontier for Jihadist Propaganda.* Retrieved from Combating Terrorist Center at West Point: https://www.ctc.usma.edu/posts/tweeting-for-the-caliphate-twitter-as-the-new-frontier-for-jihadist-propaganda

targeted because of their religious affiliation and therefore, they are in need of protection.

This idea has helped to shaped the Syrian Civil War narrative into a religious war when, for the most part, it did not start that way. While Assad is an Alawi Muslim (a type of Shi'ite) and has received support from Iran, he has ruled his country in a secular way under the control of the Ba'athist party, much like Saddam Hussein in Iraq. The Ba'athists are a secular, socialist party actually started by Michel Aflaq, a Syrian Greek Orthodox Christian. Also much like in Iraq, the victim narrative was turned on its head and the conflict has regressed into religious terminology and framing in order to serve the interests of warring parties. It is not surprising then that a majority of Syrian Christians actually support Assad's government out of fear that Islamism in the region will lead to complete Sunni dominance imposing religious law like in ISIL-controlled territory.

Aflaq

Some of Jabhat Al-Nusra's top figures are propagandists responsible for developing materials for use to spread through social media, particularly through Twitter. During the summer of 2014, the world became very aware of ISIL's activities on Twitter, from the cute and shareable pictures of jihadists holding kittens to the pictures of black-cloaked men riding jeeps holding guns in the air. Analysts were quick to spot trends in the spread of propaganda materials through Twitter, Facebook and YouTube. Many of these propaganda videos attempting to recruit or spread the messages of ISIL were notable due to their sophistication in video editing and the rather unique or "Western" manner in which the group was able to push out the materials online. The messages of ISIL centered on the idea of dissatisfaction among Muslim populations in the West, particularly with youth who felt as though they were not part of the community that they were living in. In addition to this, ISIL has taken the narrative among some Westerners that Islam, Arabs, or those who have originated in the Middle East cannot fit into Western culture since it is heavily influenced by Judeo-Christian values. These extremely complex and harsh sentiments are the cornerstone of ISIL's mission and recruitment efforts toward Western audience. The propaganda showing ISIL's military victories, life in their territory, and messages for their enemies are fuel for their online battlefield aimed at recruiting fighters and intimidating the U.S. led coalition.

Jabhat Al-Nusra's online audience is not so much Western-focused as it is focused on Syria, their surrounding neighbors, and Al-Qaeda supporters. For while ISIL is trying to gain and maintain legitimacy in the world-at-large for their mission to create a caliphate in Iraq and Syria, Jabhat Al-Nusra has zeroed in on the audience it needs to build legitimacy and support for its war against Assad. As of 2015, it was estimated that Internet penetration in Syria was about 28% and that about 5% of the population actually used the Internet.[166] Despite this seemingly low reach to Syrians themselves, Twitter's ability to disseminate information through hashtags has helped disseminate Al-Nusra's information widely. This also helps Al-Nusra to maintain a semblance

---

[166] Internet World Stats. (2015, November). *Internet Usage in the Middle East*. Retrieved from Internet World Stats: http://www.Internetworldstats.com/stats5.htm

of legitimacy among would-be allies and enemies.

There are several reports among data analysts who look at social media engagement rates that indicate the likes and re-tweeting of Twitter materials among Al-Nusra, particularly those using the hashtag #جبهة_النصرة (Jabhat Al-Nusra in Arabic). In many cases, the tweets have embedded links to YouTube showing martyrdom videos of Al-Nusra fighters and scenes from battles on the field against Syrian government forces. Some of the other most popular and most viewed videos focus on the behavior of Al-Nusra members toward the civilians in the town or city that they operate, such as protecting civilians from gunfire and explosions while also targeting soldiers they claim are those supporters of Bashar Assad's government. The framing of the content is incredibly important, again, because of its intended purpose of showing its viewers how Al-Nusra's main intent is to protect Syrian Sunni Muslims against the Assad government. The more that the group can film their actions and frame them in this manner, the more the group is able to work on developing legitimacy among the population.

The manner in which Jabhat Al-Nusra spreads its propaganda is more structured than that of ISIL. There have been several Western government attempts over the last few years to slow or completely delete and remove ISIL-created content on social media platforms. This has led to ISIL supporters and leaders having a disparate network of accounts simultaneously created and banned across Twitter. This has also been aided by the fact that ISIL is always in the news and the primary concern for most initiatives to counter violent extremism.

Jabhat Al-Nusra, on the other hand, has been flying under the radar since 2012. According to the site Vox, "Nusra has 10 official Twitter accounts through which it spreads its propaganda. Nusra's propaganda network on Twitter is split between 1 main central account and 9 other secondary accounts. The 9 secondary accounts post various kinds of propaganda from different regions in Syria." [167] The central account and media department of the group, Al-Manarat Al-Bayda, translated as "The White Minaret" in Arabic, is noted for looking very much like a news organization with branded logos, colors, and designs. [168] In order to continue to produce their content over these social media platforms, Al-Nusra has become skilled at using different hashtags to link their tweets and connect them to their supporters. VOX further proposes that Al-Nusra uses previously created Twitter accounts when their newer ones are banned, which helps them to develop ads and promote their propaganda videos using the Twitter Ads program. For those that are unable to access the Internet, they have developed CDs full of propaganda materials to distribute throughout the country.[169]

Thus, while this important fact is overlooked, the truth is that Jabhat Al-Nusra fights many of its battles online. It has to contend not only with ISIL and social media platforms' rules and regulations, but also with developing its particular jihadist content in a way to serve its purpose of promoting legitimacy among their supporters and

[167] *How Jabhat Al Nusra Uses Twitter to Spread Propaganda*. (2016, May 4). Retrieved from VOX Pol: http://www.voxpol.eu/how-jabhat-al-nusra-uses-twitter-to-spread-propaganda/
[168] Ibid
[169] Benotman, N. a. (n.d.). *Jabhat Al-Nusra: A Strategic Briefing*. Retrieved from Quilliam Foundation: https://web.archive.org/web/20150328080133/http://www.quilliamfoundation.org/wp/wp-content/uploads/publications/free/jabhat-al-nusra-a-strategic-briefing.pdf

would-be followers in and around Syria. Indeed, Al-Nusra's ability to combine their tech-savvy content promotion schemes while learning from ISIL's mistakes has helped them to stay alive and strong on Twitter and YouTube. As of now, Al-Nusra's Twitter activity analyzed indicates there are over 12,000 connections and 7,000 accounts using the Arabic hashtag #جبهة_النصرة.[170] Their content mixes videos of Nusra fighters "good deeds" done for Syrian civilians with their battleground efforts, offering an alternative to ISIL's brutal tactics.

Jabhat Al-Nusra's Battlefields

The complex situation surrounding the development of the Syrian Civil War and its primary opponents provides a unique space for Jabhat Al-Nusra. Many Western governments felt as though they were between a rock and a hard place when it came to supporting protesters throughout the region during the wave of protests during the Arab Spring; they wanted to support the protesters in hopes that it would eventually lead to the toppling of dictators in the region who, in most cases, were the primary roadblock to a series of developmental initiatives such as the institutionalization of democracy, but at the same time, those very same dictators had become strong allies bent on preventing the well-organized Islamist groups from taking hold of government institutions (these groups, of course, were primarily anti-Western oriented in their militant actions).

The case of Syria was essentially the same, but Bashar Assad's unique relationship with Iran and Russia made

[170] Barna, C. (2014). The Road to Jihad in Syria: Using SOCMINT to Counter the Radicalization of Muslim Youth in Romania. In M. Lombardi, E. Ragab, V. Chin, Y. Dandurand, V. de Divitiis, & A. Burato, *Countering Radicalisation and Youth Extremism Among Youth to Prevent Terrorism.* Milan: IOS Press

things particularly thorny for the United States and its allies. Russia's continual blocking of United Nations resolutions to condemn and act against the Syrian regime were justified by claiming Assad's regime was defending itself against terrorists, the very same claim Bashar himself gave in many of his public addresses during the war. How could the West claim to support rebels in Syria when the rebels' tactics included what they themselves counted as terrorism? And with Russian anger and disapproval lurking not far from the conflict, how could the West intervene without awaking the Russian Bear?

This indecisiveness in the conflict worked in the jihadists' favor. While the world now is intimately familiar with ISIL's rise to notoriety in Iraq and Syria due to the vacuum that opened up in both countries, Jabhat Al-Nusra's activity has not been much of a central focus during this time. ISIL's ability to attract media attention for their beheadings, mass killings, and brutal repression of minorities has worked in Al-Nusra's favor. Since Al-Nusra's inception in early 2012, they have cooperated with the many militias on the ground in Syria against the Assad regime. Their cooperation has, as aforementioned, led to an increase in recruitment as well as support among civilians.

According to Lina Khatib of *Syria Deeply*, Al-Nusra has also won favor because it is seen as a group that has taken on corruption in the aftermath of the war. [171] A few of the militant groups on the ground have suffered from infighting and the development of warlords around the

---

[171] Montgomery, K. (2015, April 13). *Jabhat Al Nusra: A Game Change in Syria*. Retrieved from World Policy Blog: http://www.worldpolicy.org/blog/2015/04/13/jabhat-al-nusra-game-changer-syri

country. Al-Nusra, on the other hand, has worked to integrate these groups ostensibly for the greater good of Syria. The groups that Al-Nusra has not attempted to integrate, however, it has challenged and battled, such as the Syrian Revolutionaries Front and the Hazm Movement. According to Khatib, Al-Nusra has claimed that it fought these groups due to corruption and affiliation with the United States, but it is most likely due to these groups posing a challenge to Al-Nusra's legitimacy. "Through alliances with certain groups, acquisitions and defeat of others, Jabhat Al Nusra aims to strengthen its footprint and widen its influence in the north, and present itself as the primary force fighting the Assad regime on the ground." [172] When the U.S. carries out airstrikes against Al-Nusra, this only further emboldens their followers.

While it is unlikely that Jabhat Al-Nusra will ever be able to militarily overcome the Syrian government's forces, they are aiming to be a viable option for Sunnis when the war finally comes to an end, much like Hezbollah has done for Shiites following the Lebanese Civil War in the early 1990s. If the recent experiences of Tunisia and Egypt following the Arab Spring revolutions are any indication of the popularity of Islamist groups as an alternative to brutal dictatorships, then Jabhat Al-Nusra may very well end up being a viable option for the beleaguered Syrian population. The Freedom and Justice Party in Egypt and Ennahda in Tunisia were very much involved in politics and even led their countries' governments in the aftermath of the Arab Spring protests.

---

[172] Ibid

Their ability to come to prominence quickly following the fall of Hosni Mubarak in Egypt and Zine Al-Abedine Bin Ali in Tunisia was most likely because these groups had developed a solid support base and were the most organized political groups, thereby filling a void leading up to the first ever democratic elections in these countries. Though these groups eventually ended up facing conflict and societal pushback in various ways, their effects are still very much felt in Egypt and Tunisia. The Muslim Brotherhood from whence both political groups emerged did a very good job of reaching out and providing services on the ground when the government often could not or would not, thereby shaping the perceptions and feelings of local populations toward the group. In the same vein, Jabhat Al-Nusra is providing these kinds of services while showing their might where it is most needed--on the battlefield--while attempting to mould the Syrian Sunni imagination to what "could be" for the future of their country when the war finally comes to its inevitable conclusion.

Since Jabhat Al-Nusra's main *modus operandi* centers around the distinction they wish to make with ISIL and other militant groups in the region, when Al-Nusra comes to town, they are not looking to violently force conversion among the civilians or slaughter them in the areas they take over, at least not initially. On the contrary, they are hoping to "win hearts and minds" by offering services, protection and a new vision for Syria's future. Al-Nusra is attempting to make life for civilians in their occupied territories as close to it was before the civil war began as possible while slowly, but surely, injecting their particular brand of Salafi Islamism into the local society. This is without a doubt a reflection of their roots in Al-Qaeda's ideology and an apparent learning of its past mistakes when trying to take over and win the support of groups in their occupied territories.

When Jabhat Al-Nusra first takes over a location, it does not immediately oust any current leaders or groups in charge of the area. Instead, it generally tries to work together to control and administer the town or city over a period of time--unless it has faced fierce opposition, such as in Druze majority areas. When Al-Nusra has garnered enough support among the population, only then will it take on any opposition remaining. "This often means beginning with *da'wa*, or proselytization, which al-Nusra frequently deploys through its publications, public events, and everyday interactions with non-members. It often launches a string of extensive *da'wa* campaigns, led by local and foreign clerics and fighters. These campaigns double as recruitment events and as platforms to promote their political project."[173]

By proselytizing, they are trying to convince the local population that if and when Bashar Assad's government falls, the only alternative must be an Islamic-run state, or caliphate. The neighborhoods campaigns aimed at recruiting also offer this vision of what Al-Nusra believes Syria could be in the region--essentially, Al-Qaeda's state. The more Al-Nusra conflates Assad's regime with chaos while simultaneously offering an alternative of an Islamic state led by jihad, the more entrenched they become in the

---

[173] Abbas, Y. (2016, May 10). *How Al-Qaeda is Winning in Syria.* Retrieved from War on the Rocks: http://warontherocks.com/2016/05/how-al-qaeda-is-winning-in-syria

local community.

This process of indoctrination among the local population happens at many levels in the society. When it comes to the children, Al-Nusra has set up academies aimed at recruiting the next generation of jihadists to fight in its army. Documentarian Medyan Dairieh was able to gain exclusive access to Al-Nusra's top leadership back in 2015 and filmed on location in parts of Syria. In this documentary produced by VICE News, Dairieh filmed and interviewed young boys taking part in Al-Nusra's jihadist academies. These young boys came from around Syria and there was even one young student who came all the way from Uzbekistan. The academy focused on teaching Arabic, religious education, and physical fitness in order to train the next generation of fighters.[174] Throughout the documentary, viewers can see instances of the boys chanting and singing songs reveling in the jihad and the wars to come. This is in juxtaposition to what is seen with the fighters on the field, who also start their day with such songs and oaths to follow Osama Bin Laden's footsteps to fight the United States and the Jews. Interestingly, while these fighters discuss the U.S. and its allies as their main source of contention, it is repeated that the main enemy at this time is actually Bashar Assad and, at times, the Lebanese Army in the south. This is indicative of Al-Qaeda's older ideology focused on destruction of the West in general and the U.S. more specifically. As much as Al-Nusra desires to infiltrate into Syrian society by directing their attacks toward the Syrian

[174] Daireh, M. (2015, November 11). *Inside the Battle: Al Nusra-Al Qaeda in Syria.* Retrieved from VICE News: https://news.vice.com/video/inside-the-battle-al-nusra-al-qaeda-in-syria

regime, their core ideology has not changed and will remain pivoting around the desire to develop a larger, global Islamic caliphate wherein they view the United States as their primary obstacle in doing so. Their leader Abu Muhammad Al-Julani even went so far as to claim he had no animosity toward the West unless they interfere in his operations against the Syrian regime.[175]

While Al-Nusra presents a particular image to the world of a "kinder, gentler terrorist group," this has not been the experience of everyone living under their rule. In Idlib province in northwestern Syria, some civilians have reported very harsh living conditions. After the group took control, many people who Al-Nusra accused of being Bashar Assad supporters or government employees were imprisoned or executed, and the group immediately began changing practices in the local community. One woman reported that they removed science and history classes from schools and changed the focus to Islamic education. She discussed how "religious police" walked the streets to make sure women and men were dressed appropriately.[176]

Obviously, people can definitely draw parallels with the activities of ISIL in Iraq and Syria. In order for these extremist groups to develop the type of society they want--which they claim is modeled after the time of the Prophet Muhammad--they feel that their only option is to make a particular action, dress or behavior mandatory among the local population. This is, of course, a type of rule and control. Al-Nusra, ISIL and other such groups control

---

[175] BBC News. (2015, May 28). *Al-Qaeda 'orders Syria's Al-Nusra Front not to attack West'*. Retrieved from BBC News: http://www.bbc.com/news/world-middle-east-32913509

[176] Hall, R. a. (2016, May 2). *The other Islamic state: Al-Qaeda is still fighting for an emirate of its own*. Retrieved from PRI: http://www.pri.org/stories/2016-04-29/other-islamic-state-al-qaeda-still-fighting-emirate-its-ow

their population under threat of punishment justified by their extreme and literal interpretation of religious texts and traditions.

In general, life under Jabhat Al-Nusra's rule is not necessarily more "preferred" than life under ISIL or under a dictatorship, but it is an interesting juxtaposition and one that must be made when analyzing these groups. In the spectrum of autocratic rule in the region, Al-Nusra's activities may be currently lies somewhere in the middle but most certainly not considered "liberal." While Al-Nusra's Al-Qaeda roots are undeniable, their repeated assurances to Syrians and the world at large that they are not Al-Qaeda and ISIL and therefore not targeting the West frames their behaviors and approach in a different light. Make no mistake, this Al-Nusra is a highly organized and well-armed and supplied militant organization whose roots and tactics stem from their Al-Qaeda past, but their ability to market themselves as "different" may very well benefit their operations in the long run in Syria, which is something that the West and other parties must take into consideration.

International Responses

While most of the world media attention has been focused primarily on ISIL's activities over the past few years, Jabhat Al-Nusra continues to expand its territory and influence within Syria, and the group presents a very peculiar problem for the international community. The very complex relationship between the U.S. and Russia has played itself out once more in this conflict, with the U.S. and Russia hesitantly making moves in Syria without an actual all-out assault against the rebel groups, even as it seems increasingly necessary in the long run for the U.S. and Russia to cooperate in their battles against Al-Nusra and ISIL as these groups dig their heels in even further among the local populations in which they operate.

The Syrian government views Al-Nusra, in many ways, the same way it views other rebel forces within the country. For Assad, Al-Nusra is an excuse to use toward the international community to exercise more extreme violence against the population wherever his government feels resistance. This plays very well into Al-Nusra's favor, since their entire premise for existing frames them as "protectors" of the country against Assad's Alawi Shi'a regime. At Syria's request, the Russian military has become increasing involved in the Syrian Civil War as well, launching air campaigns against Jabhat Al-Nusra, ISIL, and other rebel groups. One of their goals is to separate Al-Nusra from the other militant groups in the area that it is attempting to build an alliance with, such as Ahrar Al-Sham.[177] Separating Al-Nusra delays their desired collaboration with other groups, ultimately weakening their efforts in the long run. Russia, however, is very careful in its interactions in Syria, as much as it is carrying out Assad's policies in the country.

Iran's place in the Syrian conflict has ironically been one of Russian and Syrian validation, reiterating to the world that Al-Nusra, ISIL, and all of the resistance groups in the conflict are violent and bent on spreading an extremist ideology. Iran has worked with the Syrian government to provide military and intelligence support in the field

---

[177] Al Monitor. (2016, June 5). *Is Russia readying for the kill in Syria?* Retrieved from Al-Monitor: http://www.al-monitor.com/pulse/originals/2016/06/russia-syria-nusra-aleppo-qaeda-ypg-us-jihadi.htm

alongside the Lebanese Shi'a militant group Hezbollah and Iraqi Shi'a militias.[178] Since ISIL began its trek through Syria and Iraq, it has called for an increase in lone wolf attacks around the world. The United States, Canada, and many European and Asian countries have now found themselves in a very similar situation to that of the Middle East and Africa, essentially hubs of Salafi extremist activities in the world. Iran's Revolutionary Guard Corps and Hezbollah have worked very closely with the Syrian forces on the ground in their fight against Al-Nusra and the other militant groups. Quoting an Iranian military official, *Al Monitor* notes, "In fact, the real danger for the US, and the West in general, isn't Daesh but [Jabhat al-] Nusra...It's really strange how history repeats itself." [179]

For the United States, Al-Nusra has become another nuisance to deal with in the region. The U.S. and Russian approaches to terrorism in Syria and Iraq has been likened to a game of whack-a-mole, shifting focuses between ISIL and other terrorist groups around the area. As ISIL's support and hold over their territory in Iraq and Syria has decreased, Al-Nusra's has arisen in Idlib and Aleppo. When Assad crossed the U.S. designated red-line by using chemical weapons against civilians in the summer of 2013, the U.S. put itself in a precarious position. During the beginning of the Arab Spring, the Obama Administration had tried to position itself as a supporter of protesters and rebel movements against the dictatorships around the region. However, when they failed to act in

[178] Fulton, W. J. (2013, May). *Iranian Strategy in Syria*. Retrieved from Institute for the Study of War: http://www.understandingwar.org/report/iranian-strategy-syria

[179] Hashem, A. (2016, April 15). *Iranian official says Nusra, not IS, main threat to West*. Retrieved from Al-Monitor: http://www.al-monitor.com/pulse/originals/2016/04/iran-syria-palmyra-nusrah-islamic-state.htm

Syria after the extreme force of the Assad regime, the militias in the country took note, particularly Jabhat Al-Nusra. This collective international inaction was essentially the fuel Al-Nusra needed to build legitimacy with its base of supporters. They could now convincingly persuade the people that nobody else would come to their rescue. Al-Nusra aksi offered itself as an alternative to the international tension between the U.S. and Russia which held up immediate efforts to stop the violence.

During the build-up of ISIL-controlled territory in Iraq and Syria, the U.S. maintained efforts to destroy the group. There was even discussion among top leaders in the government to consider arming other groups—including Jabhat Al-Nusra—to fight against ISIL.[180] It was suggested and floated throughout the media that former CIA Director David Petraeus suggested supporting Al-Nusra against efforts ISIL because of his own experience funding militias in Iraq in 2007 when he was commander of the U.S. forces. Dealing with Al-Nusra, ISIL and other militant groups in the Syrian conflict has put the U.S. in a very difficult situation and one that also mirrors past behavior, particularly when it comes to funding militant groups.

---

[180] Harris, S. a. (2015, August 31). *Petraeus: Use Al Qaeda Fighters to Beat ISIS.* Retrieved from The Daily Beast: http://www.thedailybeast.com/articles/2015/08/31/petraeus-use-al-qaeda-fighters-to-beat-isis.htm

Petraeus

The Cold War-like approach of the U.S. and Russia has left analysts and policymakers befuddled. Analysts note that following the end of the Cold War in the late 1980s, there has been an overall decrease in international conflicts and global conflicts but a rise in civil wars around the world, as various religious, ethnic, and nationalist groups attempt to throw off the yoke of the residual effects of colonialism. In Syria, much like in other countries around the developing world, there is a long-term secular military dictator who has shown preference to some groups (Shi'a, Christians) over others (Sunnis), thus causing an upset in the balance in the region. Many analysts believe that the protests and upheaval like the Middle East experience during the Arab Spring was a long-time coming, but it was difficult to really anticipate the full extent of the chaos that ensued. The moment seemed ripe in international relations: a deadly mix of rising tension among the world's superpowers (United States, Russia), global economic problems, a steadily rising youth population, and an increase in non-state actor violent movements around the world. The Cold War may be over, but the world is still very much in the throes of a distinct phase in a new world defined asymmetric warfare between national militaries and small militant groups.

Financing and Supporting the Jihad

Militant groups cannot survive without sources of funding. Throughout Jabhat Al-Nusra's existence, Al-Qaeda has been fairly explicit in its support for the operations in Syria. Osama Bin Laden, himself a Saudi, made several connections during his time and through his own recruitment efforts. "The main group of donors is based in the Gulf area, principally Saudi Arabia, but donors also exist in other parts of the world. Some of these donors have been fully aware of the final destination of their money; others were not."[181]

---

[181] del Cid Gómez, J. M. (2010). *A Financial Profile of the Terrorism of Al-Qaeda and its Affiliates.* Retrieved from Perspective on Terrorism: http://www.terrorismanalysts.com/pt/index.php/pot/article/view/113/htm

تا حدود ۲۵ ملیون دالر جائزه   تر ۲۵ ملیون دالرو جائزه

در مقابل ارائه معلومات   دهغه معلومات په مقابل کی

موثق در باره جای بود و باش   د دغه سړیو د ژوندانه د ځای

و یا دستگیری این دو نفر   او یا نیولو په باره

An American leaflet showing Bin Laden and Zawahiri

Since the wars of colonial revolution of the 1940s and onwards in the Middle East and others parts of the Muslim world, the countries of the Arabian Gulf—Saudi Arabia, Qatar, Kuwait, and the United Arab Emirates—emerged as potential sources of funding for terrorist groups in the region. This information is not new and definitely not surprising to anyone who paid close attention to the region for some time. The leaders of the Gulf countries essentially came to power due to their ability to mix Wahabbi Islam with modern autocracy. What has emerged are several kingdoms (or "emirates") controlled by ruling families which are very much influenced by conservative Islam whose rules are mandated and enforced throughout their countries. There have been numerous reports over the years of these countries actively funding and supporting terrorist groups around the world.

For Jabhat Al-Nusra, resources in many cases have taken

the form of previously used weapons that were already purchased by Al-Qaeda or those that they have taken during their battles within Syria. In 2015, some sources reported that Qatar was encouraging Al-Nusra to break away from Al-Qaeda and operate independently.[182] These sources report discussions between Abu Muhammad Al-Julani and officials from Qatar and other Gulf states. These reports are ironic, given the fact that Qatar, Saudi Arabia, Bahrain and the U.A.E. are part of the coalition to defeat ISIL, though they actually only operate exclusively inside of Syria.

A Sunni-backed opposition to Bashar Assad would be ideal for the Gulf; political scientists view the entire region as a balancing act, each side teetering toward Shi'ism or Sunnism. Assad's strongest backer is Iran, a Shi'a majority country that has no qualms about stating its opinion on the treatment of Shi'ites and Sunnis in the Gulf and around the world. The Obama Administration has tried over the last few years to ease tensions with Iran through a few highly publicized meetings and the negotiations over Iran's nuclear program, but while relations between the two countries have not changed much, the reaction from the Gulf countries has not been positive. These countries may feel that an easing in tension between the U.S. and Iran may have real impact on the region, eventually tipping the balance once again in Iran's favor. With this in mind, the Middle East's richest leaders would certainly be concerned about their part in preventing a Shi'a takeover. These very same fears are the

[182] Karouny, M. (2015, March 4). *Insight - Syria's Nusra Front may leave Qaeda to form new entity.* Retrieved from Reuters: http://uk.reuters.com/article/uk-mideast-crisis-nusra-insight-idUKKBN0M00G620150304

same reason Qatar, Kuwait, Saudi Arabia and others have supported various militant groups over time in the region. When the Syrian Civil War began, the Gulf took notice and was perhaps even more interested in the eventual outcome of the conflict than perhaps even the U.S. and Russia.

The leaders of Turkey have also made statements nearly indicating support of Al-Nusra's efforts. Since the outset of the war, Turkey has had a vested interest in the fate of its neighbor to the south. During the early days of the conflict when analysts and politicians believed it would end just as quickly as the rebellions around the region, Turkey had supported the Muslim Brotherhood in Syria in hopes that they would take control in a post-Assad country. When that did not work out, there were reports that Turkey—like Qatar—reached out to Al-Nusra about a partnership. Ideally, this partnership would be a good balance to the Kurds in Syria that are allied with the Kurdish Workers Party (PKK), Turkey's long-time domestic militant group.[183] While Turkey has not admitted to giving financial support to Al-Nusra, there are reports that they permit safe passage of supplies to Al-Nusra through its borders from the Gulf.[184] The group appears to be one of convenience for Turkey.

As Dr. David Roberts put it in a BBC article on the matter, "Qatar has surmised, it seems, that supporting or transforming the Nusra Front, is one of the 'least worst' options."[185] As mentioned above, the U.S. even thought

[183] Stein, A. (2015, February 9). *Turkey's Evolving Syria Strategy.* Retrieved from Foreign Affairs: https://www.foreignaffairs.com/articles/turkey/2015-02-09/turkeys-evolving-syria-strategy

[184] Ibid

[185] Roberts, D. D. (2015, March 6). *Is Qatar bringing the Nusra Front in from the cold?* Retrieved from BBC News: http://www.bbc.com/news/world-middle-east-31764114

that way at one point as well. Supporting Al-Nusra is certainly not a perfect option by any means, but since they have already begun to build strong supporting among the population and have been relatively well-resourced, Qatar, Turkey, and other would-be supporters assume that Al-Nusra will be the only organized Sunni group still standing when the dust settles after the war. At this stage, there is no way of knowing if that will be the case, especially with the United States and Russia considering changing their approach to the civil war overall. What does appear to remain true is that Jabhat Al-Nusra has positioned itself as very much "the lesser of two evils" in juxtaposition to ISIL. The leaders of the Sunni countries in the region are looking for a champion to keep their own interests afloat during the chaos, but it is uncertain whether or not Al-Nusra is a group to be tamed or one to be supported from afar, much like Hezbollah's relationship with Iran.

Rebranding Jabhat Al-Nusra

In July 2016, Abu Muhammad Al-Julani announced that Jabhat Al-Nusra would formally split from Al-Qaeda and change its name to Jabhat Fatah Al-Sham, or "The Front for the Conquest of the Levant."[186] Al-Julani indicated that the name change was meant to further encourage unification of Syrian militant and revolutionary groups under one umbrella. By focusing on collaboration among Syrian fighters, Al-Nusra aims to position itself once again as a group whose sole focus is to protect the Syrian Sunni population and topple Bashar Assad's regime.

---

[186] Al Jazeera. (2016, July 29). *Al-Nusra leader Jolanie announces split from Al-Qaeda*. Retrieved from Al Jazeera: http://www.aljazeera.com/news/2016/07/al-nusra-leader-jolani-announces-split-al-qaeda-160728163725624.htm

It's apparent that by continuing to be connected to Al-Qaeda--and ISIL often referenced to in its past--Al-Nusra believed its ability to appeal more broadly to Syrians was limited. A few days prior to this statement, Al-Qaeda confirmed that the group split officially.[187] In the days following Al-Julani's announcements, various Al-Qaeda affiliated groups and leaders lauded the split from Al-Qaeda, which begs the question of why the split would be a good thing for Al-Qaeda in the first place.

U.S. officials and some experts believe that this name change and rebranding is an effort to avoid affiliation with other Western-country designated terrorist groups in hopes that they might receive support from the U.S. and others in their efforts against the Syrian regime.[188] After all, for all intents and purposes, there is no reason to believe that their tactics and approach to the civil war will be any different. Al-Nusra apparently views its current situation as a prime opportunity to consolidate power in the areas that it controls. The reaction from other militant groups in Syria seems generally positive to the break with Al-Qaeda, though there has been little indication that a larger merger of any kind is currently taking place.[189] There is likely some misapprehension because the split can be viewed with skepticism among would-be allies and long-time enemies, particularly since Al-Qaeda has financially and logistically supported Al-Nusra from its inception.

As experts look at the various reactions to the split in the

[187] Ibid

[188] Sanchez, R. a. (2016, August 1). *Syria's al-Nusra rebrands and cuts ties with al Qaeda*. Retrieved from CNN: http://www.cnn.com/2016/07/28/middleeast/al-nusra-al-qaeda-split

[189] *Opinions Divided on Nusra's Split from Al-Qaeda*. Retrieved from News Deeply: https://www.newsdeeply.com/syria/articles/2016/08/09/opinions-divided-on-nusras-split-from-al-qaida

days following the announcements, it is not hard to understand why most do not believe the Al-Qaeda split is anything more than a publicity stunt. Many of the leading Syrian militant groups have stated their hesitation to merge with Al-Nusra due to their affiliation with Al-Qaeda. The fear was that this would lead to justification among Russian and U.S. airstrikes.[190] By publicly separating from Al-Qaeda, Al-Nusra is hoping to finally realize its ultimate goal of uniting factions under its control and eventually leading to a larger, more concerted effort to finally bring down Bashar Assad's regime. The merging of terrorist groups has definitely happened before, but inevitably the issue of leadership comes to the forefront as varying personalities begin vying for control. Abu Muhammad Al-Julani and his leadership team are no doubt considering this future issue for whenever groups merge into their own. It will either be a fruitful exercise in power sharing among the jihadists or will turn out much like Al-Nusra's own origins, when ISIL split from Al-Qaeda due to a personality and ideology clash between Abu Bakr Al-Baghdadi and Al-Qaeda leadership.

Through it all, Jabhat Al-Nusra's rise to control in Syria has been a peculiar mix of learning from Al-Qaeda's past mistakes and innovative approaches to recruitment reflecting the shift of jihadist organizations to using social media tools. While it started out as a cell of Al-Qaeda in Iraq (AQI) sent by Abu Bakr Al-Baghdadi to Syria to carry out operations in the early days of the Syrian Civil War, it has since grown into a respected, well-established

---

[190] Zimmerman, K. a. (2016, July 28). *Avoiding al Qaeda's Syria trap: Jabhat al Nusra's rebranding.* Retrieved from AEI: https://www.aei.org/publication/avoiding-al-qaedas-syria-trap-jabhat-al-nusras-rebranding

and well-resourced jihadist movement on the battleground, both offline and online. Al-Nusra's makeup of predominantly Syrian fighters led by more seasoned jihadists from former Al-Qaeda operations in central Asia and around the Middle East has helped it to establish its firm and credible hold in some key locations around Syria, such as Idlib and Deir Al-Zour. Having a majority of the fighters as native Syrians has helped to assuage the fears of locals that the force is actually foreign with an agenda unconcerned with Syrian long-term stability. Al-Nusra's formal breakaway from ISIL in 2013 and from Al-Qaeda and 2016 is part of a larger attempt to slowly but surely move toward positioning itself as an entirely native operation.

Life under Al-Nusra's control is not entirely similar to that of ISIL in Iraq, as their tactics remain seemingly less harsh in comparison. In most cases, Al-Nusra works with the community leadership in the areas that it controls and implements various services, such as food delivery, medical care, and education all the while providing "protection" against the Syrian government's army. As part of their vision of protection against the Assad regime, they have instituted religious academies for recruiting and training young children to develop into jihadist fighters. They have also begun to increase the presence of religious police throughout their territory to command adherence to their interpretation of strict Sunni religious law. All of these behaviors are similar in practice to Sunni jihadi movements around the world, especially since their ultimate aim is to establish an Islamic caliphate that controls every movement and practice of the population.

The name change and recent dissociation from Al-Qaeda appear to indicate a shift in tactics. Al-Nusra leaders seem to believe that they are moving toward a ripe moment in which merging with other militant groups will bring the group to the next level of legitimacy and support among their Sunni base, even if the other militant groups remain hesitant as they have no real proof or reason to believe that Al-Nusra is not still backed by Al-Qaeda.

Meanwhile, the international community's response to the Syrian Civil War has definitely left much to be desired. The United States and Russia have once again found themselves embroiled in another conflict through proxies on the battlefield. They are each being forced to confront each other on a foreign battlefield and deal with the global backlash at home and abroad for their actions. Moreover, since the Arab Spring and rise of ISIL, there has been an increase in lone wolf attacks around the world. These attacks cause distraction in the media and among Western populations who feel even less inclined to engage with the Muslim world and welcome the ensuing waves of refugees fleeing the conflict for Europe and North America. With these complexities comes a very difficult situation for the United States. As much as it wants to get involved in the Syrian conflict and put its policy stances into action and even ponder backing Al-Nusra in efforts against ISIL and the Syrian government, Russian support for the Assad regime and Iranian and Hezbollah involvement have created a stalemate. When President Obama gave his famous "red line" speech in the summer of 2013 regarding Assad's use of chemical weapons against Syria and then failed to act when the attacks actually took place, Jabhat Al-Nusra capitalized on the situation. Repeated inaction and seemingly aimless foreign policy stances on the Syrian Civil War have played in to Al-Nusra's favor.

As much as Al-Nusra may try to show the world it is different from its rivals (particularly ISIL and now Al-Qaeda) in the region, their ideology and goals suggest otherwise. Regardless, Jabhat Al-Nusra is definitely a serious force to be reckoned with and one that the world should pay more attention to, especially as ISIL continues to be put on the defensive in Syria and Iraq. Al-Nusra is very much like Hezbollah, Hamas, and the Muslim Brotherhood in the sense that their ability to entrench themselves locally will likely assist them in the long-run. With this in mind, they may be able to turn themselves into a Muslim Brotherhood-like political, albeit armed, Islamist force in the eventual negotiations that will take place in Syria. Al-Nusra may then be able to gather supporters under its banner in the new Syrian society. Thus, if and when a post-Bashar Assad Syria finally comes to pass, Al-Nusra will definitely be a concern for the world during reconstruction efforts in the region.

Boko Haram and the Historic Social Divide in Nigeria

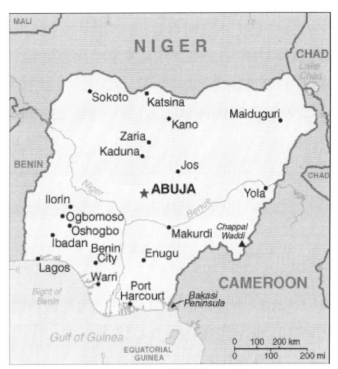

A map of Nigeria

The modern state of Nigeria, as it is recognizable today, came into being in 1914, with the creation of the British *Colony and Protectorate of Nigeria*. This was the defining moment when the vaunted British theory of *Indirect Rule* found practical expression, and the point at which the idealism of a handful of enlightened British colonial civil servants was put to the test.

The early evolution of Nigeria as a British overseas territory had followed a somewhat formularized pattern that by the end of the 19th century had been established in the wider empire, but perhaps most particularly in Africa.

In the British African context there existed fundamentally two systems of colonial rule. The first of these tended to concern those territories that offered opportunity for permanent and large scale European habitation and the second being those that did not. In this regard, South Africa was obviously recognized as the flagship British territory in Africa. It was potentially the wealthiest, it was the most strategically located in regards to British maritime interests, but, perhaps most importantly, it was climatically suitable for extensive white settlement, which, to a lesser extent was true for other British African possessions, such as Southern and Northern Rhodesia (Zimbabwe/Zambia), Nyasaland (Malawi) and Kenya.

However, there were also those territories that did not naturally lend themselves to the European temper, all of which tended to be located within the deep tropics of the continent where a combination of climate and disease rendered expatriate settlement at the very least uncomfortable and in some cases deadly. These territories were on the whole penetrated initially by Christian missionaries, acting under the impetus of faith, and arriving on the coast in the aftermath of early European maritime trading interests. The missionaries were in due course followed by the early geographic explorers, before finally both yielded to private capital interests in the form of Royal Chartered Companies, which would usually in turn be the precursor to formal colonial annexation. This last phase of African colonial expansion in Africa took place through the latter phases of the 19th century.

So in terms of the British purview at least, West Africa fell very much into the commercial and strategic fields of endeavour, with perhaps the greatest motivation for British expansion in the region being in response to concurrent French expansion.[191] And it was this, in fact, that was the basis upon which a royal charter was granted to the *Royal Niger Company*, founded by the great Victorian capitalist, Sir George Taubman Goldie; ostensibly to provide an organized bulwark against French commercial interests that were beginning to impinge on what had hitherto been a rather haphazard and disorganized British commercial dominance of the Niger delta region.

It is perhaps also worth pointing out here that the modern history of the west African region as a whole, in particular in relation to the activities of all its various European interlopers, tended to be informed in large part by the Atlantic Slave Trade, which, of course, coincided with the development and industrialization of the plantation economies of the Americas. During this period European involvement in West Africa consisted of little more than highly organized plunder, which, although lucrative, was also manifestly unsustainable. Towards the middle of the 1800s, therefore, the complexion of business in the region necessarily began to alter, in particular in the aftermath of British abolition, from which point a tendency towards more infrastructure dependent and sustainable systems of commerce required a far greater degree of organization, management and security. This was provided by the *Royal Niger Company* in exchange for extremely liberal trading rights and a more or less free hand in pacifying and establishing a basic system of European administration in the region.

As a consequence, when the Berlin Conference of

---

[191] Note: French colonial expansion in the region proceeded under not dissimilar impetus to the British and German, but in the aftermath of the loss of the first French empire, and France's defeat in the Franco/Prussian War of 1871, France tended to be more acutely conscious of prestige in her quest for imperial expansion globally, but in particular in Africa.

1884/85 was convened in order to map out European spheres of influence in Africa, and thereafter to set in motion the greatest land grab in human history, *The Scramble for Africa*, Britain was in a position, thanks largely to the efforts of Sir George Taubman Goldie, to claim the Niger delta region and its hinterland as a British sphere of influence. This preceded annexation of the territory, along with quite a large swath of what was at that time still referred to on international shipping charts as the *Slave Coast*.

Thus, with an imprimatur in hand to pacify and govern, legalized by its royal charter, the *Royal Niger Company* established a firm British presence in the region, and the era of modern Nigeria was born. At that point the coast and the northern reaches of the territory were declared separate British protectorates under Company administration, with the British imperial government itself only assuming control of the combined Niger territories in 1900. Then, in 1914, the two protectorates merged to form the *Colony and Protectorate of Nigeria*.

The logic of retaining two separate British protectorates under separate colonial administrations had been in respect of the clear social delineation between the north and the south of what would in due course become the territory of Nigeria. Broadly speaking, the territory could be divided evenly between the Christian/animist south and the Islamic north, which early colonial bureaucrats recognized as not only a cultural, but also an administrative fault line. It is also fair to say that key members of the British administration at the time, led by arguably one of the most enlightened colonial civil servants of his age, Sir Frederick Lugard, tended to have something of an exaggerated regard for native aristocracies, and the ancient, pious and scholarly aristocracies of the Islamic north of Nigeria conformed very much to this pattern.

Although there are hundreds of languages spoken in modern Nigeria, there are seven of these that dominate, and they are *Hausa, Igbo, Yoruba, Ibibio, Edo, Fulfulde,* and *Kanuri*. Among these the three principal regional languages are *Hausa, Yoruba* and *Igbo*, spoken respectively by ethnic groupings of the same name. In very general terms, the Hausa/Fulani group dominate the regions north of the Benue/Niger river confluence, and the Yoruba/Igbo group predominate in the south. The Yoruba occupy the territories west of the Niger River and the Igbo those to the east, bordering Cameroon. The Yoruba and Igbo share the single commonality of not being Muslim, which created the essential and largely irreconcilable fault line that the British found existing between the north and south of future Nigeria.

Picture of the border with Cameroon

When encountered by early colonial administrators, however, the general perception tended to be that the sultanates and emirates of the north represented the African native at his finest. It would here be instructive perhaps to quote from a London times editorial of 1904, written by Edwardian journalist and social commentator Flora Shaw, who also happened to be the wife of Lord Lugard: "The Fulani were a striking people, dark in complexion, but of the distinguished features, small hands, and fine, rather aristocratic, carriage of the Arabs on the Mediterranean coast. They were of the Mahomedan (sic) religion, and were held by those who knew them to be naturally endowed with the characteristics which fitted them for rule. Their theory of justice was good, though their practice was bad; their scheme of taxation was most elaborate and was carried even into a system of death duties which left little for an English Chancellor of the Exchequer to improve."[192]

It was this rather sycophantic regard that set the tone for the British policy of *Indirect Rule* as it applied to territories like Nigeria. In its simplest from, Indirect Rule, which was a concept conceived and implement by Lord Frederick Lugard himself, implied the devolution of all the day-to-day administrative responsibilities of government to the pre-existing traditional authority, with imperial superintendentship visible only at the center, and existing at all times within an advisory capacity. A natural corollary of this policy would be to ensure the modernization of tradition systems of government, law, tax collection and justice with the understanding that at some point they would emerge with not only their traditional identities intact, but also compatible with modern systems of government.

And in this regard, the Islamic north of Nigeria, with its long established and relatively sophisticated traditions of centralized authority, offered a perfect template. Not so the comparatively chaotic and primitive south, darker in complexion, more decentralized and disordered in their social organization, and politically fractured and individualistic. This is what Lord Lugard had to say about the Igbo, the largest ethnic group in eastern Nigeria, and arguably the most decentralized of all the tribes of the territory. "The great Ibo [Igbo] race to the East of the Niger, numbering some 3 millions, and their cognate tribes had not developed beyond the stage of primitive savagery."[193]

These were uncharitable words indeed, but forgivable

[192] Times (London). *Lady Lugard on Nigeria.* March 2, 1904, p. 12
[193] Quoted: Arinze, Josh. *Moral Anguish: Richard Nixon and the Challenge of Biafra.* Kindle Edition.

perhaps at a time immediately after the devastation of the slave trade, and before the general proliferation of Christian missionary influence and English education in the region. However, at the moment that these influences did begin to be felt in the Protectorate as a whole, it was the southern groupings, and particularly the Igbo, who embraced and absorbed the enormous advantages and potentialities that were offered by the modern world.

Conversely, the more conservative elements in the north, bound by their disdain of modern education, their resistance to Christianity and their adherence to increasingly archaic social and political conventions, began ever more to slip into an anachronistic, and indeed atavistic state of mind, maintaining their aristocratic expectations, protected as they were by the British, while at the same time yielding an ever increasing responsibility for administration and business to the educated and ambitious elements from the south, primarily the Igbo. Soon the Igbo in particular began to form large and thriving expatriate pockets in the north that daily challenged the relevance of these ancient aristocracies, breeding considerable resentment against the black south, which was, of course, an impotent resentment so long as the British remained in ultimate control.

With the grant of independence from Britain in October 1960, however, and not withstanding extraordinarily diligent efforts on the part of the British to groom Nigeria for independence, the degree and depth of ethnic tension within the colony had been grotesquely underestimated, and within five years of Britain relinquishing the territory, a boiling pot of internal contradiction erupted in a series of military coups, ethnic pogroms and ultimately civil war.

The dynamics of the Nigerian Civil War, or the Biafran War, are perhaps superficial to this narrative, it is important to understand it to the extent that it sheds light on the north/south divide in Nigeria. The essential element that triggered a war of succession in Nigeria was a series of violent, indeed perhaps even genocidal pogroms that were unleashed against Igbo expatriate communities, primarily in northern Nigeria, and Igbo elements within the military, in both cases in the immediate aftermath of two military coups that took place during 1966. Much of this had to do with general resentment against the Igbo for their apparent success and dominance in the immediate post-independence period, precipitating a move towards succession in eastern Nigeria that culminated in declared independence and the creation of the state of Biafra in the territory east of the Niger River.

The conflict was resolved in 1970 with the ultimate defeat of Biafra and the reunification of Nigeria, but lingering ethnic tensions continued to exist across religious and ethnic lines, exacerbated by the perpetuation of military rule long after the conclusion of the civil war, resulting in blatant abuses of power and ever deepening economic and political corruption, the latter in particular in terms of natural resources, with oil wealth being the most notable example, and, of course, the multiple cross currents of political patronage that naturally followed. All of this resulted in a grotesquely unbalanced distribution of wealth, widespread poverty and a great deal of burgeoning political discontent, all of which offered fertile ground for a weakening of the centre and a proliferation of lawlessness, ultimately, and almost inevitably, manifesting in an armed insurgency.

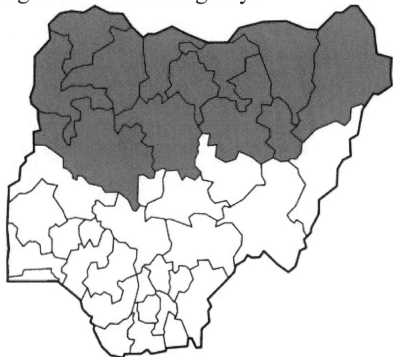

The green parts of Nigeria currently operate under sharia law.

The Rise of Boko Haram

The roots of Boko Haram can be found in the same fertile soil of many other spontaneous regional and continental African rebel and insurgent organizations, that being weak an ineffective central government, political patronage, tribalism, regionalism, unequal distribution of land resources and of course that great and most debilitating factor in African political and economic life: corruption. And moreover, it is perhaps fair to say that the religious overtones of the Boko Haram ideology, if such can be described, tends to have less to do with international jihadism than the demographic peculiarities of Nigeria as it was returned to the continent by the

British.

In quite the same way as such perennial regions of instability as the Central African remain locked in conflict thanks to the arbitrary frontier delineations of the colonial era, so the fundamentally irreconcilable differences between the Islamic north of Africa and the Christian/animist south will continue to ferment animosity and unrest in the region, as witnessed in South Sudan, Darfur and of course, more recently, in Nigeria itself.[194]

From the somewhat protected ascendency of the colonial and immediate post-colonial period, the Islamic north of Nigeria began after independence to fall increasingly behind in terms of access to wealth and political capital to the more aggressively modern south. The system of federalism that the British established prior to independence was for the most part configured to satisfy northern demands for as loose as possible a political union in order to preserve the Islamic identity of the north.[195] A separate system of justice was permitted in the north in order to accommodate Sharia as a personal status law, while the northern religious and political leader, Sir Amadu Bello, presided over a virtually autonomous administrative system.

---

[194] Note: this, of course, does not preclude tensions within the Islamic north itself, with different ethnic groups practicing Islam in different ways, and with tribal and ethnic differences often proving to be stronger than religious similarities.

[195] Note: the original Federation of Nigeria was defined by three states, North, West and East, with Lagos existing as a separate administrative district.

Bello

While this sense of inevitably autonomy fell away in the aftermath of the 1966 coups, followed by the advent of military rule, adherence to Islam, and a strong sense of separate identity, remained a powerful factor in the north.[196] Sir Amadu Bello was one of the first high profile victims of the first 1966 coup, after which the north fell under the secular rule of the military. As a consequence throughout the 1970s and 1980s a number of Islamic pressure groups began to emerge, most notable amongst them *Izala*, which was active in the late 1970s, and which called for a return to the fundamentals of Islam, followed by the *Muslim Brothers*, who, in the 1980s, were active under the slogan: '*There is no Government but Islam.*'[197]

These, however, were for the most part moderate

---

[196] Note: Pressure in the south for a more unitary system of government tended to be realized with the advent of military rule, which corresponded to the centralized command structure of the military and its tendency to respond to a strong central command.

[197] *Boko Haram and the Nigerian Insurgency [Kindle Edition]* Brendan McNamara (Author, Editor), Ryan Milliken (Author), Allen Chatt (Author), Evan Procknow (Author), Graham Plaster (Editor) *The Intelligence Community LLC*

pressure groups acting broadly speaking peacefully, and within the law, but the seeds of radical Islam also existed at the same time, with perhaps the most notable militant organization in existence at that time being the *Yan Tatsine* movement, under the messianic leadership of a radical cleric by the name of Muhammadu Marwa, or Maitatsine Hausa – *He Who Curses* – who led the first violent demonstrations in the Kano state of northern Nigeria in protest at growing corruption under military rule, and the increasing political and economic marginalization of the north.

A picture of Kano, Nigeria's biggest city

These sentiments did not ease with a return to democracy in Nigeria 1999, and the emergence of southern Christian

Olusegun Obasanjo as the first democratically elected president of the country since the 1966 coups.[198] Islamic groups in the north soon afterwards attempted to assert a somewhat separatist agenda by adopting Sharia law in twelve northern states; although in fairness a certain amount of cautious moderation accompanied the practical implementation of Sharia.

Obasanjo

This, therefore, is the soil within which the seeds of Boko Haram began to germinate. From the multiple threads of Islamic discontent under the corrupt and at times arbitrary rule of the federal government, the Boko Haram movement began to coalesce, anonymously at first, with no clear point traceable to determine its actual founding.

---

[198] Note: Obasanjo served as a military leader of Nigeria between 1976 and 1979.

Most scholars, however, are in agreement that the first identifiable root of the organization was a loose grouping of Muslim scholars who met in 1995 under the name of *Ahlulsunna wai'jama'ah hijra*, led by Islamic scholar Abubaker Lawan, and comprising for the most part a cabal of moderate, middle aged and middle class men interested primarily in the study of orthodox Islam.

Change in the organization, however, coincided more or less with democratization in Nigeria. Lawan left the country to study at the University of Medina in Saudi Arabia, relinquishing leadership of the organization to a younger and more radicalized Muslim scholar by the name of Mohammed Yusuf. Yusuf could claim only sparse formal education, but a great deal of revolutionary zeal that had been honed through a radical Quranic indoctrination acquired in neighboring Chad and Niger.[199] From Yusuf a strong militant message emerged, decrying the dilution of orthodox Islam under the influence of the political and economic patronage. This message was characterized by strong and defiant sermons that began to influence the organization, creating out of it something of a movement dominated by a single charismatic leader, followed by a withdrawal from mainstream society in order to explore a utopian version of religious life under the undiluted tenets of orthodox Islam.

---

[199] It is interesting to note that in interviews before his death, Mohammed Yusuf told the BBC Hausa Service he believed the earth was flat, and that rain was not caused by evaporation from the ground, leading to a general sense of public derision towards the group, and a tendency to not take it seriously enough to examine its aims.

Yusuf

Part of this reversionism was a complete rejection of western style education, which caused those more moderate elements within society to refer to the organization as *Boko Haram*. This, in the idiomatic form of the Hausa language, implies something to the effect of *western education is forbidden*, but literally means book, or *boko*, unlawful, or *haram*. The organization itself eschewed this name, and indeed to an extent it still does, preferring the more formal name Jamā'at Ahl as-Sunnah *lid-Da'wah wa'l-Jihād*, or *Group of the People of Sunnah for Preaching and Jihad.*

Under Yusuf, the moderate elements of the movement drifted away, being replaced by an increasingly radical membership pursuing a more vociferous and militant agenda. This message proved to have considerable resonance, and despite a certain amount of localized disquiet, Boko Haram began to attract membership from among a wide spectrum of northern Nigerians – from impoverished inner city youth to university students – and attracting support from a variety of influential sources. Mohammed Yusuf established a mosque in the Borno State capital of Maidiguri, there offering a radical if somewhat ad hoc Quranic education to all comers, which added to an already dedicated radical base.

These educational activities appeared through the early part of the new decade to occupy the energies of the group, with only sporadic clashes with police and security agencies being recorded, and generally not attracting much attention. This remained the case until about 2008/9, at which point major clashes between the group and security authorities began to generate wider popular support, culminating in major riots in 2009 after state security agents raided a Boko Haram hideout, triggering days of social unrest.

This particular episode was significant for many reasons. In the first instance, obviously, it served clear notice to any who cared to listen of the scope of popular discontent in the north, but it also elevated Boko Haram to the status of a major national security risk. However, perhaps most importantly, it resulted in the detention and extra-judicial killing of Muhammad Yusuf by police, which created the movement's first martyr, opening the way for the ascension to the leadership of Yusuf's deputy, a man by the name of Abubakar Shekau.[200]

This manifestly unstable character completed the evolution of Boko Haram from a minor thorn in the side of the Nigerian Security Services to the status of full blown insurgency, and an organization that attracted not

---

[200] Note: Abubakar Shekau is also known by the alias of *Darul Akeem wa Zamunda Tawheed*, or *Darul Tawheed*, meaning in both instance *the home of monotheism.*

only the attention, but also the concern of the United States, which was, of course, precisely the credential that Abubakar Shekau and many at the leadership of the organization desired.

Abubakar Shekau
Boko Haram's Military Capability

Religious disturbances have been a feature of the social landscape of northern Nigeria since the establishment of the Sokoto Caliphate in 1809, and thereafter sporadically throughout the phases of colonial and military rule. However, it was not until the advent of democracy in the country, and the attempt to establish Sharia Law in Kaduna State, that deadly sectarian violence flared up throughout the northern region, to the extent that it has by now become almost commonplace.

It is generally accepted, however, that Boko Haram as a militant organization did not appear as an actor in this ongoing religious turmoil until July of 2009, at which point a relatively innocuous incident involving the group catalyzed weeks of unprecedented violence that ran across several restive northern states.

There are a number of different versions in circulation regarding precisely what took place, but the most credible is simply that a group of Boko Haram members and supporters, travelling in a convoy to a funeral in the Borno State capital of Maiduguri, were stopped at a police roadblock outside the city where it was insisted that they adhere to a local law requiring the use of motorcycle crash helmets. This prompted an argument that resulted eventually in a gunfight, ending in the deaths of a number of Boko Haram members.[201] This episode immediately triggered a massive escalation of religious riots and violence that very quickly spread to Kano, Yobe and Borno, beginning a domino effect of violence and counter violence that saw Boko Haram's coming out as a fully constituted armed insurgency.

Equipped with hand grenades and small arms, groups of Boko Haram fighters took to the streets, attacking a police station in the city of Bauchi, which resulted in the deaths of between 32 and 39 militants, along with an undisclosed number of police and soldiers. At the same time, police stations in the cities of Potiskum and Wudil were also targeted, with sporadic gun battles then breaking out in

---

[201] Note: other versions of this episode suggest that the Boko Haram group were specifically targeted after intelligence had been received that they were planning a major attack.

various other locations, resulting in probably a preponderance of Boko Haram deaths, but also killing a significant number of police and security personnel.

The violence was eventually contained, but the episode considerably unnerved the federal authorities, although local public and press pronouncements tended to claim that the violence had been preempted by authorities, and that, had it not been, events might well have been significantly worse.

Then, on July 28, 2009, police surrounded the home of Ustaz Mohammad Yusuf's parents-in-law – although other reports state that Yusuf was located at a Boko Haram compound in Maiduguri – where Yusuf himself was arrested and taken into custody, and soon afterwards killed.

Again, there is a great deal of confusion over the exact sequence of events leading up to his death, but it is broadly accepted that, having escaped from police custody, Yusuf was quickly re-detained by security force elements and handed back over to the police, who, on the morning of July 30, 2009, publically executed him in the ground of the police station.

The events of July 26-30, 2009 are now broadly referred to as the *2009 Boko Haram Uprising*, marking more or less the point at which the leadership of the organization was inherited by Mohammed Yusuf's deputy, Abubakar Shekau, and likewise arguably the point at which the jihadist ambitions of the emerging leadership of Boko Haram began to define the ideological direction of what was now undeniably an armed militant group.

A note here on the personality and influence of

Abubakar Shekau might perhaps be appropriate. Mohammed Yusuf had led the organization as a militant, but none the less largely passive organization focused on a millenarianist ideology and promoting a lifestyle of orthodox Islam. Abubakar Shekau, on the other hand, emerged immediately as a radical militant jihadist with a charismatic style of leadership and a sworn agenda to punish the Nigerian authorities for the killing of Mohammed Yusuf and generally to violently propagate a reversionist agenda of returning to the pure roots of Islam and punishing a nation for its venality and corruption, and its embrace of western influences.

There are very few undisputed facts available about who and what Abubakar Shekau is. His birth date is reckoned to be anywhere from 1972 to 1981, and the location of his birth has been named as either Niger or Shekau village in the Yobe State of northern Nigeria. He has been described as both complex and paradoxical, part gangster and part theologian, and he is known in certain contexts, and among other aliases, as *Darul Tawheed*. This translates as "specialist in tawheed", taweed being the Islamic concept of oneness of Allah.[202] The sense from this that Shekau is an Islamic scholar is perhaps misleading. Despite undeniable intelligence, and fluency in several languages, Abubakar Shekau remains only nominally educated.

Nonetheless, Abubakar Shekau espouses a radical form of Islam that Nigerian academic, Barkindo Atta of the School of African and Oriental Studies in London, describes as "a spill over from the Sunni-Salafi doctrine that the temporal proximity to Prophet Mohammad is

[202] *Profile of Nigeria's Boko Haram leader Abubakar Shekau*. BBC News. 22 June 2012.

associated with the truest form of Islam."[203]

In this case, temporal proximity implies simply a closer adherence to the original tenets of Islam, with Shekau, along with a number of other Salafi jihadists, freely advocating the use of violence, even violence against fellow Muslims and Salafi purists and activists who in one way or another deprecate violence or advocate any sort of participation in political processes and dialogue.

In this context, Boko Haram appears to ally itself with those Sunni-Salafi jihadists who are calling for and utilizing violence as a means of ensuring a reversion to the original forms of Islam, and the subsequent rejection of everything that can be deemed as *un-Islamic*. The foundations of Boko Haram's ideological propaganda, therefore, and the fundamentals of its recruitment message, and indeed its strategic and organizational structure, are all based on the principal of rejecting western influence, with the ultimate objective of building a society or caliphate based strictly on core Islamic values. [204] In this case, western influence is characterized primarily by the Nigerian federal government, but also elements within the state governments and the Islamic establishment that are deemed un-Islamic for one reason or another, or influenced by un-Islamic tendencies.

An identifying characteristic of Boko Haram that differentiates it from more international jihadist organizations is the fact that, despite occasionally claiming to be linked into the international radical Islamic networks, Boko Haram has to date acted upon no wider

---

[203] tonyblairfaithfoundation.org - Boko Haram: Ideology, Ethnicity and Identity

[204] Ibid.

regional or international objective than its fundamental opposition to the Nigerian government. There is evidence, however, that Boko Haram has received some logistical and technical assistance, and perhaps training from *al-Qaeda in the Islamic Maghreb* (AQIM), and other organizations, but so far claims that the movement is strategically linked to any transnational organization remain unproven.

Boko Haram has taken to using the same flag used by the Islamic State

There are, however, a number of anecdotal factors that will indicate at least a degree of logistical direction from larger and more sophisticated organizations, and an example of this is the recent use of improvised explosive devices (IED), and more specifically, vehicle bourn IEDs (VIED), and indeed the selection and training of suicide bombers, in particular female suicide bombers. On February 24, 2015, for example, a female suicide bomber, reported to be aged no more than seven, detonated an explosive device in a crowded market in the northern town of Potiskum, killing five and wounding dozens, followed later in the day by two further suicide bombers detonating explosive devices at bus terminus, the first in Potiskum and the second in Kano, this time collectively killing at least 27 people.

The first recorded Boko Haram suicide bombing was in fact recorded as early as 2011, which at the very least implies an aspirational link without outside organizations, and indeed, more recently, Boko Haram's printed and video propaganda material has come more closely to resemble that of the Islamic State (ISIS), which implies again at the very least an aspirational link, while reports of foreign looking and speaking militants visible in the ranks of Boko Haram again suggests the beginnings of a wider field of interest, and the possibility that Boko Haram is beginning to attract foreign jihadists.

Much of this information, however, originates from Nigerian intelligence sources, and there is naturally much to be much to be gained by the Nigerian federal government at least *claiming* that Boko Haram has morphed into an international organization, with increased financial and security aid from the international community being perhaps the most important inducement. Indeed, in the aftermath of the failed attempt to rescue hostages Chris McManus and Franco Lamolinara in March 2012, the details of which will be discussed later, Nigerian President Goodluck Jonathan began to place a far greater emphasis on the link between Boko Haram and international terrorism, to which the US State Department responded by obligingly placing Abubakar Shekau on the list of *Specially Designated Global Terrorist*, along with deputies Khalid al-Barnawi and Abubakar Adam Kambar.[205]

Al-Barnawi

Boko Haram's Tactics and Operations

Having eventually regained control of Maiduguri and other northern cities in the aftermath of the 2009 Boko Haram Uprising, police and security services embarked immediately on a brutal and bloody and punitive purge of the Boko Haram's members, and indeed anyone in the wider community suspected of being a supporter or a sympathizer. This forced those surviving members of the organization to flee the country, most either to Niger or Cameroon, although it was at that point that a handful of prominent members of Boko Haram were tracked to

---

[205] Note: Khalid al-Barnawi, also known as Mohammed Usman, is an erstwhile high ranking member of Boko Haram and current leader of splinter faction Ansaru with known links to al-Shabab. Abubakar Adam Kambar was reported killed by Nigerian security forces prior to this designation.

training camps in Algeria and Somalia, and according to the United Nations Security Council, a handful at least also received terror training in a Tuareg rebel camp in Mali.[206] What is clear, however, is that the hiatus that occurred for the remainder of 2009, and for the first half of 2010, were not idle months for Boko Haram, and towards the middle of 2010 members of the group began to reappear in Maiduguri, where they immediately began a campaign of assassinations.

Initially these attacks where quite unsophisticated and random, characterized by motorcycle gunmen targeting police checkpoints in hit-and-run operations in both Borno and Yobe states. Additional targets were local civic and political leaders who had been singled out for corruption, or for having informed on Boko Haram members during the purges of the year before. Individuals who had been apportioned homes and property formerly belonging to escaped Boko Haram members were also targeted and killed. Other operations included the September 2010 attack by about 50 gunmen on the central Bauchi prison, which resulted in the release of 721 prisoners.

On Christmas Eve 2010, the stakes were raised significantly when a series of bomb blasts targeted churches and a market in two districts of Jos, killing scores of people. These incidents were not initially attributed to Boko Haram, and were in fact attributed to another Nigerian militant organization, *Movement for the emancipation of the Niger Delta* (MEND), and indeed Henry Okah, a former leader of MEND, currently in custody in South Africa, still faces charges in Nigeria for

---

[206] *What Is Boko Haram?* United States Institute of Peace, Special Report.

one of those attacks.[207] The same was true on New Year's Eve when an open air fish market in Abuja was targeted, the second bomb attack in Abuja in three months, for which Boko Haram was not initially suspected.

Okah

An FBI assisted investigation ultimately revealed similarities in construction between the devices used in Jos and those in Abuja, at which point suspicion began to fall on Boko Haram. This, of course, was a significant tactical advance on the random assassinations and terrorist actions in and around Maiduguri, with the organization proving itself now able to extend its reach as far as Abuja, and moreover displaying a willingness to target civilians in high profile attacks aimed primarily at causing large numbers of civilian casualties.

There was also a paradoxical element of gangsterism associated with Boko Haram's activities at this time, with targets also being selected for the potential that they offered for extortion, kidnapping and simple robbery,

[207] *What Is Boko Haram?* United States Institute of Peace, Special Report.

which accounted in the early stages of the insurgency for much of Boko Haram's funding. Banks, cash in transit convoys and businesses were all becoming targets, justified as the spoils of war.

According to Abubakar Shekau himself, the killing of civilians "for the purpose of conquering and taking their money follows verses of the Qur'an." Here he is making reference to *ghanima*, or khums, meaning loosely the spoils of war but also taxation payable to a Sultan or Caliph from booty collected from non-believers in the aftermath of war. Thus, "we take from our enemies in the battle we fight in the name of Allah."[208]

On June 16, 2011, an enigmatic bomb attack was launched against police headquarters in Abuja when a car laden with explosives was driven into a secure compound in the wake of a convoy of senior officers in Abuja's government district. The vehicle was directed by security staff to the rear of the building where the explosives were detonated, killing the bomber himself and a single traffic policeman.

A great deal of speculation surrounded this attack. It is thought that the principal target was the Inspector General of Police whose convoy the bomber had followed into the compound, but it was not immediately clear whether the attack had been intended as a suicide bombing, or whether the driver had simply been delayed in Abuja traffic and was therefore unable to escape the blast himself. If, however, this had been an intended suicide bombing, then it would be the first such incident in the short history of the insurgency.

---

[208] CTC Sentinel – *Leadership Analysis of Boko Haram and Ansaru in Nigeria* By Jacob Zenn

This question, however, was answered two months later in what was something of a coming of age attack for Boko Haram. On Friday, August 26, 2011, a vehicle crashed two security barriers and succeeded in ramming into the reception area of the main United Nations building in Abuja before detonating a quantity of explosives that killed the driver and a further 23 people in what would prove to be the most serious and successful terrorist attack in Nigeria to date. It was also the first Boko Haram operation that targeted an international institution, which represented a widening of its campaign. In the opinion of many intelligence analysts, it was through this attack that Boko Haram proved it was receiving international assistance.

The frequency, sophistication and brutality of Boko Haram attacks continued into 2012, escalating to the point where more attacks took place in the opening months of 2015 than had taken place in the whole of 2014. This is a clear indication of a massive escalation in Boko Haram's scope and reach, with the movement's funding network growing, and its access to sophisticated weaponry and operational intelligence exceeding in many respects the Nigerian security force's ability to respond. Civilian victims of Boko Haram totaled 6,347 during 2014, amounting to the largest number of civilian casualties of war recorded on the African continent that year.[209]

The largest and most deadly series of operation to date occurred between January 2-7, 2015, in a coordinated sequence of attacks against the town of Baga, in the extreme northeast of Nigeria, bordering Cameroon. The

---

[209] The Guardian Friday 23 January 2015 - *Nigeria suffers highest number of civilian deaths in African war zones.*

operation began on January 3 as Boko Haram elements overran a military base containing a *Multinational Joint Task Force* comprising troops and support personnel from Chad, Niger and Nigeria, which was followed by mass killings in and around the city that left possibly as many as 2,000 civilians dead, often in horrific circumstances.[210]

Responsibility for the episode was claimed by Boko Haram in a propaganda video that was released soon afterwards. In the video, Abubakar Shekau, in a lengthy rant, revealed large quantities of captured weaponry and equipment, threatened renewed attacks against targets in Cameroon and Chad, and condemned the actions of Nigerian president Goodluck Jonathan in joining solidarity marches in Paris supporting international outrage at the *Charlie Hebdo* killings.[211]

---

[210] Note: These figures were proffered by Amnesty International, but have since been disputed by the Nigerian government, which claims a more accurate figure is 150. This, however, bearing in mind newsreel and satellite imagery, in very unlikely.

[211] Note: On 7 January 2015, two Islamist gunmen forced their way into and opened fire in the Paris headquarters of Charlie Hebdo, killing twelve and wounding eleven, four of them seriously.

Goodluck Jonathan

Indeed, the preceding weeks and months, a number of deadly attacks had been launched against both Chad and Cameroon, prompting each to weigh in with troops and support in what is in effect an internationalization of the insurgency. In December 2014, a Cameroonian soldier was killed in an attack that followed a series of earlier attacks against Cameroonian civilians, resulting collectively in an estimated 30 fatalities. Two days later, Cameroonian troops repelled four simultaneous Boko Haram raids on the towns of Makary, Amchide, Limani, Guirvidig, Waza and Achigachia, located in Cameroon's Far North Region. A number of militants were killed in a Cameroonian counterattack, with authorities estimating the number of Boko Haram members involved at over 1,000.

Similar threats and attacks have been launched against both Chad and Niger, with some suggestions that Boko Haram members have been active alongside AQIM in Mali, although in general it has been observed that Boko Haram attacks beyond Nigerian border have been confined primarily to the region defined as the old Bornu Caliphate which the movement seeks in some manner of form to replicate.

The extent of the insurgency within Nigeria, and its gradual internationalization, has prompted a great deal of discussion, handwringing and international anxiety. However, only limited military and intelligence assistance to Nigeria began to accrue from a number of sources, most notably the United States. America has provided to date a small amount of financial and counter-terrorism assistance under the umbrella of the Anti-terrorism Assistance Program and the Trans-Sahara Counterterrorism Partnership.[212] However, it is perhaps also worth noting that former U.S. Ambassador to

---

[212] http://www.state.gov/r/pa/prs/ps/2014/05/226072.htm

Nigeria, John Campbell, who is now a Council on Foreign Relations senior fellow for Africa policy studies, has on frequent occasions warned the White House to resist the temptation to characterize Boko Haram as simply another foe in the global war on terrorism, since the group's grievances have been to date, and fundamentally remain, primarily local.[213] According to Campbell, "The Boko Haram insurgency is a direct result of chronic poor governance by Nigeria's federal and state governments, the political marginalization of northeastern Nigeria, and the region's accelerating impoverishment. Rather than fighting the militant group solely through military force, the U.S. and Nigerian governments must work together to redress the alienation of Nigeria's Muslims."[214]

---

[213] Council on Foreign Relations, November 2014 – *U.S. Policy to Counter Nigeria's Boko Haram.*

[214] Council on Foreign Relations, November 2014 – *U.S. Policy to Counter Nigeria's Boko Haram.*

Campbell

Campbell advised that a more viable strategy for Washington to pursue in Nigeria would be to leverage what influence it had to ensure free, fair and credible elections in Nigeria in 2015, and for the government of Nigeria to curb the blatant human rights abuses that have so far characterized the official Nigerian response to the insurgency, and to meet the needs of refugees and persons internally displaced by the ongoing fighting in the northeast.

This, however, despite being extremely sage advice in the context of avoiding direct engagement, and in quantifying the insurgency as less an international terrorist threat and more a manifestation of understandable grievances within a tottering system, seems also to be somewhat forlorn when considering the complete inability of the Nigerian security services to adequately come to grips with the insurgency, and its subsequent tendency to lash out in all directions, targeting the wider civilian population in a misdirected and largely ineffective counter-insurgency (COIN) operation.

The Nigerian Counter-Insurgency Response

The quality of an army, or indeed any armed force, can only really be quantified in relation to the quality of its enemy, and perhaps the most interesting ramification of the Boko Haram insurgency has been the way in which it has demonstrated tremendous deficiencies in the ability of Nigerian military to respond to what really amounts to a very limited regional insurgency, and one that enjoys only very limited mainstream popular support.

From its origins as a battalion of the Royal West African Frontier Force, the Nigerian armed forces have evolved very much according to British and Commonwealth traditions, with a majority of senior officers at independence being Sandhurst trained and handpicked by the British themselves. Thus, they are supposed to represent not only the very cream of Nigerian manpower but also characterize the strengths of British military training and tradition, and, perhaps most importantly, to ensure to the greatest extent possible that the armed forces of a newly independent British colony would pose the lowest risk possible of indiscipline.

The British, therefore, invested an inordinate amount of

time and treasure into training and arming the new Nigerian army, which ultimately suffered the same failing as the country as a whole: ethnic divisions and rivalries that ultimately tore the force apart. One of the first compromises made was to configure the various regiments and battalions along ethnic lines in the aftermath of the first 1966 coup, and to deploy them more or less according to the delineations of their home regions.

The first major test of independent Nigerian military capability was the civil war of 1967-70, which revealed a great deal of form and procedure, but much tactical dilettantism as well, alongside clear evidence of a tendency towards ethnic equalization and a high tolerance of human rights abuses. Federal forces won that contest less as a consequence military prowess than its overwhelming logistical advantage occasioned by almost universal international political support, and a great effort on the part of the British to ensure that the federation that they had created survived.

The next major military challenge for Nigeria came with its majority involvement in the Economic Community of West African States (ECOWAS) peacekeeping efforts in Liberia and Sierra Leone, under the aegis of the Economic Community of West African States Monitoring Group (ECOMOG), which devolved into a blatantly corrupt scramble to seize its share of the natural and economic spoils of two nations in absolute crisis. Indeed, the popular local interpretation of the acronym ECOMOG became "Every Car or Moving Object Gone."

It therefore comes as no particular surprise that the armed forces of Nigeria have manifestly failed to come to grips with Boko Haram. Perhaps the most telling hint of Nigeria's lack of military preparedness or integrity comes from the result of the failed hostage rescue attempt to secure the freedom of British and Italian hostages Chris McManus and Franco Lamolinara. The operation, undertaken by the British Special Boat Service, in cooperation with unspecified Nigerian armed force units, attempted in March 2012 to storm a house in the northern city of Sokoto in the extreme northwest of Nigeria. They were hoping to free the hostages after reports of their imminent movement and killing were intercepted by British intelligence agencies. The attempt, undertaken in broad daylight, failed, and the two hostages, alongside two militants, were killed.

Anecdotal reports suggest that much of the failure of the operation had to do with the diplomatic necessity of British Special Forces cooperating with the Nigerians, combined with leaking of information and prior warning being given to the militants.[215] While this remains anecdotal, and in the absence of a tactical analysis of the operation, the facts of its failure will likely remain unknown for some time to come, but the deficiencies of the Nigerian COIN response have been fairly well documented.

A fundamental principal of counter-insurgency is the question of "hearts and minds," which was established as part of the Briggs Plan in Malaya during the Malayan Uprising of 1948-60, during which the earliest precepts of dealing with popular uprisings and 'People's War' were

---

[215] Note: Militants in this instance belonged to a suggested splinter group of Boko Haram, *Ansaru*, or *Jamā'atu Anṣāril Muslimīna fī Bilādis Sūdān* (Vanguard for the Protection of Muslims in Black Lands)

evolved. These were then collected and refined in various campaigns ranging from the Mau Mau Uprising at more or less the same time to the Portuguese colonial wars in Africa and the Rhodesian and South African wars of liberation.

The Boko Haram insurgency conforms to the classic definition of asymmetric warfare, meaning there are two opposing forces with vastly different military capabilities. One (for the most part) represents the state in a conventional configuration, and the second represents the militant expression of a popular movement, usually responding to deep-seated discontent leveled against the government. This is broadly the case in northern Nigeria. The Nigerian method of winning hearts and minds, as with the case of many conventional responses to popular movements, seeks to avoid recognition of authentic political grievance, removing, therefore, from its mandate any obligation towards social improvement and instead relying on a reapplication of terror in order to terrorize the terrorists.

In a September 2014 report entitled "Welcome to Hellfire," Amnesty International drew attention to systematic human rights abuses being perpetrated by the Nigerian armed forces in pursuit of Operation Flush, a deeply questionable counter-insurgency operation implemented in 2009 as the Boko Haram operational profile began to include attacks against security forces, schools, churches and civilians. Initially, a Joint Task Force (JTF) was established, comprising personnel from all of the various security services. This operated under a state of emergency that had been declared in 15 northern

Local Government Areas (LGAs) by President Goodluck Jonathan, initially in January 2012, and extended in May 2013 to include Adamaw, Borno and Yobe states. This State of Emergency has since been extended twice.

In 2013, the JTF was dissolved and operational command of security operations was handed over to the Army Chief of Staff, at which point a tactical shift saw the formation and deployment of a Civilian Joint Task Force (CJTF). The CJTF is essentially a state-sponsored civilian militia with powers to arrest suspected Boko Haram members or sympathizers. And of course, under wide ranging emergency laws, the security forces themselves enjoy sweeping powers to arrest and detain anyone suspected of terror related offences.

The result of all of this has been an effective and officially sanctioned reign of terror as mobs of sparsely trained (if at all) local youth, empowered by almost total impunity, descend on local communities with arbitrary powers to select and interrogate any individuals who upon any basis at all might be deemed members of, sympathetic to, or in some way associated with Boko Haram. Mass arrests, beatings, torture and killings have both been reported and recorded, with a great deal of graphic video and photographic evidence surfacing that implicates state security agents in a number of horrific and blatant human rights abuses, many of which constitute de facto war crimes. Perhaps the most shocking evidence has been a variety of amateur videos taken of the extra-judicial killing of a number of civilians whose throats were individually cut before being tossed into a mass grave by elements of the Nigerian military assisted by members of the CJTF.

Although difficult to deny, the Nigerian government has nonetheless attempted to do so. The claim has been made that the executions were perpetrated by members of Boko Haram masquerading as Nigerian soldiers, which has indeed taken place on several occasions, but in this case there is clear evidence on video of the incident that proves that this was not so. Perhaps the most compelling is the result of an analysis of visible rifle markings that identify a weapon in the possession of a soldier as belonging to a specific Nigerian battalion.

Much of this has been revealed by a handful of Western media outlets, including PBS *Frontline* and the British Channel 4 *Dispatches,* each of which produced revealing and deeply disturbing documentaries illustrating, not only the Nigerian security services, in particular the police and army, but also the CJTF implicated in random and widespread human rights abuses, running the gamut of beatings, arbitrary arrest and detention, mass killings and public executions. Alongside this was testimony taken from a number of former members and currently serving members of the CJTF confirming mass atrocities against civilians, which also revealed the ad hoc nature and extreme brutality exercised by what is in effect an undisciplined mob of largely unemployed and disaffected teenagers, crudely armed, empowered and acting with almost absolute impunity.

Military operations documented by Amnesty International and various other sources describe a pattern of mass arrests and screenings of people, many identifiable as children, in towns and villages, typically as a consequence of fairly random identification, and usually thereafter involving beatings and other violent abuse. Those detained as suspected members of Boko Haram are often held incommunicado in local or smaller military camps without access to family or legal representation for long periods. Torture and other ill-treatment by the soldiers has been routine – either at the time of, or immediately after arrest, or while detained – often to punish them for their alleged links with Boko Haram, and indeed large numbers of people have simply disappeared, with many later turning up dead.

Needless to say, there has been no serious attempt on the part of the Nigerian authorities to investigate or act upon allegations brought against the military and police by, in particular, Amnesty International. When contacted for comment upon the release of the Channel 4 documentary *Nigeria's Hidden War,* the Nigerian High Commissioner in London dismissed purported cases of human rights abuses and war crimes. He asserted "nothing of the sort is being perpetrated in Nigeria. This is because there has to be a war before you talk about war crimes. What is happening …is an effort ...to stamp out insurgency…[Where] possible collateral damage could be experienced. The Nigerian Government … is a signatory to many international human rights instruments, … is doing everything possible within the ambit of law… [The] Government … or its agencies cannot be said to be targeting unprotected civilians as a matter of policy."[216]

More focused Amnesty International attempts to raise concerns with the Nigerian government and military have

[216] *channel4.com* - Nigeria's Hidden War: Channel 4 Dispatches. August 18 2014

resulted in a tacit acceptance of mass arrests and torture as a broad strategy, but rationalizing it as means justifying ends: "It's a natural reaction by the army to cordon off an area to search when we don't get adequate information about particular acts... We also have challenges in investigating or detecting the truth. So we have to make do with the crude method we have. These extra measures are necessary for the context we operate in."[217]

In August 2014, the office of the National Security Officer in Nigeria wrote to Amnesty International and conceded, "Our security and law enforcement agencies are committed to abiding by the Geneva Conventions and all standard operating procedures designed to maximize the protection of civilians when fighting an armed and hidden insurgency, which blends in with the local population. That said, however, there have indeed been abuses committed where our security and law enforcement operatives failed to abide by those important standards. We are however determined to do better and happily with each passing day we are doing better."[218]

Those claims aside, the weight of anecdotal evidence alone is sufficiently compelling to conclude that a violent and indiscriminate campaign was, and in many instances still is, being waged in the northeast of Nigeria in an attempt to stamp out popular support for the Boko Haram movement.

The World's Reaction to Boko Haram

It is interesting to note that it was in the immediate aftermath of Chibok kidnappings that calls for some sort

---

[217] Amnesty International's meeting with senior military officers at Defense headquarters in Abuja, 31 July 2013.
[218] Letter to Amnesty International from the Office of the National Security Adviser, 7 August 2014.

of an international intervention were most loudly spoken, and most universally acknowledged. In May 2014, a month after the kidnappings, a summit meeting between French and affected African heads of state was held in Paris to explore ways and means of coordinating a campaign against Boko Haram. A great deal of people articulated the international threat and called for action. One of the most notable was Senator John McCain, who called for an American military operation to rescue the kidnapped girls, but ultimately there remains great international reluctance to actively intervene against Boko Haram.[219]

A picture of damage done to the school where the girls were kidnapped

[219] McCain's call was based on humanitarian and not strategic rationale.

A picture of some of the girls' parents crying after the kidnapping

Nigeria lies within what might be regarded as the British sphere of influence, given that it is a former British colony and an Anglophone country, but the likelihood of an international response, if any, would in all probability originate in France. West Africa, broadly speaking, exists within the French sphere of interest more than it does any other colonizing power. French defense agreements with a majority of her ex-colonies have seen French military interventions in Gabon, Chad, CAR, Comoros, Zaire, Djibouti, Republic of Congo and more recently in Côte-d'Ivoire, Libya and Mali. However, France did not directly interfere in the Biafran War of 1967-70, but likewise neither did Britain, and the only significant intervention by Britain in the region since then has been Operation Barras, which was a special force operation that took place in Sierra Leone on September 10, 2000 to release five British soldiers of the Royal Irish Regiment who had been held by a local militia group. American intervention, if held back during the depth of the Rwandan, Liberian and Sierra Leonean crisis, is unlikely to be forthcoming in Nigeria, in particular in the aftermath of the disastrous intervention in Somalia.

The likelihood, therefore, of any direct outside military action in Nigeria to confront Boko Haram is extremely remote. The integrity of the Nigerian state is not at risk, and although there is very little practical hope that the Nigerian security forces will ever regain full control over what is traditionally a wild and lawless region, there is also no risk of an imminent coup d'état, or any other such hazard to the central government.

There is also the question of Nigeria's almost mind-numbing levels of corruption and the obvious excesses in its counter-insurgency efforts, as demonstrated by the unpalatable evidence of extreme human rights abuses being perpetrated against the civilian population of the north. Some of these have been anecdotally classified as war crimes, which make any international dealings with Nigeria diplomatically tricky to say the very least.

Part of this has to do with the fact that Boko Haram's creed continues to focus locally, as well as the fact that the organization's opposition against the Nigerian government is understandable in the sense that the Nigerian forces have committed atrocities. In fact, some of the worst excesses of violence perpetrated by Boko Haram are not that much worse than the worst excesses of the security establishment in responding to the crisis. Thus, the primary diplomatic challenge must be for

Western governments to first bolster the democratic institutions of Nigeria, assist with the eradication of corruption, and help professionalize the military by attempting to build the necessary trust and empathy between them and the population that they purport to defend.

Boko Haram's Uncertain Future

According to former U.S. Ambassador to Nigeria, John Campbell, Boko Haram poses no direct security threat to the U.S. homeland, but its attacks on Nigeria, and Abuja's response that is characterized by extensive human-rights violations, does challenge American interests in Africa.[220] There exists a significant risk that if Boko Haram is actively pursued with the same arsenal of political, financial and military options being deployed against such organizations and ISIS, al-Qaeda, al-Shebaba and AQIM, Boko Haram will by association be elevated to that status and will begin to attract the interest, recruitment and funding of international jihadists. In a sense, this would create the very problem that the international community seeks to avoid. At the same time, it's probably safe to assume some elements of Boko Haram are ambitious enough to seek associations with foreign terror franchises to boost their own image internationally.

There are no definitive studies available detailing the organization and leadership structure of Boko Haram, which more than anything else underlines the shadowy nature of the movement and its leadership. It is recognized, however, that as the organization has matured

---

[220] International Business Times January 18 2015 – *Boko Haram: United States Intervention In Nigeria Is Complicated, Officials Say.*

in the five or six years since it has been operational, complex leadership structures have evolved along the lines of an independent cell structure under the broad umbrella leadership of a *Shura Council*, headed, nominally at least, by Abubakar Shekau. That said, there is by no means unanimity in intelligence or academic circles that he is either the only or the absolute leader of the group.[221]

According to U.S. Congressional research, the core group of Boko Haram numbers in the hundreds rather than the thousands, with a much wider field of informal support available primarily within the Kanuri tribal group. Abubakar Shekau belongs to this group, which geographically overlaps the four corners region of Nigeria, Niger, Chad and Cameroon. This is the region which also defines, incidentally, more or less the borders of the old Bornu/Sokoto Caliphates which Boko Haram, at least ideologically, is committed to bringing back.

Even the within the Shura Council itself, the leadership is disperse and remote, offering a degree of anonymity but also leading to a fractured decision making process and the tendency for confusion and miscommunication. Individual members of the Shura Council rarely meet, instead communicating through human liaison and cell phones, and in this way controlling a system of individual cells that are responsible for different roles and functions within the organization, as well as specific geographic areas. For example, certain cells specialize in and are

---

[221] Note: *Shura* is an Arabic word implying inclusive consultation. The Quran, and indeed Muhammad himself, encourage all Muslims to decide their affairs in consultation with those affected by any decision. A Shura Council, therefore, is a standard organizational/administrative body in the Islamic world, with Shura Councils, or consultative councils, existing in one form or another in most predominantly Islamic countries.

responsible for the racketeering aspects of the group's activities, including the bank and cash in transit robberies, money laundering and the acquisition of vehicles and general equipment. Others are responsible for providing intelligence services, including the selection and research of targets and modes of operation, and yet others are more combat oriented, others more technical. There are, for example, bomb makers, as well as those for funding cells, propaganda and media, external relations and welfare/medical. The latter is responsible for the care of wives and families of deceased members and relatives of suicide bombers.[222]

There are reported to be at least 30 individual cells, each overseen and commanded by a different council member, with overall decisions made within the council. On occasion, there's a propensity for Abubakar Shekau to act independently and autonomously, which again adds to the tendency towards miscommunication and division. In essence, any definitive statement issued by the organization might not be wholly representative of group opinion or determination.[223]

It would appear also that Abubakar Shekau maintains very little contact with the operative structures of Boko Haram, dealing instead with only a handful of select cell leaders. This leads to a degree of operational unpredictability, but it also makes it much more difficult to negotiate with a group that appears to have many individual heads, each to some degree independent of the

[222] Sahara Reporters July 15 2012 - *Boko Haram Reportedly Has Complex Organizational Structure.*

[223] Walker, Andrew. *United States Institute of Peace*, June 2012, *What is Boko Haram?*

other.

It is inevitable, therefore, that the organization would be subject to internal divisions, and in key policy aspects, would be seen to be pulling in different directions. Like other sectarian Muslim groups, its ideological premise has compelled Boko Haram to lash out frequently at fellow Muslims. In fact, a majority of Boko Haram's victims have been northern Nigerian Muslims, with the movement even targeting those within its own membership and support base in order to settle internal factionalism and disagreements.[224]

It might perhaps be instructive in concluding an examination of the Boko Haram leadership to dwell briefly on the nature of these internal divisions, for they determine to a significant extent the general ambiguity of the organization, and indeed the tendency towards internationalization as the movement itself matures away from its established, founding leadership.

Perhaps the most extreme example of internal contradiction occurred in January 2012, when a group claiming to be a moderate breakaway faction of Boko Haram released a video tape to the Nigerian Television Authority offering terms of negotiation. Four days later, men claiming to be Boko Haram publicly beheaded six people in Maiduguri. Indeed, according to the U.S. Institute of Peace, when Boko Haram kills their own, they behead them, and reports of beheadings seem to go up when there are talks of negotiation.[225]

---

[224] U.S. House of Representatives Committee on Homeland Security September 13, 2013 - BOKO HARAM: A Growing Threat to the U.S. Homeland.

[225] *Ibid.*

Internal divisions within the movement are also premised to some extent on ethnic lines. The Boko Haram base of operations spreads over a wide geographic area, and differing ethnic groups are not only targeted by the group but also inducted. This means the ethnic composition of the upper ranks and leadership begins to dilute. The Kanuri ethnic group that makes up the majority within Boko Haram occupies a limited geographic area in the northeast of Nigeria, and it is significantly outnumbered within the wider region of Islamic influence in northern Nigeria by the Hausa/Fulani group. Both groups practices Islam in different ways, and on the wider religious/political stage in Nigeria, the Hausa/Fulani are significantly more influential. According to one report from STRATFOR Global Intelligence, "As Boko Haram attacks began to kill more Hausa-Fulani, a backlash among western Nigerian Muslims has been mounting, particularly in Kano, Nigeria's second largest city and the country's northern commercial hub."[226]

Perhaps the most significant impact of internal division and leadership contradictions within Boko Haram is the potential ideological merger between Boko Haram and the wider diaspora of Islamic jihadist organizations. In a highly detailed study of the Boko Haram leadership by Jacob Zenn, a respected African and Eurasian Affairs analyst, the author details a number of Mohammed Yusuf's "disciples," including Abubakar Shekau, each with differing views on the strategic and ideological direction of the movement and each tending to pull in different directions. One such member is Mamman Nur,

---

[226] *Ibid.*

who masterminded the 2011 UN bombing in Abuja, and who, also known as Abu Usmatul al-Ansari, was a founder member of Ansaru. Nur is a Cameroonian with significant contacts to international terrorist organizations such as AQIM, al-Shabaab, MUJAO, al-Qaeda Central, and other militant groups in Africa. What is interesting about him is the fact that he fled Nigeria in the aftermath of the 2009 uprising in the direction of East Africa, finding refuge and ultimately training and ideological direction from al- Shabaab in Somalia. When he returned, he was highly motivated to regionalize the Boko Haram agenda.[227]

Nur

Mention has already been made of Khalid al-Barnawi and Abubakar Adam Kambar (the latter of whom is probably dead), each of which exerted a strong influence towards regionalization and internationalization of the Boko Haram insurgency. This is suggestive of other

---

[227] Note: it ought not to be assumed from this that Abubakar Shekau lacks interest in being absorbed into a foreign jihadist franchise, or indeed franchising Boko Haram itself. There simply appears to be significant limitations to Shekau's leadership ability, notwithstanding his apparent firm grip on the organization at present. There is evidence that Shekau is not taken seriously outside of Nigeria, and there may be a reluctance on the part of outside organizations to invest in a movement that is led by an individual displaying evidence of instability and erratic leadership, which may well changed at some point in the future when control of the organization is passed on.

strong influences within the organization, and perhaps to a degree its future direction. As a result, when trying to chart its future course, the question to be answered is one of leadership, because regardless of its rapid advances in scope and capability, Boko Haram remains proscribed by the limitations of its current leadership. According to Jacob Zenn, "Boko Haram's future trajectory may depend on Mamman Nur. Due to Nur's ideological influence on Ansaru and operational connections to AQIM, al-Shabab and the late Kambar, Nur may be the "Boko Haram" leader communicating with AQIM, al-Shabab, al-Qa`ida in the Arabian Peninsula (AQAP), the Islamic Movement of Uzbekistan (IMU) in Pakistan and other al-Qa'ida affiliates."[228]

Currently, it is recognized that Boko Haram is an affiliate of al-Qaeda, and associated on some level with al-Shabaab, which is itself more closely associated with al-Qaeda. However, all of those links, along with Boko Haram's associations with militant organizations in North Africa, remain imperfectly understood, suggesting that a full association is still off in the distance rather than already here. The future leadership question is vexed, however. Shekau remains a divisive leader, but he enjoys legitimacy based on his ethnic origins, his grassroots support, and his credentials as Mohammed Yusuf's second-in-command. Any leadership change would likely see Khalid al-Barnawi assuming operational control of Boko Haram and Mamman Nur assuming ideological control, at which point, thanks to the latter's connections but also to the increasingly robust tactical capability of the

---

[228] CTC Sentinel - *Leadership Analysis of Boko Haram and Ansaru in Nigeria*, by Jacob Zenn

organization, is a scenario to be taken very seriously indeed.

Indeed, whatever limitations there might be on the ideological proliferation of Boko Haram, what is inescapable is that it is growing in tactical capability and is gradually acquiring an impressive arsenal of military equipment despite the localized success claimed against it by the Nigerian security services. The recent Libyan conflict has made available military hardware that has the potential to significantly amplify the current level of threat. Among these are a number of variants of SA-7B MANPAD missile systems, which could be used to target both civilian and military aircraft. In addition, the organization is now in a position to deploy between 500 and 1,000 militants in any ground operation, supported by captured ordnance including 81mm mortars and a variety of armored vehicles and armored troop carriers along with a fleet of converted civilian vehicles.

Thus, in every respect, Boko Haram is a force both to be recognized and feared, and while it lacks the capability at the moment to fatally compromise the existing government in Abuja, it definitely retains the capacity to increase insecurity in the north. It may even be possible for the group to carve out its desired caliphate and hold territory in an increasing tenuous and lawless region of Africa. All the while, even though there is still no direct evidence that Boko Haram has morphed into an international terrorist organization, it now possesses the ability and a stated interest in attacking Western interests, which would simply require a modest leadership and ideological realignment to achieve.

Further Reading
Al-Qaeda

Austrian Centre for Country of Origin and Asylum Research and Documentation (ACCORD). *Clans in Somalia.* December 2009. http://www.refworld.org/docid/4b29f5e82.html.

Baldauf, Scott. "The 'Cave Man' and Al Qaeda." *The Christian Science Monitor.* October 31, 2001. http://www.csmonitor.com/2001/1031/p6s1-wosc.html.

Benotman, Noman and Roisin Blake. "Jabhat al-Nusra." *Quillam Foundation.* http://www.quilliamfoundation.org/wp/wp-content/uploads/publications/free/jabhat-al-nusra-a-strategic-briefing.pdf.

Bergen, Peter L. *The Osama Bin Laden I Know.* New York: Free Press, 2006.

Bin Laden, Osama . *CNN.* By Tayseer Alouni, *CNN.* February 5, 2002. Transcript available at http://web.archive.org/web/20061206081331/http://archives.cnn.com/2002/WORLD/asiapcf/south/02/05/binladen.transcript/index.html.

Carter, Shan and Amanda Cox. "One 9/11 Tally: $3.3 Trillion." *The New York Time.,* September 8, 2011. http://www.nytimes.com/interactive/2011/09/08/us/sept-11-reckoning/cost-graphic.html.

Cole, Juan. "'Too Extreme for Al Qaeda': Al Zawahiri Disowns ISIL." *Mideast Posts.* May 2, 2014. http://mideastposts.com/middle-east-politics-analysis/extreme-al-qaeda-al-zawahiri-disowns-isil/.

Dolan, Kerry A. "The Secret Of Al Qaeda In Islamic Maghreb Inc.: A Resilient (And Highly Illegal) Business Model." *Forbes.* December 16, 2013. http://www.forbes.com/sites/kerryadolan/2013/12/16/the-secret-of-al-qaeda-in-islamic-maghreb-inc-a-resilient-and-highly-illegal-business-model/.

Fisk, Robert. *The Great War for Civilisation: The Conquest of the Middle East.* New York: Vintage House, 2005.

"Full Transcript of Bin Ladin's Speech." *Al Jazeera.* November 2, 2004. http://web.archive.org/web/20070613014620/http://english.aljazeera.net/English/archive/archive?ArchiveI d=7403.

Hoffman, Bruce. "Al Qaeda, Trends in Terrorism and Future Potentialities: An Assessment." *Studies in Conflict and Terrorism* 26, no. 6 (2003): 429-442.

Hubbard, Ben. "The Franchising of Al Qaeda." *The New York Times.* Jan 25, 2014. http://www.nytimes.com/2014/01/26/sunday-review/the-franchising-of-al-qaeda.html.

Joscelyn, Thomas and Bill Roggio. "Shabaab Formally Joins Al Qaeda." *The Long War Journal.* February 9, 2012. http://www.longwarjournal.org/archives/2012/02/shabaab_formally_joi.php.

Kingsley, Patrick. "Egypt Faces New Threat in Al-Qaida-Linked Group Ansar Beyt Al-Maqdis." *The Guardian.* January 31, 2014. http://www.theguardian.com/world/2014/jan/31/egyp

t-alqaida-terrorist-threat-ansar-beyt-almaqdis.

Laub, Zachary and Jonathan Masters. "Al-Qaeda in the Islamic Maghreb (AQIM)." *Council on Foreign Relations.* January 8, 2011. http://www.cfr.org/terrorist-organizations-and-networks/al-qaeda-islamic-maghreb-aqim/p12717.

Lewis, Jessica D. "Al-Qaeda in Iraq Resurgent: The Breaking the Walls Campaign, Part I." *Middle East Security Report* 14 (September 2013): 1-41.

McCabe, Thomas R. "The Strategic Failures of Al Qaeda." *Parameters.* (Spring 2010): 60-71.

Pool, Jeffrey. "Zarqawi's Pledge of Allegiance to Al-Qaeda: From Mu'asker Al-Battar, Issue 21." *The Jamestown Foundation Terrorism Monitor* 2, no. 24 (Dec 2004): 4-6.

Qutb, Sayyid. "Milestones." In *Political Dissent: A Global Reader: Modern Sources*, edited by Derek Malone-France, 211-244. Plymouth: Lexington Books, 2012.

Rashid, Ahmed. "The Taliban: Exporting Extremism." *Foreign Affairs.* November-December 1999. http://www.foreignaffairs.com/articles/55600/ahmed-rashid/the-taliban-exporting-extremism

Riedel, Bruce. "The World After 9/11 – Part I." *The Brookings Institution.* September 6, 2011. http://www.brookings.edu/research/articles/2011/09/06-after-911-riedel.

Robbins, James S. "Al-Qaeda Versus Democracy." *The Journal of International Security Affairs* 9 (2005): 53-59. Available at

http://www.afpc.org/publication_listings/viewArticle
/56%20/true.

Roggio, Bill. "Wuhayshi Imparted Lessons of
AQAP Operations in Yemen to AQIM." *The Long
War Journal.* August 12, 2013.
http://www.longwarjournal.org/archives/2013/08/wu
hayshi_imparts_les.php.

Schmitt, Eric. "As Al Qaeda Loses a Leader, Its
Power Shifts From Pakistan." *The New York Times.*
June 7, 2012.
http://www.nytimes.com/2012/06/08/world/asia/al-
qaeda-power-shifting-away-from-
pakistan.html?_r=3&partner=rss&emc=rss.

Stewart, Scott. "Al Shabaab's Threat to Kenya."
Stratfor Global Intelligence. April 26, 2012.
http://www.stratfor.com/weekly/al-shabaabs-threat-
kenya.

Windrem, Robert. "Al-Qaida Timeline: Plots and
Attacks." *NBC News.* Accessed June 12. 2014,
http://www.nbcnews.com/id/4677978/ns/world_news
-hunt_for_al_qaida/t/al-qaida-timeline-plots-
attacks/#.U6I33fmSySp.

Wright, Lawrence. *The Looming Tower: Al-Qaeda
and the Road to 9/11.* New York: Random House,
2006.

*The 9/11 Commission Report: Final Report of the
National Commission on Terrorist Attacks Upon the
United States,* official government edition.
Washington, DC: U.S. Government Printing Office,
2004.

U.S. Library of Congress. Congressional Research

Service. *Al Qaeda: Profile and Threat Assessment,* by Kenneth Katzman. CRS Report RL33038. Washington, DC: Office of Congressional Information and Publishing, August 17, 2005.

U.S. Library of Congress. Congressional Research Service. *Terrorist Attack on USS Cole: Background and Issues for Congress*, by Raphael Perl and Ronald O'Rourke. CRS Report RL20721. Washington, DC: Office of Congressional Information and Publishing, January 30, 2001.

U.S. State Department. Office of the Coordinator for Counterterrorism. *Country Reports on Terrorism.* April 28, 2006. http://web.archive.org/web/20070711072535/http://www.state.gov/s/ct/rls/crt/2005/65275.htm.

Whitlock, Craig. "Gates: Al-Qaeda Has Assembled a 'Syndicate' of Terror Groups." *The Washington Post.* January 20, 2010. http://www.washingtonpost.com/wp-dyn/content/article/2010/01/20/AR2010012001575.html.

Zenn, Jacob. "Leadership Analysis of Boko Haram." *CTC Sentinel* 7, no. 2 (February 2014): 23-29.

Zimmerman, Katherine. "Testimony: AQAP's Role in the al Qaeda Network." *Critical Threats.* September 18, 2013. http://www.criticalthreats.org/al-qaeda/zimmerman-testimony-aqaps-role-al-qaeda-network-september-18-2013.

ISIS

"2 Most Wanted Al Qaeda Leaders in Iraq Killed by U.S., Iraqi Forces." *Fox News.* April 19, 2010. http://www.foxnews.com/world/2010/04/19/iraqi-al-qaeda-leader-killed-countrys-intelligence-team-pm-maliki-says/.

Aarja, Hadil. "ISIS Enforces Strict Religious Law in Raqqa." *Al-Monitor.* March 21, 2014. http://www.al-monitor.com/pulse/security/2014/03/isis-enforces-islamic-law-raqqa-syria.html.

"Al-Qaeda Confirms Iraq Leaders' Deaths." *The Telegraph.* April 25, 2010. http://www.telegraph.co.uk/news/worldnews/middleeast/iraq/7632630/Al-Qaeda-confirms-Iraq-leaders-deaths.html.

"Al-Qaeda Spiritual Leader Labels Islamic State as 'Deviants.'" *Ammon News.* July 1, 2014. http://en.ammonnews.net/article.aspx?articleno=25875#.U7NcdPmSySo.

Ali, Abdallah Suleiman. "ISIS Announces Islamic Caliphate, Changes Name." *Al-Monitor.* June 30, 2014. http://www.al-monitor.com/pulse/security/2014/06/iraq-syria-isis-announcement-islamic-caliphate-name-change.html.

"All You Need to Know about ISIS and What Is Happening in Iraq." *RT News.* June 20, 2014. http://rt.com/news/166836-isis-isil-al-qaeda-iraq/.

"Another Militant Group Opposes BISP." *The News.* April 10, 2009. http://www.thenews.com.pk/TodaysPrintDetail.aspx?ID=171651&Cat=7&dt=4/9/2009.

Atwan, Abdel Bari. *The Secret History of Al Qaeda.* Berkeley: University of California Press, 2006.

Ayad, Christophe. "Abou Bakr Al-Baghdadi, Le Nouveau Ben Laden." *Le Monde.* May 29, 2014. http://www.lemonde.fr/proche-orient/article/2014/05/29/abou-bakr-al-baghdadi-le-nouveau-ben-laden_4428636_3218.html.

Baker, Aryn. "Why Al-Qaeda Kicked Out Its Deadly Syria Franchise." *TIME.* February 3, 2014. http://time.com/3469/why-al-qaeda-kicked-out-its-deadly-syria-franchise/.

Baroud, Ramzy. "ISIL and Iraq's Pandora's Box." *Middle East Eye.* June 15, 2014. http://www.middleeasteye.net/columns/isil-and-iraq-s-pandora-s-box/817321027.

Bassil, Yousif, Mohammed Tawfeeq and Cal Perry. "Iraq TV Airs Alleged Confession of Terrorist Leader." *CNN.* May 18, 2009. http://www.cnn.com/2009/WORLD/meast/05/18/iraq.alleged.terror.confession/index.html?iref=24hours.

Benotman, Noman and Roisin Blake. "Jabhat al-Nusra." *Quillam Foundation.* http://www.quilliamfoundation.org/wp/wp-content/uploads/publications/free/jabhat-al-nusra-a-strategic-briefing.pdf.

"Bomb at Italian Police HQ in Iraq Kills 26." *Fox News.* November 12, 2003. http://www.foxnews.com/story/2003/11/12/bomb-at-italian-police-hq-in-iraq-kills-26/.

Brisard, Jean-Charles and Damien Martinez. *Zarqawi: The New Face of Al-Qaeda.* Cambridge:

Polity Press, 2005.

Bush, George W. "The President's State of the Union Address." Speech, Washington DC, January 29, 2002. The White House Archives. http://georgewbush-whitehouse.archives.gov/news/releases/2002/01/20020129-11.html.

Cole, Juan. "'Too Extreme for Al Qaeda': Al Zawahiri Disowns ISIL." *Mideast Posts.* May 2, 2014. http://mideastposts.com/middle-east-politics-analysis/extreme-al-qaeda-al-zawahiri-disowns-isil/.

Cosgrove-Mather, Bootie. "Poll: Talk First, Fight Later." *CBS News.* January 23, 2003. http://www.cbsnews.com/news/poll-talk-first-fight-later/.

Darwish, Adel. "Abu Musab Al-Zarqawi." *The Independent.* June 9, 2006. http://www.independent.co.uk/news/obituaries/abu-musab-alzarqawi-481622.html.

"Description of the Abbottabad Documents Provided to the CTC." *The Washington Post.* http://www.washingtonpost.com/r/2010-2019/WashingtonPost/2012/05/03/Foreign/Graphics/osama-bin-laden-documents-combined.pdf.

Faraj, Caroline. "Al-Zarqawi Group Claims Allegiance to Bin Laden." *CNN.* October 18, 2004. http://www.cnn.com/2004/WORLD/meast/10/17/al.zarqawi.statement/.

Franks, Tommy. *American Soldier General Tommy Franks.* New York: Regan Books, 2004.

Froomkin, Dan. "Failing to Reassure." *The*

Washington Post. May 24, 2007.
http://busharchive.froomkin.com/BL2007052401145
_pf.htm.

Gambill, Gary. "Abu Musab al-Zarqawi: A
Biographical Sketch." *The Jamestown Foundation.*
December 15, 2004.
http://www.jamestown.org/single/?tx_ttnews%5Btt_
news%5D=27304.

Gritten, David, Lucy Rodgers and Emily Macguire.
"Syria: The Story of the Conflict." *BBC News.* March
14, 2014. http://www.bbc.com/news/world-middle-
east-26116868.

Guidère, Mathieu. *Historical Dictionary of Islamic
Fundamentalism.* Plymouth: Scarecrow Press, 2012.

Hall, John. "The ISIS Map of the World." *Daily
Mail.* June 30, 2014.
http://www.dailymail.co.uk/news/article-
2674736/ISIS-militants-declare-formation-caliphate-
Syria-Iraq-demand-Muslims-world-swear-
allegiance.html.

"How Did It Come to This?" *The Economist.* June
19, 2014. http://www.economist.com/news/middle-
east-and-africa/21604627-crisis-iraq-has-roots-going-
far-back-history-recently-folly.

Hunt, Emily. "Zarqawi's 'Total War' on Iraqi Shiites
Exposes a Divide among Sunni Jihadists." *The
Washington Institute.* November 15, 2005.
http://www.washingtoninstitute.org/policy-
analysis/view/zarqawis-total-war-on-iraqi-shiites-
exposes-a-divide-among-sunni-jihadists.

Joscelyn, Thomas. "The Islamic State's Rivals in

Syria Reject Announced Caliphate." *The Long War Journal.* July 1, 2014. http://www.longwarjournal.org/archives/2014/07/the_islamic_states_r.php.

Joshi, Shashank. "Abu Bakr Al-Baghdadi: The World's Most Wanted Man." *The Telegraph.* July 1, 2014. http://www.telegraph.co.uk/news/worldnews/middleeast/10935790/Abu-Bakr-al-Baghdadi-The-worlds-most-wanted-man.html.

Kearney, Frank. "Abu Du'a." *TIME.* April 23, 2014. http://time.com/70832/abu-dua-2014-time-100/.

Kirdar, M. J. "Al Qaeda in Iraq." *Center for Strategic and International Studies* (June 2011): 1-15.

Krauthammer, Charles. "Charlie Gibson's Gaffe." *The Washington Post.* September 13, 2008. http://www.washingtonpost.com/wp-dyn/content/article/2008/09/12/AR2008091202457.html.

Leiken, Robert S. "Who Is Abu Zarqawi?" *CBS News.* May 18, 2004. http://www.cbsnews.com/news/who-is-abu-zarqawi/.

Lewis, Jessica D. "Al-Qaeda in Iraq Resurgent: The Breaking the Walls Campaign, Part I." *Middle East Security Report* 14 (September 2013): 1-41.

McCoy, Terrence. "How ISIS Leader Abu Bakr Al-Baghdadi Became the World's Most Powerful Jihadist Leader." *The Washington Post.* June 11, 2014.

http://www.washingtonpost.com/news/morning-mix/wp/2014/06/11/how-isis-leader-abu-bakr-al-baghdadi-became-the-worlds-most-powerful-jihadi-leader/.

"Morocco's Militants." *The Economist.* Feb 21, 2008. http://www.economist.com/node/10733039.

Moukalled, Diana. "Opinion: The Western ISIS and Its Second Rebirth." *Asharq Al-Awsat.* July 1, 2014. http://www.aawsat.net/2014/07/article55333827.

Mount, Mike. "Reward for Wanted Terrorist Drops," *CNN.* May 13, 2008. http://edition.cnn.com/2008/WORLD/meast/05/13/pentagon.masri.value/index.html.

Napoleoni, Loretta. "Profile of a Killer." *Foreign Policy.* November 9, 2005. http://www.foreignpolicy.com/articles/2005/11/09/profile_of_a_killer?page=0,2&hidecomments=yes.

Noueihed, Lin. "Qaeda-Linked Group in Iraq Denies Head Captured." *Reuters.* May 12, 2009. http://www.reuters.com/article/2009/05/12/us-iraq-baghdadi-idUSTRE54B4WI20090512.

Peterson, Scott. "Picture of a Weakened Iraqi Insurgency." *The Christian Science Monitor.* June 16, 2006. http://www.csmonitor.com/2006/0616/p01s04-woiq.html.

Pool, Jeffrey. "Zarqawi's Pledge of Allegiance to Al-Qaeda: From Mu'asker Al-Battar, Issue 21." *The Jamestown Foundation Terrorism Monitor* 2, no. 24 (Dec 2004): 4-6.

"Profile: Islamic State in Iraq and the Levant

(ISIS)." *BBC News.* June 16, 2014. http://www.bbc.com/news/world-middle-east-24179084.

"Report: True Identity of 'Islamic State of Iraq' Leader Revealed, Photos Aired." *CBS News.* May 7, 2008. http://www.cbsnews.com/news/report-true-identity-of-islamic-state-of-iraq-leader-revealed-photos-aired/.

Roggio, Bill. "Islamic State of Iraq – An AL Qaeda Front." *The Long War Journal.* July 18, 2007. http://www.longwarjournal.org/archives/2007/07/islamic_state_of_ira.php.

Roggio, Bill. "Letters from Al Qaeda Leaders Show Iraqi Effort Is in Disarray." *The Long War Journal.* September 11, 2008. http://www.longwarjournal.org/archives/2008/09/letters_from_al_qaed.php.

Roggio, Bill. "US and Iraqi Forces Kill Al Masri and Baghdadi, Al Qaeda in Iraq's Top Two Leaders." *The Long War Journal.* April 19, 2010. http://www.longwarjournal.org/archives/2010/04/al_qaeda_in_iraqs_to.php.

Roggio, Bill. "Who Is Abu Omar Al Baghdadi?" *The Long War Journal.* September 14, 2008. http://www.longwarjournal.org/archives/2008/09/who_is_abu_omar_al_b.php.

"Saddam Hussein Captured 'Like a Rat' in Iraq Ten Years Ago Today." *Fox News.* December 13, 2013. http://www.foxnews.com/world/2013/12/13/saddam-hussein-captured-like-rat-in-iraq-ten-years-ago-today/.

Schemm, Paul. "Iraqi Al Qaeda Group Leader Still In Custody: Iraqi FM." *Huffington Post.* May 13, 2009. http://www.huffingtonpost.com/2009/05/13/iraqi-al-qaeda-group-lead_n_202995.html.

Schifferes, Steve. "US Names 'Coalition of the Willing." *BBC News.* March 18, 2003. http://news.bbc.co.uk/2/hi/americas/2862343.stm.

Siegel, Pascale Combelles. "Mujahideen Leader Appeals to Scholars and Professionals to Defeat U.S.-Iranian Plot to Subjugate Iraq." *The Jamestown Foundation.* April 30, 2009. http://www.jamestown.org/single/?tx_ttnews%5Btt_news%5D=34926&no_cache=1#.U7AmRvmSy18.

Simcox, Robin. "The 'Islamic State of Iraq'." *The Wall Street Journal.* July 31, 2012. http://online.wsj.com/news/articles/SB10000872396390443477104577550500445383554.

"Tanzim Qaidat al-Jihad fi Bilad al-Rafidayn (QJBR)." *Terrorism Research and Analysis Consortium (TRAC).* http://www.trackingterrorism.org/group/tanzim-qaidat-al-jihad-fi-bilad-al-rafidayn-qjbr-al-qaeda-land-two-rivers-see-separate-entry.

Tilghman, Andrew. "The Myth of AQI." *Washington Monthly.* October 2007. http://www.washingtonmonthly.com/features/2007/0710.tilghman.html.

"Transcript: Lawrence Eagleburger on FNS." *Fox News.* August 19, 2002. http://www.foxnews.com/story/2002/08/19/transcript

-lawrence-eagleburger-on-fns/.

"Two Arab Countries Fall Apart." *The Economist.* June 12, 2014. http://www.economist.com/news/middle-east-and-africa/21604230-extreme-islamist-group-seeks-create-caliphate-and-spread-jihad-across.

U.S. State Department. Office of the Coordinator for Counterterrorism. Country Reports on Terrorism. April 30, 2007. http://www.state.gov/j/ct/rls/crt/2006/82738.htm.

Western, Jon. *Selling Intervention and War: The Presidency, the Media, and the American Public.* Baltimore: The John Hopkins University Press, 2005.

"Who Was the Real Abu Omar Al-Baghdadi?" *Asharq Al-Aqsat.* April 20, 2010. http://www.aawsat.net/2010/04/article55251030.

Wright, Lawrence. *The Looming Tower: Al-Qaeda and the Road to 9/11.* New York: Random House, 2006.

The Nusra Front

Abbas, Y. (2016, May 10). How Al-Qaeda is Winning in Syria. Retrieved from War on the Rocks: http://warontherocks.com/2016/05/how-al-qaeda-is-winning-in-syria/

Al Jazeera. (2016, July 29). Al-Nusra leader Jolanie announces split from Al-Qaeda. Retrieved from Al Jazeera: http://www.aljazeera.com/news/2016/07/al-nusra-leader-jolani-announces-split-al-qaeda-160728163725624.html

A-Monitor. (2016, June 5). Is Russia readying for the kill

in Syria? Retrieved from Al-Monitor: http://www.al-monitor.com/pulse/originals/2016/06/russia-syria-nusra-aleppo-qaeda-ypg-us-jihadi.html

Barna, C. (2014). The Road to Jihad in Syria: Using SOCMINT to Counter the Radicalization of Muslim Youth in Romania. In M. Lombardi, E. Ragab, V. Chin, Y. Dandurand, V. de Divitiis, & A. Burato, Countering Radicalisation and Youth Extremism Among Youth to Prevent Terrorism. Milan: IOS Press.

BBC News. (2014, September 24). What is the Khorasan Group? Retrieved from BBC New: http://www.bbc.com/news/world-middle-east-29350271

BBC News. (2015, May 28). Al-Qaeda 'orders Syria's Al-Nusra Front not to attack West'. Retrieved from BBC News: http://www.bbc.com/news/world-middle-east-32913509

Benotman, N. a. (n.d.). Jabhat Al-Nusra: A Strategic Briefing. Retrieved from Quilliam Foundation: https://web.archive.org/web/20150328080133/http://www.quilliamfoundation.org/wp/wp-content/uploads/publications/free/jabhat-al-nusra-a-strategic-briefing.pdf

Byman, D. L. (2015, February 24). ISIS vs. Al Qaeda: Jihadism's global civil war. Retrieved from Brookings Institution: https://www.brookings.edu/articles/isis-vs-al-qaeda-jihadisms-global-civil-war/

Daireh, M. (2015, November 11). Inside the Battle: Al Nusra-Al Qaeda in Syria. Retrieved from VICE News: https://news.vice.com/video/inside-the-battle-al-nusra-al-qaeda-in-syria

del Cid Gómez, J. M. (2010). A Financial Profile of the

Terrorism of Al-Qaeda and its Affiliates. Retrieved from Perspective on Terrorism: http://www.terrorismanalysts.com/pt/index.php/pot/article/view/113/html

Fanack - Chronicle. (2015, July 1). Jabhat Al-Nusra Tries to Look Like a Moderate Terrorist Group. Retrieved from Fanack - Chronicle of the Middle East & North Africa: https://chronicle.fanack.com/specials/extremism/jabhat-al-nusra-tries-to-look-a-moderate-terrorist-group/

Farag, N. (2014). Between Piety and Politics: Social Services and the Muslim Brotherhood. Retrieved from Frontline - PBS: http://www.pbs.org/wgbh/pages/frontline/revolution-in-cairo/inside-muslim-brotherhood/piety-and-politics.html

Fulton, W. J. (2013, May). Iranian Strategy in Syria. Retrieved from Institute for the Study of War: http://www.understandingwar.org/report/iranian-strategy-syria

Gartenstein-Ross, D. a. (2013, August 22). How Syria's Jihadists Win Friends and Influence People. Retrieved from The Atlantic: http://www.theatlantic.com/international/archive/2013/08/how-syrias-jihadists-win-friends-and-influence-people/278942/

Habeck, M. (2014, June 27). Assessing the ISIS - Al-Qaeda Split: The Origins of the Dispute. Retrieved from Insite Blog on Terrorism & Extremism: http://news.siteintelgroup.com/blog/index.php/categories/jihad/entry/193-assessing-the-isis-al-qaeda-split-the-origins-of-the-dispute-1

Haid, H. (2016, August 9). Opinions Divided on Nusra's Split from Al-Qaeda. Retrieved from News Deeply: https://www.newsdeeply.com/syria/articles/2016/08/09/opinions-divided-on-nusras-split-from-al-qaida

Hall, R. a. (2016, May 2). The other Islamic state: Al-Qaeda is still fighting for an emirate of its own. Retrieved from PRI: http://www.pri.org/stories/2016-04-29/other-islamic-state-al-qaeda-still-fighting-emirate-its-own

Harris, S. a. (2015, August 31). Petraeus: Use Al Qaeda Fighters to Beat ISIS. Retrieved from The Daily Beast: http://www.thedailybeast.com/articles/2015/08/31/petraeus-use-al-qaeda-fighters-to-beat-isis.html

Hashem, A. (2016, April 15). Iranian official says Nusra, not IS, main threat to West. Retrieved from Al-Monitor: http://www.al-monitor.com/pulse/originals/2016/04/iran-syria-palmyra-nusrah-islamic-state.html

How Jabhat Al Nusra Uses Twitter to Spread Propaganda. (2016, May 4). Retrieved from VOX Pol: http://www.voxpol.eu/how-jabhat-al-nusra-uses-twitter-to-spread-propaganda/

Internet World Stats. (2015, November). Internet Usage in the Middle East. Retrieved from Internet World Stats: http://www.Internetworldstats.com/stats5.htm

Karouny, M. (2015, March 4). Insight - Syria's Nusra Front may leave Qaeda to form new entity. Retrieved from Reuters: http://uk.reuters.com/article/uk-mideast-crisis-nusra-insight-idUKKBN0M00G620150304

Montgomery, K. (2015, April 13). Jabhat Al Nusra: A Game Change in Syria. Retrieved from World Policy Blog: http://www.worldpolicy.org/blog/2015/04/13/jabhat-al-nusra-game-changer-syri

Prucha, N. a. (2013, June 25). Tweeting for the Caliphate: Twitter as the New Frontier for Jihadist Propaganda. Retrieved from Combating Terrorist Center at West Point: https://www.ctc.usma.edu/posts/tweeting-for-the-caliphate-twitter-as-the-new-frontier-for-jihadist-propaganda

Roberts, D. D. (2015, March 6). Is Qatar bringing the Nusra Front in from the cold? Retrieved from BBC News: http://www.bbc.com/news/world-middle-east-31764114

Roggio, B. (2006, October 16). The Rump Islamic Emirate of Iraq. Retrieved from The Long War Journal: http://www.longwarjournal.org/archives/2006/10/the_rump_islamic_emi.php#

Sanchez, R. a. (2016, August 1). Syria's al-Nusra rebrands and cuts ties with al Qaeda. Retrieved from CNN: http://www.cnn.com/2016/07/28/middleeast/al-nusra-al-qaeda-split/

Schatz, B. (2016, August 5). Meet the Terrorist Group Playing the Long Game in Syria. Retrieved from MotherJones: http://www.motherjones.com/politics/2016/08/syria-al-qaeda-nusra-battle-aleppo

Stein, A. (2015, February 9). Turkey's Evolving Syria Strategy. Retrieved from Foreign Affairs: https://www.foreignaffairs.com/articles/turkey/2015-02-09/turkeys-evolving-syria-strategy

yalibnan. (2015, March 19). Al Qaeda forces Druze of Idlib Syria to destory their shrines and convert. Retrieved from YaLibnan: http://yalibnan.com/2015/03/19/al-qaeda-forces-druze-of-idlib-syria-to-destroy-their-shrines-and-convert/

Zimmerman, K. a. (2016, July 28). Avoiding al Qaeda's Syria trap: Jabhat al Nusra's rebranding. Retrieved from AEI: https://www.aei.org/publication/avoiding-al-qaedas-syria-trap-jabhat-al-nusras-rebranding/

Free Books by Charles River Editors

We have brand new titles available for free most days of the week. To see which of our titles are currently free, click on this link.

Discounted Books by Charles River Editors

We have titles at a discount price of just 99 cents everyday. To see which of our titles are currently 99 cents, click on this link.

Printed in Poland
by Amazon Fulfillment
Poland Sp. z o.o., Wrocław